Wisdom Crieth Out!
Words of Inspiration for Everyday People

Demetrice M. Gates

DENVER, COLORADO

Bible references from King James version of the Bible

The opinions expressed in this manuscript are solely the opinions of the author and do not represent the opinions or thoughts of the publisher. The author has represented and warranted full ownership and/or legal right to publish all the materials in this book.

Wisdom Crieth Out!
Words of Inspiration for Everyday People
All Rights Reserved.
Copyright © 2013 Demetrice M. Gates
v1.0

Author photo: by Bricen T. Andrews Sr. at Photography by Bricen

This book may not be reproduced, transmitted, or stored in whole or in part by any means, including graphic, electronic, or mechanical without the express written consent of the publisher except in the case of brief quotations embodied in critical articles and reviews.

Outskirts Press, Inc.
http://www.outskirtspress.com

ISBN: 978-1-4787-0642-7

Outskirts Press and the "OP" logo are trademarks belonging to Outskirts Press, Inc.

PRINTED IN THE UNITED STATES OF AMERICA

Contents

INTROLOVETION v
CHAPTER 1: LEND HIM YOUR EAR 1
CHAPTER 2: ALLOW HIM TO SPEAK 70
CHAPTER 3: TAKE HEED 125
CHAPTER 4: HEAR YE! HEAR YE! 162
CHAPTER 5: THINK ON THESE THINGS 202
CHAPTER 6: APPLY THINE HEART 244
ABOUT THE AUTHOR 330

INTROLOVETION

"In the beginning God created the heaven and the earth" (Genesis 1:1). What did God use to create it all? He used the greatest and the most ancient tool to date; He used wisdom (Proverbs 3:19). When God created Adam and Eve, He used wisdom. We need wisdom to make the greatest decisions in life such as deciding on the right mate or just deciding on what outfit to wear to a job interview. *Wisdom Crieth Out!* is doing just that today on Mother Earth. The heaven and earth that God created in the beginning is a far cry from perfection today. Wisdom is crying out each and every day in the news, in people, etc. God put this book upon Demetrice M. Gates's heart, not just for the scholar or blue-collar worker, but for the everyday person as well. Wisdom has no age, race, creed, or level of intelligence. Wisdom is for all walks of life. God put this book upon his heart with that in mind. In this candid, yet easy-to-read book, Demetrice M. Gates explains the love and care that God has for us. He also encourages us to remain faithful and true to Him by how we treat our fellow man. God's heart is heavy in this day and age, and His wisdom is crying out. "Wisdom is the principal thing; therefore get wisdom: and with all thy getting get understanding" (Proverbs 4:7).

CHAPTER 1

LEND HIM YOUR EAR

A TRUE FRIEND

God is love. He is so special to me. Whenever I call on Him, He's always there to answer me. God is the Lord of hope. He is the God of many great wonders, but most of all, a true friend.

"Have mercy upon me, O Lord; for I am weak: O Lord, heal me; for my bones are vexed" (Psalm 6:2). Whenever you are weak, God will be there to make you strong. When you are sick, He's your remedy. He will heal you from anything. All you have to do is believe in Him and accept His Son Jesus Christ as your personal Savior. God is real; He's in our everyday life. When we cry at night, God is there.

"I will both lay me down in peace, and sleep: for thou, Lord, only makest me dwell in safety" (Psalm 4:8). The only time I feel peace is when I'm in the presence of God. The Lord is our bodyguard; He is our protector, especially from the evil forces of Satan. He won't allow evil to come near us (Psalm 91:7). Whenever evil approaches, God will quickly destroy it because He is a powerful force. I take our relationship seriously because God takes our relationship seriously. He makes me feel special, He makes feel worthy, He honors and cherishes me. He shows me unconditional love.

"I will praise thee, O Lord, with my whole heart; I will shew forth all thy marvellous works" (Psalm 9:1). As long as I live, I will continue to praise God. I will continue to spread His great name at any place that I go. Whenever I'm lonely, He's always there to keep me company. Sometimes we may forget that God has enough love to go around, but He is equally a true friend to each and every one of us.

A STRENGTH BUILDER

I love the Lord because He is constantly in my life. Every day, the Lord smiles down on all of His children. The Lord is a true strength builder; He gave David the strength to defeat Goliath, and He gave Noah strength and confidence to build the ark. God is not a comic book or action movie hero, but a real hero in the time of real trouble for a real need.

"Though I walk in the midst of trouble, thou wilt revive me: thou shalt stretch forth thine hand against the wrath of mine enemies, and thy right hand shall save me" (Psalm 138:7). There is no situation or trouble so big that God cannot handle it. God will help you with all of your problems. He will bring you out of your suffering. When the disciples started to lose faith, and Jesus saw the storm and the fear in His disciples, He spoke to the winds and the sea and there was a great calm (Matthew 8:23–27). God is powerful and a strong force in the day of trouble.

In our sorrows He will be there to comfort us. When we lose hope, He will be our confidence. "My flesh and my heart faileth: but God is the strength of my heart, and my portion for ever" (Psalm 73:26). The closer you get to God, the more trouble that Satan is going to try to put you through; however, I'd rather be with God and go through trials and tribulations than to be with Satan. At the end of a trial or tribulation, the children of God are going to rejoice in His holy name. We know that the Almighty God has something great in store for us. That's why it's worth going through trials and tribulations because the ending will be victorious, and we will come out stronger.

BE A SOLDIER

If we are going to be a part of God's army He wants us to be soldiers. He wants us to be tough. God doesn't have any room for murmurers and complainers. God gets frustrated when we complain and murmur all the time. He says to Himself, "Why do they have so little faith?" In John 16:33, Jesus said, "In the world ye shall have tribulation." Jesus is telling us while we are in this world we are going to face tribulations and hard times because we are not of the world.

I used to cry all the time. I had little faith, but once I gave God my whole heart, mind, and body, eventually the crying ceased. When you give God all of you, your tears of sorrow will become tears of joy. God doesn't put sorrow in your heart. He puts joy within.

When you are going through a tribulation, hold on to God and be tough. If you can't have faith in God through your tribulations, what are you going to do when the holy war between good and evil really breaks out? You have to put all your faith and trust in God. Don't let your mind waiver.

Become and remain strong in the midst of your tribulations. Be like Job and be patient. Always remember that God is on your side, no matter the situation. We can not let Satan take control of us, our families, or any of our loved ones. Hold on to your faith and be a soldier in the army of the Lord!

DON'T WORRY ABOUT YOUR ENEMIES

"Through God we shall do valiantly: for he it is that shall tread down our enemies" (Psalm 60:12). God will not let your enemies touch you. It is He who shields and protects you when you are walking in the valley of death (Psalms 23:4). Continue to walk toward God as though nothing will stop you.

"That He would grant unto us, that we being delivered out of the hand of our enemies" (Luke 1:74). God is our Deliverer. He will deliver us from any form of an enemy. Whether it's drugs, alcohol, smoking, overeating, bullying from your peers, or even your boss, He will deliver you from all your enemies, especially Satan. We also must know that Satan has, is, and will always be, part of any enemy that we face, and must know or remember it's Satan that is the root of that enemy (Ephesians 6:12).

My brothers and sisters, God has a special place for us. He's getting all of us prepared for it. Any trial that you face, count it all as joy.

God uses your trials to strengthen you. He never fails at doing His job. God always has your back, so don't worry about your enemies.

DON'T BE AFRAID

Many of us may say we are not afraid, but the truth is, we are. There is no reason for you to be afraid because the Lord is with you. I used to be afraid too, but when I became strong in the Lord, my spirit of fear went away. "For God has not given us the spirit of fear; but of power, and of love, and of a sound mind" (2 Timothy 1:7).

"God is our refuge and strength, a very present help in trouble" (Psalm 46:1). The Lord will be there to protect you from any danger. He won't let anything hurt or harm you. Wherever you go, just remember the Lord will be there. God is your Spirit and bodyguard. He will always be there to help you in time of need.

"Yea, thou I walk through the valley of the shadow of death, I will fear no evil: for thou art with me; thy rod and thy staff comfort me" (Psalm 23:4). The Lord is your rod and staff. He will destroy any evil that approaches you. Just like a tornado, God will fling your fear into the pits of hell. He won't leave any evil behind for the search team to look for you because the Lord doesn't leave trouble behind.

My dear friends, always remember that the Lord is your knight in shining armor. With His sword, He will slice all of your feared enemies. God doesn't want you to fear any man or anything. "So that we may boldly say, The Lord is my helper, and I will not fear what man shall do unto me" (Hebrews 13:6). On that note, my friends, don't be afraid.

GENTLE SPIRIT

The Lord loves those who are humble. Like Him, a person who is humble is slow to anger. A person who is humble also has a gentle spirit. When you have a gentle spirit, people enjoy being around you. They feel peace when they are in your presence.

When people need you, don't turn your back on them. The Lord is always there for His children whenever they cry out for Him. Just like a pillow, the Lord is a comforter for all of His children. His voice is so gentle that it can calm a ferocious beast.

"Comfort your hearts, and stablish you in every good word and work" (2 Thessalonians 2:17). No matter what people say or do to you, don't make them feel bad. It's not good to hold grudges. Do less arguing and more compromising, because fussing and fighting doesn't help a relationship grow. Let God be the mediator of your household.

In the world today, we need more people with a gentle spirit. The violence in this world is growing. I'm praying that everyone accepts Jesus Christ as his or her personal Savior because He is the sole provider of a gentle spirit.

GOD IS IN CONTROL

My brothers and sisters, don't worry about your life for God is in control. When God is in control, everything goes smoothly, even when you are going through hell. You're able to relax and let God handle His business when you know He is in control. It feels so good to be shielded by Him.

God will build you into a powerful soldier. Demons would be afraid to go near you when you decide to serve Him and allow Him to take full control.

When God is in control, you don't have to worry about anything. He will help you pay your bills. He will help you get a house or a car. He will repair a broken relationship. God will supply you with everything that you need. He's almighty for a reason.

God controls the time. He decides when He wants to bless you. All you have to do is be patient. It's that simple. God is not asking you to do much. You have to be willing to do something for God and trust that He will do for you.

My brothers and sisters, you should be praising God for the marvelous works that He displays. Don't limit yourself when it comes to blessing God. Be glad to serve the Lord. Always keep God on your mind. Most important, remember that He's in control.

HONOR HIM

The Lord is a God of many great wonders. He is a revealer of dreams. God is that force that understands what goes on in your mind and heart. He is a majestic God; therefore, you should honor Him.

"Thou art worthy, O Lord, to receive glory and honour and power: for thou hast created all things, and for thy pleasure they are and were created" (Revelation 4:11). God created man in his own image. When He created us, He didn't make any mistakes. We should all give thanks to God for doing a marvelous job. God is a righteous King.

"O come, let us worship and bow down: let us kneel before the Lord our maker" (Psalm 95:6). God is worthy to be praised. We should not take Him for granted. Although we may sin, He is always there to forgive us. No matter what we do, God will always love us.

"God is a Spirit: and they that worship him must worship him in spirit and in truth" (John 4:24). The only way to worship God is in the spirit because the Lord doesn't dwell with the flesh. When you worship the Lord, you will gain strength. Worship God in truth because He doesn't deal with liars. All you have to do is be honest with God and yourself.

We should all give thanks to God for being in our lives. He is good to everyone. The Lord loves everyone. He knows that we all make mistakes. My brothers and sisters, continue to honor the Lord for He is a holy King that always rewards His servants.

IN DUE TIME

There is no secret that people of today have become a "I want it now" generation. They want everything to happen in such a fast or swift pace. There are even those of the older generation who may "want it now" as well. Some of us just don't have enough patience to wait. We say that we trust in God, but our actions are saying, "Hurry up, Lord!" My brothers and sisters, just relax, because in due time, God will bless you.

God does not lie (Numbers 23:19). If He said He is going to bless you, believe Him that it shall come to pass. God has many blessings in store for you. It is up to you to be patient until He opens the storage room and supplies you with your blessings.

God has hope for all of us. Love God like He loves us. He never quits on His children. It is we that quit on Him. God is willing to bless us. We have to be willing to bless Him. Show God how much you love Him because He is going to show you how much He loves you. In due time all of your desires are going to be fulfilled, so give thanks and glorify Almighty God.

JUST PRAY

My brothers and sisters, we all go through hard times. It's how we face those hard times that make us bold or weak. Face the storm that comes upon you in your life. All you need to do is just pray, and God will be there to help you. When you pray, you have to believe. You have to have faith that the Lord will be there to help you. He is a trustworthy God whom everyone can depend on. Open your heart to Him. I promise you He won't fail you.

"And this is the confidence that we have in him, that, if we ask any thing according to his will, he heareth us: And if we know that he hear us, whatsoever we ask, we know that we have the petitions that we desired of him" (1 John 5:14–15). Those who have confidence in the Lord know that He will be there for them. Your heart and mind must be without doubt. When you ask the Lord for something without doubting, it makes Him feel good. It lets Him know that you are trusting in Him to do all things.

The Lord never breaks a promise. He never forgets His promise. God hears your every cry, and believe me, He will be there to comfort you. "Blessed be God, even the Father of our Lord Jesus Christ, the Father of mercies, and the God of all comfort" (2 Corinthians 1:3). God is the one who is going to bless you. He is the one who is going to heal you from all of your pain. Believe in God and trust in Him. And when all else fails, just remember to pray.

LEAN ON GOD

God is a graceful Father. He gives us the strength that we need to make it through each day. He is a God that has high hopes for us. What makes it more wonderful is that He is going to help us along the way. That's why we should all lean on Him.

The more you lean on God, the easier your life will be. He will handle all of your worries. God will strengthen your mind. He will speak for you. God doesn't want any of us to fail. He is going to uplift us the way that He wants us to be. Man doesn't uplift the children of God; the Holy One does.

"I will deliver thee, and thou shalt glorify me" (Psalm 50:15). When you lean on God, He will deliver you from all evil. There is nothing more powerful than God. While you are still worrying about the same thing, God has already fixed it. Please don't try to fix things yourselves because they will stay broken. Let God be your plumber and fix your heart when it is leaking. God will replace your heart with a pure heart. He will cleanse you from all of your sins.

Don't call yourselves getting upset with God because it won't work. You didn't make God; He made you. God will take care of everything for you, so just be patient. Sometimes I may get impatient, but God is there to remind me to stay patient. Always keep God on your mind and heart because He keeps you in His mind. You are never alone. God is present even when you think He's not. Continue to walk in God because He is a great Father to lean on.

LEAVE IT IN GOD'S HANDS

How are you doing, my brothers and sisters in Christ Jesus? Jesus is a delightful shepherd. I just love the way that He leads us sheep. His Father God is the Master Shepherd who is leading all of us through. My brothers and sisters, I just want to tell you that whatever problem you are having, leave it in God's hands.

First of all, when you leave it in God's hands, everything will work out for you. God will never mishandle your problems. He will take care of your every need. God will take your pain away. The problem that you are facing, someone else is facing it as well. What makes you think that God can't handle it? There is no problem that is too big for God. He is the problem solver.

Moreover, once you leave it in God's hands, it will take a lot of weight off of your shoulders. He will leave you experiencing huge relief. God wants you to leave everything to Him. He is the one who is going to make everything all right. God doesn't want you to worry about a thing.

My brothers and sisters, God loves you with a passion. Don't depend on anyone but God. He is the one that is going to lead you to the place where you belong. Trust in God, depend on God, and love God so He can do wonderful works for you, and through you. Just leave it in God's hands and, trust me, He will never close them.

LEND A HELPING HAND

One thing I try not to be is selfish. God doesn't appreciate a selfish person. You have to be willing to do things for people, like God is willing to do things for you. Lending a helping hand should be one of the most important things on our minds. It shows a great quality that we Christians can possess. The Heavenly Father blesses those who do such a good thing. It also shows that you have good character.

When you help someone out, it makes that person feels good. I love to see a smile on a person's face when I lend him or her a helping hand. Be a cheerful giver because the Almighty loves a cheerful giver. "Every man according as he purposeth in his heart, so let him give; not grudgingly, or of necessity: for God loveth a cheerful giver" (2 Corinthians 9:7).

Moreover, people know that you have kindness in your heart for you are willing to help them. You not only make yourself look good, but most important, you make God look good. He was the one that anointed you with a helping spirit, so don't forget about Him. God will do anything for His people, so He expects you to be the same way if it's for the right reason.

Furthermore, help your neighbor because some day you may need them to help you. That's why it's not good to be selfish, because at some critical stage, you may need someone. "He that despiseth his neighbour sinneth: but he that hath mercy on the poor, happy is he" (Proverbs 14:21). There is no man on this earth wealthier than God. We can let all the rich men put their money, jewels, and possessions together, and they still won't have greater riches than God, so if God can lend a helping hand, they can also do it. God doesn't belittle anyone. He treats everyone the same, and you should be the same way, so be kind and lend a helping hand.

LISTEN TO GOD

Trust me, people, because sometimes I know you feel like giving up. I get so sick and tired of Satan trying to attack my mind. That's why you've got to have God on your side, because you can't fight Satan alone. Satan is a pest. Whatever you do, my friends, always listen to God.

First of all, when you listen to God, He will guide you the right way. One thing God does not do is mislead people. God is the truth and the light. As you are walking in the valley of the shadow of death, God will shine His light upon you. He knows that you get weak. The minute you get weak, He whispers something in your ears for you to become strong.

Moreover, never close your ears to God. As soon as you close your ears to God, Satan will attack. He attacks when you let your guard down. Satan is sneaky. That's why the Holy Word refers to him as a snake. You see, Satan fears God. He knows when God is present. When God is present, Satan flees in another direction. He doesn't like it when you talk about God. You know he hates it when you listen to God.

"I lead in the way of righteousness, in the midst of the paths of judgment" (Proverbs 8:20). When you are led by God, nothing can stop you from reaching your goals. God will knock anything down that steps in your way. He is leading you down the path of righteousness, so just continue to follow Him. The minute you slip, that's when Satan slides on in, but get back up and follow God. Almighty God is the perfect teacher who teaches great things, and that's why I say you should listen to Him.

LISTEN TO THIS

My brothers and sisters, listen to this. Almighty God is a tremendous God. We can count on Him. God poured His breath into our nostrils so that we can live. It's time that we recognize God and count the blessings that He has poured down upon us.

"For great is our God above all gods" (2 Chronicles 2:5). There is no god like our Almighty God. He is the one who created all things. He is the one who nature obeys. If only we would obey God like nature does, the world would be a much happier place, but we want to be disobedient. Hearken unto the Lord's voice, obey His voice, and respect His voice. Trust me, God won't lead you astray. I have been serving God my entire life, and He has never forsaken me. It is we who forsake Him.

When did you ever hear that God is good to just a couple of people? "The Lord is good to all: and his tender mercies are all over his works" (Psalm 145:9). The Lord loves all of us equally. He doesn't treat anyone better than the next. He does have amazing grace for all of us. He gives us plenty of chances to do the right things in life. God never gives up on His children. He has confidence in us. That's why I'm going to continue to serve God, because it makes me feel good to have someone that is always beside me.

I'm glad that you took heed to listen to this. I hope these words influence you to continue to worship and praise God. He is the one who gives all of us mercy. Fellowship with others and tell them how God has been wonderful to you. As you do that, watch how your Heavenly Father blesses you more and more because you recognize Him.

LIVE IN HONESTY

I love God because He is fair to everyone. God doesn't belittle anyone. God is always there, even when you think He's not. He wants you to recognize Him. He also wants you to live in honesty.

God created man in His own image, which means that He wants us to live the right way. He wants us to seek after His righteousness. The right way to live is to stay truthful. As long as you are honest, you are not going to dig yourself into deep holes. Fibbing doesn't do anything but cause trouble. Many relationships fail because the couples lie to each other. Talk to a couple who has been married for twenty or forty years and ask them how their marriage lasts that long. They will tell you because of honesty.

When you are truthful, God will bless you. He does not deal with liars. Fibbing doesn't do anything but cause destruction. God wants you to be honest with people just like you are honest with Him. He knows when you are telling a lie or telling the truth. God knows everything that goes on in this earth. Anyone who thinks that he or she can fool God is fooling him or herself. If man can catch you in a lie, what do you think God can do? To be truthful, my brothers and sisters, live in honesty because you will go a long way in life.

MEDITATE ON GOD

Be silent for a moment and listen to your spirit. What kind of spirit do you have? What kind of spirit controls your mind? Think about that. If Satan controls your spirit, I know a way you can make him stop. Get to know God, and let Him control your spirit. Please just meditate on God.

When you meditate, it is important that you clear your mind of negative thoughts. Keep your mind on God, and God only. Tell God how much you love Him. He will show you guidance. He will give you peace. At all times think positive, even when you are going through hell. If God brought Jesus out of hell, He can bring you out as well.

While you are meditating, ask God for strength. He will be willing to give it to you. God already knows what your heart desires. He loves you with a passion. Let God use you as a vessel to help pull more souls into the kingdom. Don't be selfish; help someone get to know God; besides, someone helped you.

My brothers and sisters, God will bless you with a calm mind and a calm spirit. God will enlighten you with joy. He will make you be a light for other people. Trust in God, and know that He won't mislead you. God loves you too much to do that. If your mind is troublesome, He will give you peace, and that's why I say you should meditate on God.

NEVER LOSE SIGHT

Good morning, my friends. It's nice to see another day. This is a wonderful day that the Almighty God has created. He is a great God. This world that He created is beautiful. Don't take God for granted, and never lose sight of Him.

"There is a way that seemeth right unto a man, but the end thereof are the ways of death" (Proverbs 16:25). When you try to do things on your own, it won't work. No one on this earth is greater than Jesus Christ. Jesus Christ had help from God. What makes you better than Jesus that you don't need help from God? I ask God for help every day because I know I can't make it alone. If you know anyone that made it without the help of God, introduce me to him. If you know anyone greater than God, introduce me to him.

"He that handleth a matter wisely shall find good: and whoso trusteth in the Lord, happy is he" (Proverbs 16:20). Happy is he or she because they kept their sights on God. When you keep your sights on God, He will fulfill you with blessings. When you keep your sights on God, He will fulfill you with joy. When you keep your sights on God, He will fulfill you with peace. God never breaks a promise. God gives all of us grace, and He is the Lord of forgiveness.

"A wicked doer giveth heed to false lips; and a liar giveth ear to a naughty tongue" (Proverbs 17:4). Children of God, please separate yourselves from people like that. God knows you are willing to help them, but how could you help them when they are not willing to help themselves? I'm telling you, don't hang around them because you may pick up their ways. When you pick up their ways, you will lose sight of God. When you lose sight of God, you will be falling into the same pit with those wicked doers. You will also find yourself slipping off the pathway. Keep your sight on God, and bless His holy name.

OPEN UP YOUR HEART

It's not easy being a servant of the Lord. That's why I thank Him for giving me strength. I thank Him for blessing me to have peace in my heart. Having peace in my heart gives me the opportunity to open up my heart to others.

First of all, when you open up your heart to others, you show them how much love you have for them. Many people in this world need love. They are not getting love from their home, or anywhere else. Always offer your love to someone because they would appreciate it. Don't turn anyone down. Have you ever seen Almighty God turn His love down from anyone? No, you did not. God loves everyone. He doesn't have hate in His heart.

Moreover, love people like God loves you. Sometimes it may be hard to show love to some people. In a situation like that, you pray for that certain individual and leave it up to God. God is the problem solver, and He will do anything to lift up that individual.

My dearly beloved friends, don't give up on an individual. Don't forget that you used to be weak. Someone was there to open up his or her heart to you. We all need love. We all have to love each other like our Heavenly Father loves us. God doesn't put hate in our heart; He puts love in it, so be like God and open up your heart.

PERSONAL SAVIOR

We all wonder about things. We wonder about how we get up in the morning, and if there is life on another planet. I know who wakes me up in the morning. It is the Almighty God. You know God is a good God. It is good to know that you have someone that you can depend on. God is that someone I can depend on. He never turns His back on me. At times I may be down, but God will be there to encourage me.

God loves all of us. If He did not love us, He would have not sent His only begotten Son to save us from our sins (John 3:16). It's time that we praise God to the fullest. It's time that we stop being selfish and let God use us the way that He wants us to be used. We are all special to God, and there is a purpose why each of us is on the earth. God gave each of us a job to do, and that job is to help Him and each pull other souls in. That's why we go through trials and tribulations, because God is testing our faith and love for him. "And not only so, but we glory in tribulations also: knowing that tribulation worketh patience; and patience, experience; and experience, hope" (Romans 5:3–4).

My brothers and sisters, remember to pray because it is important. When you pray, you get closer to God. Be consistent with your prayers, which means, pray every day. Don't talk to God in weakness but in boldness. "Let us therefore come boldly unto the throne of grace, that we may obtain mercy, and find grace to help in time of need" (Hebrews 4:16). As a witness, I can tell you what I experience in my everyday life. I pray daily, and as I pray, I get closer to Him. So stay encouraged in the Lord and know that He is your personal Savior who will be there to help you in times of need.

PROBLEM SOLVER

Who is the problem solver? Almighty God is the problem solver. He handles all my problems. He brings me out of all my troubles. God blesses me with everything that I need.

"Many are the afflictions of the righteous: but the Lord delivereth him out of them all" (Psalm 34:19). The Lord delivers all of His children out of afflictions. Satan has many devices that he throws at the children of God. That's why we all have to stand tall in the Lord because we can't overcome evil without the help of Him. Anyone who says that he or she can defeat Satan without Jesus Christ is a liar. Satan would just look at you and laugh.

We all have to be prepared for the days of battle. It's not easy being a servant of the Lord. It takes a lot of hard work and praying. When you pray, ask the Lord for strength because living in a world of sin, you are going to need it. We all have problems, but the Lord will take care of them because He is the great problem solver.

PROVIDER OF JOY

I'd rather be happy than to be sad. I'd rather be happy than to be mad. Living in this world, God knows there are going to be times that we are going to be mad and sad. He just wants to help you control your sadness and madness. Let God make you free from being sad and mad because the Lord is the provider of joy.

"My soul shall be satisfied as with marrow and fatness; and my mouth shall praise thee with joyful lips" (Psalm 63:5). When Almighty

God provides you with joy, you will become slow to anger. With the joy that Almighty God is going to provide you with, there won't be any time for you to get mad. Your problems will become overshadowed by the joy that Almighty God is going to provide you with. Instead of you worrying about your situations, you will be rejoicing in His holy name.

"For our heart shall rejoice in him, because we have trusted in his holy name" (Psalm 33:21). All you have to do is invite Jesus Christ into your hearts. When you invite the Lord into your heart, He will handle everything for you. The Lord will bless you with a calm spirit. He will take away all of your worries. The joy that the Lord is going to provide you with is real powerful. His joy is so powerful that He can make King Kong shout his name with gladness.

"They that sow in tears shall reap in joy" (Psalm 126:5). There will be no more sad tears once the Lord blesses you with joy. He will fill the whole inside of your body with joy. Many will wonder why you smile and laugh all the time. Some may even think you are crazy and always up to something. Those who feel why you smile and laugh all the time will know why—because you've been joymatized by the provider of joy which is the Almighty God.

SMOOTH OPERATOR

The Lord is a marvelous God. He does everything in a perfect way. God makes sure that His animals are fed and His plants are watered. He does a great job taking care of the nature. The Lord is a smooth operator.

First of all, God does a great job motivating His children. He makes certain that their hearts are filled with confidence. God just wants His children to have faith which "is the substance of things hoped for, the evidence of things not seen" (Hebrews 11:1). The Lord wants us to see things in the spiritual realm. If you are of the Lord, you don't live in the flesh but in the spirit. "For ye are all the children of God by faith in Christ Jesus" (Galatians 3:26).

Moreover, God blesses His children with patience. To get any gift or reward from God you've got to have patience. Don't be in such a hurry to get things because God will supply you with everything that you need. "That ye be not slothful, but followers of them who through faith and patience inherit the promise" (Hebrews 6:12). The Lord wants you to have faith and believe in Him that He will bless you. "For ye have need of patience, that, after ye have done the will of God, ye might receive the promise" (Hebrews 10:36).

The Lord loves all of His children. He blesses us in a special way. Everything that He created is unique. God is that dream that we hope to see come true. My friends, God is just a smooth operator.

STAND TALL

God is a merciful Lord. He is a great Father to all of His children. His blessings are poured down on us like rain. Whenever we make the right decisions in life, God rejoices. There's nothing that we can do to make God stop loving us. His love lasts eternally. My earth family, God just wants us to stand tall.

Even though you are living in the world, don't live of the world. God knows it's not easy because of the sinful nature that it contains. In the midst of our temptations, He wants us to hold on to Him. There are many things in the world that tempt us to do ungodly things, but don't give in to it. Just remember that God is always with you.

My beloved sisters and brothers, I love you. As your brother, I'm going to continue to talk to you through the pages of this book. Love God with all of your heart. Finish the work of Jesus Christ with your whole heart. Jesus Christ died for all of your sins. He was the ultimate sacrifice. Since Jesus Christ took such a horrendous punishment for us, we should at least stand tall against the principalities of Satan because he is the ruler of sin.

STAY POSITIVE

Whatever you do, my brothers and sisters, stay positive. There is nothing that can stop you from reaching your goals. "I can do all things through Christ which strengtheneth me" (Philippians 4:13). Always keep that in your hearts. Know that the Lord is on your side. Know that the Lord won't forsake you.

Staying positive gives you confidence. In your heart, you feel that you can do anything. The God that you serve is positive so you should be positive. Don't be associated with those that are negative. The only thing they would do is bring you down. When you are positive, you will draw attention. Others will love to be around you. With your positive spirit, you make people feel good. By you being positive, it helps them feel positive.

The more people come around you, the better that they feel. It's just like when you are around the Almighty God. He makes you feel great. He shows you love. God doesn't make anyone feel bad for He loves all of us. God wants all of us to be a light, so stay positive and let your light shine throughout the world.

THE GREATEST BOOK TO BE IN

We always hear people talk about how they would love to be in a Hall of Fame book, magazine, and newspaper article. I'm not saying that those things are bad because I would like to be in them too. I just would like to tell you in the name of Jesus Christ what's the greatest book to be in: the Book of Life. The Book of Life is the most famous book in the universe besides the Holy Bible. It contains the names of those who are going to inherit the kingdom of heaven. It contains the names of those who are joint heirs with Christ. While they were living on earth, they showed God and Jesus Christ love. They are the ones who truly allowed the Holy Spirit to guide them.

The Book of Life is written by Almighty God. The names are written in red, that is, the blood of Jesus Christ. Jesus Christ is waiting to see the ones whose names are written in the Book of Life. He is just waiting to have fun with them for all eternity. God is telling Jesus to be patient, for the time is going to come for Him to see them. My brothers and sisters, I believe that your name is written in the Book of Life. Be happy that your name is written in it. Your name is in there with Abraham, Moses, Sarah, Paul, David, Daniel, the Hebrew boys, Noah, and the rest of the great people of God in the Bible. Start praising God for the Book of Life.

Thank Jesus Christ for dying for your sins and for God raising Him from the dead. If it weren't for Jesus Christ coming to this earth and dying for your sins, you would have no place in heaven or the Book of Life. The name of the book is the Lamb's Book of life. The Lamb represents Jesus Christ, so don't wait until God open the gates of heaven to rejoice. Begin rejoicing now, for you already know that you are in the Lamb's Book of Life, the greatest book to be in!

THE HOLY KING

There is a King who is the ruler of everything. This King sits high and looks low. He also makes perfect decisions. The King whom I'm referring to is the Almighty God. Heaven is His throne; the place where He looks upon all of His children. Like a shepherd, He protects His sheep, which are His children. He won't allow anyone or anything to harm them.

The Almighty God is a holy King. He treats His servants with great love and respect. He also gives everyone an equal opportunity to seek Him. The great thing about the holy King is that He will help you along the way. "In all thy ways acknowledge him, and he shall direct thy paths" (Proverbs 3:6). The King of Peace will guide you through life's troubles. He will instruct you to make the right decisions in life. When you make a mistake, He will be there to correct it.

"For this God is our God for ever and ever: he will be our guide even unto death" (Psalm 48:14). The Lord will direct you to the path of righteousness. His way is the key to eternal life. God will be your navigator along the pathway. With the light of His salvation, He will brighten the path for you.

There is no other king like the Almighty God. He is a King who welcomes everyone to His throne. The Lord wants everyone to celebrate with Him. Hope that the Lord chooses you to be among the celebration because He is the holy King.

THE HOLY ONE

Who is the Holy One? The Almighty God is the Holy One. Through a virgin, He sent His only begotten Son to save us from all of our sins. "And the angel answered and said unto her, The Holy Ghost shall come upon thee, and the power of the Highest shall overshadow thee: therefore also that holy thing which shall be born of thee shall be called the Son of God" (Luke 1:35).

God is in the midst of the church, so we should not be ashamed to praise Him. "Wherefore God is not ashamed to be called their God: for he hath prepared for them a city" (Hebrews 11:16). Just like Abraham, Sarah, Abel, Noah, Joseph, Moses, Enoch, and Isaac, God will prepare a city for us, and He will not be ashamed of us if we will have faith in Him.

Jesus Christ rebuked Satan and told him that His Father is already rich. When a storm passes through, the Almighty God keeps our house standing. When we are hungry, He feeds us. When we are thirsty, He gives us something to quench our thirst, but like the Israelites, we still want to tempt God.

Never be afraid of what Satan can do because the Holy One is on your side. He will be there to shield and protect you. Some of us just don't know that the Holy One has already prepared a place for us. All we have to do is seek Him. God is a rewarder of them that diligently seek Him. "Be silent, O all flesh, before the Lord: for he is raised up out of his holy habitation" (Zechariah 2:13).

THE PROMISE KEEPER

Smile, for God loves you. Rejoice, for He created you. One thing God doesn't do is lie. Sometimes you may feel that things are not going to happen for you. I'm here to tell you, *don't worry* because things *are* going to happen for you. Whatever God say He is going to do for you, He is going to do it because He is the promise keeper.

First of all, you have to believe in God. Believe that God will make a way for you. Believe in God with passion. God just wants the best for His children. Sometimes you may feel that God is too slow. God is not a slow-moving God. He just wants you to be patient. God is always on time, and His time is the best time. He knows the time better than anyone in this world.

Moreover, you have to hold on to God. Friends, time will get rough for you. When times get rough, you have to keep your faith in

God. Satan is going to do many things to tackle your mind, but you have to rebuke him. Keep pressing toward God with all your strength and heart. He will be there to help you throughout your life. Hold on to God because He has all the power to defeat Satan.

My beloved friends, get to know God each day as you live. He has been a wonderful Father to me. Trust in Him with all your mind, heart, body, and soul. "Ask, and it shall be given you; seek, and ye shall find; knock, and it shall be opened unto you: For every one that asked receiveth; and he that seeketh findeth; and to him that knocketh it shall be opened" (Matthew 7:7–8). Now, by you believing in God, holding on to Him, and reading those two verses in Matthew, you should know that He is the promise keeper; a God who never breaks a promise.

THE TRUE SHOT CALLER

Check out the Almighty God. He is so fabulous by the way He works things out. God makes small blessings into bigger blessings, and large blessings into larger blessings. Trust me, God can do anything. God is the true shot caller. He calls the shots on everything. He tells the sun where to set. God tells the rain when and where to fall. He tells the natural disasters what places to skip over. I mean God is amazing.

Everything He does is for the good. Many people think that God does not exist. I'm here to tell you that He does exist. Who puts the breath in your body so you can live? Who gave you those legs so you can walk? Who gave you that mouth so you can talk? Almighty God gave you those things. God created you, and He can break you. He created you out of dust, and He will put you back in the dust.

Continue to hold on to God because He will be happy to bless you. God has many blessings to give everyone if they would just believe in Him. God doesn't beg anyone to do anything. I love God, and I will do anything that He tells me to do. We all have to be that way. Once you open up your heart to God and walk in His ways, watch how everything good happens for you. God is the true shot caller who always calls the perfect shots.

THE ULTIMATE JUDGE

It's great when you are serving someone like the Almighty God, the one who provides you with everything that you need. God has enough love for everyone. His love lasts eternally, which means forever. The Lord is not only our master, but He is also the ultimate judge.

God looks at everything that each of us does. He takes records of the good things and records of the bad things that we do. He knows our every thought and feeling that we have in our hearts. There is nothing that you can do behind closed doors without God knowing it. No one can hide from God. No one can keep secrets from Him. God is everywhere that you go.

There shouldn't be any excuse for anyone not to make it to heaven. God's Word, which is the Bible, tells and shows us how we should live our life. The Bible is our guide to eternal life, but we have to be willing to obey God's commandments. His only begotten Son made the sacrifice for us, and the majority of us are still not grateful. All God wants us to be is a living sacrifice for Him.

It's funny, but sad, when people think that they have more power than God. God is different from these earthly judges. The innocent ones are the ones going to heaven. God gives everyone a chance to plead their case when He reveals their life to them. God's sentence is not a jail cell, but hell—which is worse than any prison on earth, so submit yourselves therefore to God because He is the ultimate judge who always makes the final decisions.

TRUST IN THE LORD

Many Christians today are double-minded. They can't make up their mind about who to serve. Just because they are Christians doesn't mean that they serve God. Most of them sin more than they bless God. It's great to read the Bible, but you have to live according to it. When I read the Bible, I live according to it because I trust in the Lord.

The Lord will make everything good for you if you would just trust Him. Many of us have faith one minute, then the next minute, we lose it. How could the Lord bless you if your mind is wavering? He is just asking you to do two simple things: have faith and trust in Him. "Blessed is that man that maketh the Lord his trust" (Psalm 40:4)." The man who makes the Lord his trust doesn't worry because he relies on God. When you rely on God, He will handle all your problems. When you rely on God, watch how all your blessings start flowing. At the twinkling of an eye is how fast God will bless you.

Whatever you do, have faith in God. "They that trust in the Lord shall be as mount Zion, which cannot be removed, but abideth for ever" (Psalm 125:1). When you have faith in the Lord, nothing can stand in your way. The Lord will be your rod and staff. "The Lord is good, a strong hold in the day of trouble; and he knoweth them that trust in him" (Nahum 1:7). For example, some of us may say that a brother is getting blessed with everything that he asks for. He is getting blessed with everything that he asks for because he trusts in the Lord. God will do the same thing for you if you would just trust Him. God treats everyone fairly. "Trust in the Lord, and do good; so shalt thou dwell in the land, and verily thou shalt be fed. Delight thyself also in the Lord: and he shall give thee the desires of thine heart. Commit thy way unto the Lord; trust also in him; and he shall bring it to pass" (Psalm 37:3–5).

WILLING TO FOLLOW

Jesus Christ doesn't have any hate in His heart. The only thing He hates is evil. Jesus Christ is our source to getting closer to God. With Jesus as your source, you are going to pass the course to getting closer to God, but you have to be willing to follow Him.

First of all, God gives you a choice to either serve Him or Satan. He doesn't force you to do anything. If you serve God, you are going to live eternally. God is the provider of everlasting joy. He is the one who you should worship daily. God is the epitome of holiness.

"The Lord is with you, while ye be with him; and if ye seek him, he will be found of you; but if ye forsake him, he will forsake you" (2 Chronicles 15:2).

It's quite simple; the more you seek after God, the closer you are going to get to Him. Everywhere you go, God will be there. He will never forsake you. You are never alone as long as you keep God in your heart. God will be your shield in the days of battle.

"The Lord is good unto them that wait for him, to the soul that seeketh him" (Lamentations 3:25). God loves those who are patient. Those who are patient receive the greatest blessings. God wants all of your attention. Everyone should spend time with Him each day.

I love God because He's been so great to me. He never forsook me. I want everyone to serve God. God has enough blessings for everyone in this world. He loves each and every last one of us, so draw nigh unto Him and be willing to follow.

WORK HARD

One thing I try my best to do is work hard. God loves children that work hard. You not only have to work hard for God, but you have to work hard for the ones that He appointed over you. If you disobey your boss on earth, you are disobeying God, and that's not good. "Servants, be obedient to them that are your masters according to the flesh, with fear and trembling, in singleness of your heart, as unto Christ; Not with eyeservice, as menpleasers; but as the servants of Christ, doing the will of God from the heart" (Ephesians 6:5–6).

First of all, God blesses those who work hard. "The Lord shall open unto thee his good treasure, the heaven to give the rain unto thy land in his season, and to bless all the work of thine hand: and thou shalt lend unto many nations, and thou shalt not borrow" (Deuteronomy 28:12). God is not lazy, so you should not be lazy. Now, there's a difference between lazy and resting. *Lazy* means unwilling to work; moving slowly; sluggish. To *rest* means to cease from all work, activity, or motion. God allows us to rest because He rested when He finished His work. "And God blessed the seventh day, and sanctified it: because that in it he had rested from all his work which God created and made" (Genesis 2:3).

Furthermore, what makes you better than God that you should not work? I had to realize that for myself because I know that I'm not greater than He. I have a long way to go to reach Him. Even His Son Jesus Christ worked. "Jesus saith unto them, My meat is to do the will of him that sent me, and to finish his work" (John 4:34). There should not be any excuse for anyone not to work hard for God. The only way to get to God is through Jesus Christ. If you don't get to Jesus, there is no way you are going to get to God. Whatever you may do, work hard and bless God because He deserves all of your attention.

YOU ARE NEVER LONELY

What's going on, everybody? How are you all doing? You know today is a wonderful day to serve the Lord. Every day is good to serve the Lord for He blesses you to see another day. I just want to tell you that you are never lonely as long as you have God in your life.

"I will not leave you comfortless: I will come to you" (John 14:18). The Almighty God will be there with you every step of the way. When you are feeling low, He will be there to uplift you. God will put a smile on your face so bright that it will light up the whole room. The Almighty God is a Lord of comfort. He will be there to comfort you in your weakest hour.

The Lord will take heed to your cry. Just like the great Father that He is, He will be there to dry your tears. God will talk to you and help you make it through your problems. He will not leave you in sorrow. The Lord is filled with everlasting joy. He will shower you with His love, kindness, and tender mercies.

My brothers and sisters all over the world, get right with God. Whatever ungodly thing that you are doing, stop doing it because traveling to hell is not a good idea. I know some of you do those things so that you can have friends. However, once you put God in your life, you don't have to worry about making friends. God will bring people to you. Some days you are going to feel alone, but remember, you are never lonely because God is there with you at all times.

A CLOSE RELATIONSHIP

The best thing to have is a close relationship with God. God understands all things. He understands why things happen. When you experience something bad, God will be there to lift you up. When you are feeling sad, He will enlighten you with joy. He has plenty of time to spend with everyone for He is the Lord. God will never neglect you. If you have anything on your mind that's troubling you, take it to God for He will ease it. When you need encouragement, God will be there. When you need strength, He will be there. When you need love, He will be there. That's why I have a close relationship with Him. God has everything that you need. That's why He says you should not want for anything. He already knows what you need. All you need to do is stay focused on Him. When you focus on God, you don't worry about anything for you know He will take care of everything. God is a king who is always there to provide His servants with riches. If there is something that you don't understand, call on God for He will help you, and that's why I say the best thing to have is a close relationship with Him.

A DAILY DELIGHTMENT

Good morning, my brothers and sisters. Today is a lovely day. Did you thank the Lord for blessing you to see this lovely day? God has given you another chance to see His marvelous creation. The brightness of the sun is so amazing. The heights of the trees are so unique. The depths of the seas are so astonishing. Who created these beautiful features? Your Heavenly Father, the Almighty God. Show God how much you appreciate His works. Give God the praise that He most absolutely deserves. He is perfect in everything that He does. He loves those who keep Him in their minds and hearts. Don't get me wrong; God loves everyone. His love is everlasting. Whatever you do, keep His commandments because keeping God's commandments lets Him know that you love Him. God just wants you to know that He is always by your side. My brothers and sisters, God is a daily delightment.

A GOOD APPEARANCE

My brothers and sisters, you know it's important to have a good appearance. Wherever you go, keep yourself looking good. Your Heavenly Father God wants you to look good. My friends, you are representing God. Just because you want to have a good appearance doesn't mean that you think you are all that. Don't worry about what people have to say about you. There are going to be people that say you are stuck on yourself, but don't let that get you down; continue to look good. Show everyone the grace that God has given to you. You are not only good on the inside, but also good on the outside. Those who are jealous can't handle that. Jesus Christ was a handsome man. He had many people talk about Him, but He kept going. Have some good class about yourself. Just because you may be from the ghetto doesn't mean you have to act like it. God wants His children to have a good appearance. He trains His children to have a good appearance. You can't go to a job interview dressed any kind of way and expect to get hired. You have to go to a job interview looking good. My brothers and sisters, remember to have a good appearance, for it shows you have respect for your Heavenly Father and yourself.

A GREAT GIVER

Every day I think about how God has been so great to my family. He has brought us from a long way. God has poured down His blessings on all His children. He is truly a great giver. He has given us the ability to preach and to teach. God is willing to share His blessings with all of us. He has so many blessings that they can cover the whole earth. God has anointed all of those who really desire to do His works. He takes care of His children. He blesses us with a nice place to stay and a car that can take us from place to place. The best things that I like that God has given to us are a pure mind and a pure heart. With a pure mind, we keep ourselves on positive thoughts. We keep our mind on God. With a pure heart, we open ourselves to others. We are willing to love others and share with them. The greatest thing I love that God has given to us is Jesus Christ. Jesus Christ made a way for us. He sacrificed Himself by dying for our sins. Now do you understand why I say that God is a great giver? God had given up His begotten Son to be our sacrifice.

A LETHAL WEAPON

God is a powerful force. When it comes to His children, He shields and protects them. He doesn't like anyone bothering His children. His children are His sheep who He pastures 24 hours each day. God is a lethal weapon. Remember what happened to those men who carried Shadrach, Meshach, and Abednego to the fiery furnace? They were burnt to death (Daniel 3:22). Instead of Daniel being eaten by the lions, the men who were responsible for him being thrown in the lions' den were eaten along with their wives and children (Daniel 6:24). Remember how God destroyed the city of Sodom and Gomorrah (Genesis 19:24–25)? There is no man, army, or beast on this planet that can stand up to God. There is no one who can defeat God. The fight won't last for a second. There is no one who can hide from God. There is no one who can run from God. God can destroy everyone on this planet by just snapping His fingers. He shows all of us mercy. With His kindness, He blessed us to be beautiful creatures. "When the angels sinned, God did not spare them: he sent them down to the underworld and consigned them to the dark underground caves to be held there till the day of Judgment" (2 Peter 2:4). With that in mind, you should be convinced that God is a lethal weapon.

A MARVELOUS GOD

I love the Lord. Jesus Christ is my friend. Every day He blesses me with gifts. He blessed me with the gift to write. God is my Heavenly Father. When I call on Him, He is always there to answer me. He is a marvelous God. God blesses the earth with trees to help us breathe. He blesses the earth with plants to make the air smell good. God blesses the earth with steel to help us build. The way that He feeds the earth is so unique. With His rain, He feeds the creatures in the sea, nature, and the human race. Without God, this earth will not survive. That's why I'm glad that He holds it in His hands. With the sun, He keeps us warm. With the wind, He keeps us cool. Whenever a storm approaches, He shields us from it. When we are walking into danger, He warns us. When we are stressed, He relieves us. Now do you understand why I say He is a marvelous God?

A POWERFUL FORCE

What is the definition of a powerful force? I can define that with one word: God. God is a powerful force. He treads upon His enemies like a tornado sweeps through a city. Everything He does is perfect. Which means, God doesn't make any mistakes. When God controls your mind and heart, nothing can go wrong. Everywhere that you may go, you have to believe that He's with you. All you have to do is say the blood of Jesus, and He will be right there. Let God be your light just as He was with the Israelites, as He led them out of the land of Egypt (Exodus 13:21). As you pursue God, He will light His pathway for you. The path is not going to be easy because Satan is going to try his best to block you from getting closer to God. That's why you've got to have faith in God and believe in Him, that He won't allow Satan to give you a detour off the pathway. When God touches you and speaks, it is powerful even when He whispers. To all of my Christian friends, God is also powerful when He is silent.

A POWERFUL SHIELD

God is a powerful shield. He is a shield that protects His children 24 hours a day. God is always there to protect His children from any danger. With His force field, he stops any evil force from entering His children. He won't let any evil force harm them. Any ungodly thing that approaches them will immediately get shocked. He shields His children daily. It is a huge mistake to mistreat His children. Those who interfere with the children of God will have to pay for it. I hope they don't think that they are going to get away with it, because it doesn't work that way. You mess with the children of God, you have to deal with Him, and believe me, it won't be a pretty sight. You can't get mad if we serve God. Not only that, He created us, but also created you. Who do you think you are? I tell you this, if you continue to mess with the children of God, He will destroy you because He is a powerful shield that never lets his guard down. "Our soul waiteth for the Lord: he is our help and our shield" (Psalm 33:20).

A SHINING STAR

God is a just Father. God builds His children with strength. He knows when they are feeling low. God is a shining star. Every place that He goes to, he stands out. The enemy knows when He is present. When God is present, the enemy scatters away. God is all about peace. He speaks peace, eats peace, drinks peace, and rests with peace. To sum it all up, He is peace. God is that streetlight that is on when you are walking at night. He is that second wind that gives you a push when you are working out. He loves it when He is acknowledged by His children. He loves to be appreciated. God shines on every scene. He shines in the darkest places on earth. Before you fall asleep, look out of your window and check out the shining star, which is the Almighty God.

A SPIRITUAL CONVERSATION

A spiritual conversation is a good conversation. It's when the children of God talk about their Heavenly Father and personal Savior. All you hear is positive speaking. There is nothing profane that comes out of the children of God's mouths as they talk about God and Jesus Christ. When you are having a spiritual conversation, your mind and speaking is pure. It pleases God when His children talk about Him. God looks down upon His children and smiles as they acknowledge Him. He knows that His children love Him for He searches their minds and hearts. God says to Jesus, "Listen to the way that my children talk about us. It's a good thing that we created them." When you are having a spiritual conversation, it expresses the way that you feel about God and His Son. The best thing I love about a spiritual conversation is that you don't hear curse words come out of people's mouths. The conversation is pure not filthy. As you talk about God and His Son, you get that wonderful feeling inside of you. You feel that you are being anointed. God blesses those who appreciate Him. My brothers and sisters, continue to have a spiritual conversation for it shows that you are blessing your Heavenly Father.

A STRONG TOWER

Check this out, my brothers and sisters. It makes God feels so good when you do the right things in life. God rejoices as you continue to go down the right pathway. He loves bragging about His children. Just remember that God is a strong tower. He stands tall with might and power. You can lean on Him in your weakest hour. He's the Creator whose blessings pour showers. One thing God won't do is give up on you. No matter what you do, God will always love you. He is an unselfish God. Anything that you need, He will provide it for you. Any trouble that you get into, He will bring you out of. Any mistake that you make, He will gladly correct. God is a merciful Father. He gives all of His children grace. God is a stone wall that no one can run through, not even Superman. He's a ship that can't be sunk. God is a tree that can't fall down. He will protect you from all of your enemies, and that's why I say He is a strong tower.

A TRUE EXAMINER

Listen, everyone, I just want to tell you all that God is a true examiner. He examines everyone's heart. He knows if your heart is clean or polluted. God knows if you care about Him or not. He knows if you are doing things from the heart or doing things just to glorify yourself. "O lord, thou hast searched me, and known me. Thou knowest my downsitting and mine uprising, thou understandest my thought afar off" (Psalm 139:1–2). The Lord knows your every thought. He knows what you are thinking about. He examines your mind to see if your thoughts are pure. When it comes to examining, God is serious. He is not going to dwell inside of an unclean vessel. He has to examine you to see what He needs to work on. It is for your own good. When you go to the clinic, the doctor gives you an examination to see what he needs to work on. God does the same thing when He examines your spirit, so don't get upset. He is only here to help. He has to make sure that you are doing fine. God doesn't want you to have a handicapped heart, mind, or spirit. God wants you to be well equipped. He wants you to be prepared because when you go to war, He doesn't want you to be overtaken by the enemy. If you are not ready, God is not going to send you out. Otherwise, the enemy will slaughter you. Trust me, God always knows what He is doing. "Search me, O God, and know my heart: try me, and know my thoughts: And see if there be any wicked way in me, and lead me in the way everlasting" (Psalm 139:23-24).

A TRUE MINISTER

God is a true minister. He ministers to all. He is someone you can count on to lead you the right way. God *is* the right way. He will lead you to the path of eternal life. God is eternal life. God does not lie. He is not a hypocrite. He is a perfect and just God. He knows everything about life. God knows the struggles that you face. He knows the pain that you are going to have. God is here to help you. Listen to Him. He will not mislead you. Put all of your trust in Him. Serve God with your whole heart. He is a minister of guidance. He works great with those who are patient and those who are willing to follow Him. God tells you the whole story. He does not tell you half of it. He will counsel you with any problem that you have. He is a great guidance counselor. The best part about it is that He won't try to get money out of you. God is willing to help you get through any problem or situation that you are having. If you want to know anything or have something on your mind, take it to God for He is a true minister who can help you with everything.

A TRUE SOLDIER

Check this out, my brothers and sisters. It is very important that you know this. Many of us claim that we are soldiers, but are we true soldiers? A true soldier is one who is willing to serve God in no matter what storm he or she goes through. A true soldier does not complain; he or she gets the job done. He or she follows the orders of God. A true soldier knows that God is the head in charge. A true soldier is not afraid to die for God. He or she is ready for war. God is the missile that is going to destroy the evil military. He equips His troops for battle. He makes sure that they are armed and ready. God is the generator of toughness. He trains His troops to be tough. When He puts His soldiers out on the battlefield, they destroy every evil thing. God commands His troops to destroy them all. He does not want any evil to be standing. He is a mighty God, and He wants His soldiers to be mighty. My brothers and sisters, strive to be true soldiers because it is an honor being on the battlefield of the commander in chief of the holy army.

ALL THINGS ARE POSSIBLE

What's up, my friends? What's going on? I just want to tell you that all things are possible. You serve the Almighty God. Through Him you can do anything. Through Him you can become successful. With God you are successful There is nothing too hard for God. I'm talking about the God who gave man the authority to rule over the beasts of the field. Set your goals and go after them. Don't limit yourself. Use every gift that Almighty God granted you with. Don't let your gift be in vain. Show the world how God has been good to you. Any obstacle that you face, count it all as joy for you know the Lord will help you through it. All you have to do is believe in Him, and His begotten Son Jesus Christ. Prove to God how much you love Him. Show God that you are ready to make it to the next level and remember that "with God all things are possible" (Mark 10:27).

ALWAYS BE ON GUARD

What's up, my friends? How are you doing? I'm doing great because I have a great Father. I'm here to remind you to always be on guard. As soon as you step out of your home, Satan is waiting for you. Just like God has children, Satan has his. Satan is everywhere. He's at the jobs, schools, churches, homes, and in high places. That's why we have to be ready for him. God has given us the tools to be prepared for Satan. It is up to us to use the tools. We all have to be strong in the Lord and the power of His might because that is the only way to triumph over Satan. Satan is not weak; he is powerful, but not more powerful than Almighty God is. Don't forget that Satan was in heaven. He knows how powerful God is. That's why he is trying his best to destroy the children of God. Satan doesn't love anyone. He doesn't love the people who worship him or himself. All he does is use them to do his evil work. All he does is prey on innocent people. Friends, continue to read your Bible because it has power. The more you read the Bible, the stronger you get. It is your guide to getting closer to God. Satan is a snake, and that's why we always have to be on guard to snap that snake's head off.

AN ADORING FATHER

God is an adoring Father. He provides His children with anything that they need. He provides them with love, peace, happiness, wisdom, knowledge, and understanding. He is a caring Father. Whenever His children weep, He dries their tears. He gives His children great advice. God raises His children in the way that they are supposed to be raised. He knows that they are not perfect. God always forgives His children whenever they do something wrong. He knows that they are going to make mistakes. God puts a roof over His children's heads. He provides them with transportation so they can handle their business. His children don't have to beg for anything. God already knows what their hearts desire. He is a true provider. God whispers pure words in His children's ears. He pours His comfort into their hearts. He quenches their every thirst for righteousness. I mean, God is truly amazing. He knows when His children are troubled for He watches their every coming and going. He searches their minds and hearts to see if everything is okay. He is a great Father that rewards His children for doing the right things in life. My brothers and sisters, God is an adoring Father who always cares for His children.

AN UNSELFISH GOD

God is an unselfish God. Look at the way that He blesses His children. He blesses His children to be healthy. He blesses His children to become successful. God gives His children comfort. Look at the way He blesses the animals. He gave the animals ponds to drink water from. He gave the animals plants to eat. He gave the animals a good outer covering to match the changes of the weather. Look at the way that God blesses nature. He blesses nature with the sun, and rain to help the trees and the flowers grow. He is a wonderful God. That's why I say the earth can't survive without Him. We all need God. God is full of love and compassion. He is merciful. He shows everyone and everything how great His love is. Just like God blesses us, we also have to bless Him. We have to bless God with praises. We have to bless God by paying our tithes and offerings. The more you bless God, the more He is going to bless you, and that's why I say He is an unselfish God.

BE COMMITTED

For us to be strong in God, we have to be committed to serving Him. "If they obey and serve him, they shall spend their days in prosperity, and their years in pleasures" (Job 36:11). The children of God have to be a strong army to go up against the principalities of Satan. When God calls us to do something, we should not be hesitant to do it because He is not a slow-moving God. "And we know that all things work together for good to them that love God, to them who are the called according to his purpose" (Romans 8:28). We have to be willing to do the works that the Almighty commands us to do. The Lord never does anything to harm us because He loves His children. The Lord never gives us too much that we can't handle. It's time that we have faith and trust in God. The Lord will heal you when you are sick. He will also be your shield in the day of battle, so why not be committed to an awesome force like Him?

BE FIRED UP FOR GOD

Good morning, my brothers and sisters. What a joyous day that God Almighty has created! I mean, He is a joyful God. My brothers and sisters, I challenge you to be fired up for God. Fired up for God means being pumped up for Him. When you praise God, be fired up for Him. When you talk about God, be fired up for Him. He is not a God of sadness. He is not a God of hindrance. You should be happy to be fired up. When a prophet tells you that God is going to wonderfully bless you, you get fired up. Why can't you get fired up to bless God? I'm not trying to judge you, I'm trying to motivate and encourage you. The more you get fired up for God, the more He shines in you. Even when you are having problems, be fired up for God, for He is bigger than your problems. Your neighbor will look at you and say, "Man, that sister or brother is fired up in the Lord." Don't let anybody stop you from being fired up for God. Continue to praise, bless, and be encouraged in Him. God will say to Jesus and the Holy Spirit, "It feels good living in this individual." For now on, my brothers and sisters, stop complaining about your problems and situations, and come unto the Lord fired up.

BE HAPPY FOR OTHERS

It feels so good to have God in your life. God is a happy God, and He wants you to be happy. My brothers and sisters, happiness cries out. Be happy, my brothers and sisters, even if you have to force yourself to be happy. Be happy when you get blessed and be happy for others. God not only wants to bless you in the name of Jesus, He wants to bless others. Be happy for others. Thank God for blessing others. Do they deserve to get blessed? They work hard just like you do. Be happy when God blesses others with a car and a house. Be happy when others move on top of the ladder. They love God just like you do. By you being happy for them, it makes them feel good. I remember when my childhood basketball teammate walked to me and told me that he made it to the National Basketball Association League (NBA), and I was so happy for him. By me being happy for him, it put a big smile on his face. Instead of being jealous of others, be happy for them because that is a great example of being Christ-like people.

BE PROUD TO BE MEN AND WOMEN OF GOD

My brothers and sisters, I just would like to tell you to be proud to be men and women of God. It feels good to be that way. There's nothing wrong being proud men and women of God; just don't forget who created you. I'm not talking about proud as being arrogant because God hates arrogance. I'm talking about proud as being confident and happy. Just like when you saw Jesus Christ in the Triumphal Entry, He was proud of who He was. He presented Himself as a king because

He is a king. My brothers and sisters, recognize that you are not only men and women of God, but also kings and queens. We are men and women of honor. God does not want us walking with our heads down. The world wants us to be in bondage. We have to refuse to be in bondage. We have a higher power helping us. We have a higher power guiding us. It is time for us to recognize who we are and the power that we have. Our Father created this world. Our Father created this universe. We have the right to be proud. Greet each other with love. Honor each other with respect. Let the world know that God raises great people. You see the worldly ones walk with their heads up high. Why can't we walk with our heads up high? So be it if they call us arrogant. So be it if they say we think that we are all that. You're right, we are all that, for God created us and brought us up right. God is worth more than houses, cars, and money. He has the richest throne in the universe. He rejoices when His people walk with authority. He breathes off of authority and honors Himself with love. My brothers and sisters, just be proud to be men and women of God for your Father is proud of creating and nourishing you.

BE SLOW TO ANGER

Good morning, my friends. I'm glad that Almighty God blesses you to see another day. He does everything in an amazing way. It lets you know that you are special to Him. I just want to remind you to be slow to anger. What do you gain by being angry? Satan wants you to get angry. He knows that if you get angry you are capable of sinning. That's why Almighty God says, "Be ye angry and sin not: let not the sun go down upon your wrath: Neither give place to the devil" (Ephesians 4:26–27). God knows that sometimes you are going to get angry. Being angry is not a sin, but He wants you to be careful so your anger doesn't cause you to sin. Many people out there in the world dwell in anger. They let the spirit of anger control them, but you don't have to be like them. Those are the ones who provoke you to get angry. Let God control your spirit. Always remember that "A soft answer turneth away wrath: but grievous words stir up anger" (Proverbs 15:1). My beloved brothers and sisters, don't cause anyone to get angry. If anyone tries to get you upset, just be polite to him or her. It lets your Heavenly Father know that you are slow to anger.

CALL ON GOD

God is the most wonderful force in the universe. His perfection surpasses everyone. His love is better than anyone. God is that friend you need to call on. His phone line is never busy. You can talk to God about anything. He will feel your pain. God knows everything about you. He knows what you are facing in life. God will help you make it through anything. His power is so unique. Take a look at the clouds; they are so wonderful. Take a look at the stars; they are tremendous. Now if God can create something so unique like that, what makes you think that He can't help you make it through life's challenges? Take time to meditate on God. Open up your mind and heart to God. Please don't let your mind be wavering. "The just shall live by faith" (Romans 1:17). To please God you've got to have faith. Trust me because sometimes I know it's hard to have faith, especially when you keep failing at something, but hold on to God because He won't leave you hanging. You have to be a puppet for God. When you are a puppet for God, He controls your life. When you are a puppet for Satan, the strings get tangled. My friends, just call on God because He will always answer your call.

CONTINUE TO DO GOOD

The children of God have a marvelous Father. They don't have to worry about anything. All they have to do is continue to do good. The Almighty God is good so He expects His children to be good. God doesn't discipline His children to be bad. He is the greatest role model in the universe. He controls everything. The children of God have to abide by God's commandments. Whenever He tells us to do something, we have to do it. He is our Heavenly Father so we have to respect Him. When we do good, it shows our Father that we obey Him. You can't be a knucklehead and expect to get blessed. You should want to do good for God is always watching. Impress God by helping others. Show Him that you are concerned about others. Some people just care about themselves. They don't have others on their minds. They don't care about others. How do you expect to get into the kingdom of heaven if you are selfish? God deals with people who care. He nourishes those who care. "Wherefore let them that suffer according to the will of God commit the keeping of their souls to him in well doing, as unto a faithful Creator" (1 Peter 4:19).

DO WHAT YOU HAVE TO DO FOR GOD

My brothers and sisters, I challenge you to do what you have to do for God. Don't worry about what God is going to do for you because He always does His part. Whatever you do for God, stay faithful to it. If you preach, sing, write, play drums, or dance, stay faithful to it. God is faithful to you, so you be faithful to Him. Whatever you do for God, do it with gladness. Don't hate to do it, but love to do it. God doesn't hate what He does for you. The God that we serve is awesome. He would do anything to please His children. Doing what you have to do for God is a great thing. It's a great thing because you are working for the greatest boss in the universe. When this boss rewards you, it is huge. My brothers and sisters, don't do what you have to do for God just for His rewards, but do it because you love Him. He is a God with high hopes for you. He is a God with many great wonders. God will not hassle or hinder you; He will encourage you so do what you have to do to honor Him.

DON'T BE ASHAMED

You say you serve a wonderful God, but why are you ashamed of Him? It wouldn't hurt you to tell other people about Him. You can talk about everything else, but when it comes to God, you stay silent. He is the greatest Father to talk about. I never had a boring conversation about God. I have fun when I talk about God. God gives you joy. He is an interesting God. There are too many fake people out there in the world. There are too many fake Christians out there. I'm just telling the truth. One minute you are for God, and the next minute you are mad at Him. Make up your mind about who you want to serve. You don't have that much time left. We are living in the last days. I'm talking about the people who serve God, but are ashamed of Him. Jesus said, "For whosoever shall be ashamed of me and my words, of him shall the Son of man be ashamed, when he shall come in his own glory, and in his Father's, and of the holy angels" (Luke 9:26). Talk about your Heavenly Father. Tell others how He has been blessing you. The more you talk about God, the more blessings He is going to send down. You should be happy to talk about God for He is a great master to serve, so don't be ashamed.

DON'T BE JEALOUS

Feel me on this. The same Spirit created us all, which is Almighty God. Why do some of us want to be jealous? The person that you are jealous of is no better than you. You never know, that person that you are jealous of can give you great advice. He or she can be a great blessing for you, but you chose to be jealous. Instead of being jealous of one another, why can't we use our gifts that God has given to us and help each other out? Be positive toward one another and not negative. God created us to love each other and not to be jealous of each other. Don't get me wrong, sometimes I'm a jealous person and have to get over my egotistical ways. God knows that we are not perfect, but we should help each other reach that point. It's okay that you don't have good looks like the next person. It's okay that you don't have a house or car more expensive than the next person. God still loves you. He loves all of us the same. My brothers and sisters, just continue to work hard and don't be jealous.

DON'T BE SELFISH

My brothers and sisters, whatever you do, don't be selfish with God. God is the one who wakes you up every day. He is the one that protects you from all of your enemies. He is the one that showers blessings down upon you. Promise God that you won't be selfish with him. Please God by serving Him, and by blessing others. Look at the beautiful children that God blesses you to have. Look at the nice home that God blesses you with. Look at your family members that God delivered and saved. My brothers and sisters, I'm talking about a

God that loves you no matter what you do. His loves is so extraordinary. My brothers and sisters, just feel me on this. When you were all alone, who was there for you? When you were sick, who was there for you? When you were hurt, who was there for you? It was the love of God. Give God thanks of appreciation. Praise God with joyfulness. Let God know how much you admire Him. It hurts me when someone speaks badly against God. That person needs to understand that God was the one that created him or her. That person needs to know that God is the one that truly loves him or her. Be compassionate toward God. Love, honor, and adore Him. He sent His Son to die for you. Selfish is not in His vocabulary for He is an unselfish God. My brothers and sisters, let us all bow down to God to let Him know that we are not going to be selfish and we respect Him.

DON'T FORGET ABOUT GOD

What's up, saints of God? What's going on? All the best things start to happen for you when you put your trust in the Lord. I know that was the best decision you have made in your life. I just have to remind you to not forget about God. All you have to do is keep God on your mind. Bless God by paying your tithes and offerings. Praise Him each day as you live. Tell more people about Him. Tell them how God made you into what you are today. I personally get so sick and tired of people who forget about God. All their life they cry and complain about not getting blessed, but once they get blessed, they forget about God. God just sits in heaven and shakes His head. There is no one that exists or has existed on this planet that is above God. There is no one who has more power or riches than He. It won't hurt you to open your Bible and read it. It won't hurt you to brag about God. God was the one who blessed you to be successful. My brothers and sisters, please don't forget about God.

DON'T GIVE UP

Hello, everyone, it's me again. Rejoice, for the Lord blesses you to see another day. I'm always doing great because the Lord is everywhere I go. Whatever you do, have faith in God and don't give up. Life is a challenge only the strong survive. Each day you are facing a new challenge. The children of God face a challenge every day because Satan is out there waiting for us. Satan is very evil, and he would do whatever it takes to destroy the children of God. That's why we have to be equipped with the armor of God. "Evil men understood not judgment: but they that seek the Lord understand all things" (Proverbs 28:5). Now, there are going to be people who are going to be against you. That comes with the territory of being a child of God. Look what happened to Jesus. He had stones thrown at Him (John 10:31–39). The Jews rejected Him. Continue to walk as children of the light. Show your Father that you do have faith in Him. When you do the right thing, you make Him feel proud. My friends, continue to walk boldly in the Lord and don't give up because you are a conqueror.

DON'T MESS WITH GOD'S INVESTMENT

This is for the people who act like they don't know. God is a tough God. He isn't afraid of anyone. Fearless is His nickname. He doesn't let anyone push over Him. To all of those who think that they are big and bad, try messing with God or His investment, and watch your results. It won't be a pretty sight. God's investment is His people. His people are bought with a price, which is through Jesus Christ, His remarkable Son and right-hand man. If you don't believe me, read the book of Exodus, 14:21–31. God took the Egyptians out for messing with His investment, the children of Israel. For those of you who act like they don't know who's God's investment, I'm going to tell you. It's that person you see loving his or her neighbor. It's those you see preach and teach the holy Word of God. Just to break it down, it's those who worship God in spirit and in truth. Don't mess with them. What you need to do is be a part of the investment. Turn from your wicked ways and ask God for forgiveness. Follow after Jesus Christ and grow in grace. Love, adore him, and tell your enemies don't mess with me because I'm God's investment, an investment you don't want to tamper with.

DON'T PLAY WITH GOD

Let me give you all a warning; don't play with God. God is nothing to play with. He is a force that can, and will, destroy you. Remember what he did to Aaron's sons, Nadab and Abihu. He devoured them with fire (Leviticus 10:1–2). I mean, God does not play. There are too many people in the world misleading others, but they are going to pay for it. Do you think that God is going to let you get away with misleading His children? I pity the fool who thinks that. God is not going to let the antichrist, false prophets, and the deceivers get away with anything. He is going to destroy them all. Instead of trying to play with God, let Him use you the way that you are supposed to be used. Let God control your life and mold you into a powerful soldier. Those who live in God are joint heirs with Christ. They are going to share the kingdom with Him. Those who think that God is a joke are going to suffer the fiery furnace forever. Do you want to be a part of the kingdom, or suffer in the fiery furnace? In the kingdom there is peace, love, happiness, joy, and eternal life. In the fiery furnace there is death and suffering. Those who are serious with God are going to inherit the kingdom so if you want to be a part of that, don't play with God because He is the ultimate judge, someone you should be afraid of.

DON'T SIT IN THE SEAT OF JUDGMENT

I know you hear that all the time. My brothers and sisters, don't do it. There is only one God. He is the one who judges all. When He judges, he does it fairly and righteously. That's our problem today; instead of minding our own businesses and living our lives, we intend to judge others. When you judge others, God will judge you by the same measure. My brothers and sisters, just live your life. God didn't put us down here to judge one another; He put us down here to help each other. You are judging that person because he or she may be on crack. That person that you are judging God can save, and that person can be a help to you. That person can join you in helping God save souls. Many of us try to be God. God doesn't need your help to be Him; He created you. All you have to do is what God tells you to do, and judging others is not one of His commandments. What you need to do is continue to read your Bible and help others get to know God. Each of us has a job to do, but it does not include judging others. You all know that I'm not talking about sitting in the courtroom, and that person sitting on the bench gives a verdict. I'm talking about when you judge someone for not living the way that you think that they should live. It is up to that person if they decide to live the wrong way or the right way. You just continue to do what you are doing for God. You just make sure that you are a faithful servant to God. The more you judge a person, the more they are going to continue to do what they are doing. My brothers and sisters, don't sit in the seat of judgment because God knows that you don't want anybody judging you.

DON'T WORRY

Why do you continue to put pressure on yourself? Why do you continue to stress yourself? Most of all, why do you continue to bug God about your future? God is saying don't worry. You worry about everything. You worry about when your husband or wife is going to come. You worry about whether you are going to make it. It is in God's blood for you to make it. God will not let you down. My saints and friends, you are going to make it. You are destined to make it. You are tough. God loves you because you have a never say die attitude. Just relax and allow God to work with you. He knows what you desire to do. He knows what you are hungry for. Just follow after Him and He will guide your steps. Don't be anxious, but be patient. God is at work. He's setting everything up for you. Once He places you there, you will be ready. So be glad and rejoice. Like my mother says, trouble doesn't last always. Don't put trouble on yourself. Don't stress your family. Continue to do what you are doing. Rely on God. Give all of your burdens to Him. I'm speaking to you straight from the heart. Ask God to bless you to get your mind, body, and soul right. Let God prepare you so you don't have to worry about anything. I get fearful, but I ask God to help me out on everything. It doesn't feel good walking around with worry on your heart. My brothers and sisters, give God everything, and don't take it back, for you will find yourself worry free for a successful and prosperous life.

FULL OF COMPASSION

It's wonderful when you are serving someone like the Almighty God. A Lord who blesses you every day. He shows everyone love except evildoers. God is full of compassion. When we sin, He forgives us. When we are alone, He is there to comfort us. I love everything about the Lord. He is an unselfish God. When He blesses me, He blesses my family. God is that pillow you lay your head upon. He is that fresh spring water that you drink. When His children are depressed, He gives them joy. God hears your every cry. He answers your every call. He has a remedy for every sickness. When you have a disease, He is your cure. As you are lying in the hospital bed, He is there to tell you to hold on. "He hath made his wonderful works to be remembered: the Lord is gracious and full of compassion" (Psalms 111:4).

GET WITH THE PROGRAM

God is an amazing God. He performs awesome miracles. I just desire to tell you all to get with the program. The program is serving God. Let God program your mind to serve Him. Once God programs your mind to serve Him you will have peace, which surpasses all understanding. My brothers and sisters, we are living in the last days, so get right with God. There are many deceivers out there in the world. There are many false prophets. You have to be careful of the ones who talk because they can mislead you. You have to read the Bible for yourself. You have to get to know God. God is not an evil God; He is a good God. He doesn't bring harm to anyone. He showers His children with love. Put all of your trust in Him. Let God train your mind to live in righteousness. He will not mislead you. God is the most powerful prophet in the universe. Everything He says comes to pass. Take heed to His voice. Follow His voice for He is leading you to the way of righteousness. Show God that you can endure until the end of time. Get with the program for you will see it will have a great and eternal reward for you.

GIVE GOD SOME TIME

Let me ask you a question. Why do so many Christians fail to give God some of their time? He is the one that provides you with time. God is the one that blesses you to have time to handle your business. You should give God some of your time. Give God some of your time by thanking Him for waking you up in the morning. Every morning I thank God for blessing me to see another day. It is He that wakes us up each day. While you are taking a break from your studies or from work, meditate on God. Talk to God; His ears are always ready for a conversation. You can talk to God about anything. He is a friend that understands. He is a friend that will give you His full attention. God will help you understand life because He is life. He will let you know why things happen. Don't just give God time when you are sad or feeling low. Give God some time while things are going well for you. Like I say, I want God to be a part of my everyday life. I want to live with God eternally. Continue to read your Bible and give God some time because He does hold the world in His hands.

GOD IS ALL THAT MATTERS

I'm just going to get right to the point. God is all that matters. It's not a bad thing to have on your mind. Those who are in God know that it's a good thing. God wants you to enjoy life. He wants you to be prosperous and successful, but He wants it to be by His way. God wants to guide your mind, body, and soul. He loves you and wants the best for you, but you have to realize that God is all that matters. Please don't think God is selfish, arrogant, and stuck on Himself because He is not. If God was stuck on Himself, He would not think about blessing you. Knowing that God is all that matters is for your benefit. He already knows that He is all that matters; that's why He's in heaven, a place that He also wants you to be. God created you to worship Him. He created you to praise and honor Him. Once you realize that you will see that it's fun praising God. Not the fun meaning to play with Him, but the fun meaning happy to do it because God is in your life. Acknowledge God by speaking to your heart through the spirit. Tell him that you love Him. Tell others about Him. Give yourself a pat on the back for walking that Christ-like walk, for you realize that God is all that matters and reap all the wonderful spiritual benefits of knowing that.

GOD IS AWESOME

Check this out, my brothers and sisters. God is awesome. Remember the way that He helps those who were in the Twin Towers to survive? Remember how He helped you get out of that abusive relationship? I'm talking about a God who builds His people with strength. The time that His children are on the verge of fainting He redeems them with strength. God is a tremendous God. He is the only true God. He makes sure His enemies feel His wrath. God builds His church on the basis of the fruit of the spirit, which is through His beloved Son Jesus Christ our Lord and Savior. If you don't believe me that God is awesome please do so now. God was the one that helped you get out of trouble. God was the one that helped you get a high school diploma, GED, and all those college degrees that you have on your wall. Recognize God for just the name that He has. By His name that should tell you that He's awesome. The *g* stands for great one. The *o* stands for omnipotent. The *d* stands for delightment. My brothers and sisters, give God the praises for He is the awesome force that made you in His image.

GOD IS GOING TO WORK IT OUT

Please stop whatever you are doing and relax. Stop pacing back and forth across your room, and please stop worrying your ministers, for God is going to work it out. Whatever you are going through, God is going to work it out. Do you think God is going to leave you in that situation that you are in? Do you think God is going to let that problem hinder you? My brothers and sisters, you belong to God. He will not let anything get the best of you. He's going to help you get that job you desire. He's going to help your children graduate from high school and college. He is going to help whatever family member or friend that you are worrying about get off drugs, alcohol, or cigarettes. Your bills are going to get paid. Your marriage is going to get restored. Your spirit is going to get fulfilled. If I were you, I would be rejoicing for God is going to work out everything, for working things out is part of His nature.

GOD IS MIGHTY

Many people don't understand God. God operates in ways that you can't imagine. He makes the weakest men the strongest, and the poorest men the richest. That's why I try not to question God because there is nothing too impossible for Him to do. God is mighty. He can appear in any form or anything that He chooses. He can appear in many different ways that you can't even imagine. He talked to Moses through a burning bush, and He saved Daniel from the lions' den. If I continue to tell you all the miraculous things that God has done, I would be writing the Bible all over. I'm talking about the God who rules the kingdom of heaven, and He is offering us an opportunity to dwell with Him. All of us should take His offer and meet the challenge because Satan is going to set a pit for us to fall in. The amazing part about serving the Lord is that He won't allow you to fall in the pit. Everyone should be ready to jump on the bandwagon to sojourn to heaven. God can just snap His fingers, and Satan can be destroyed. Satan knows His time is almost up. That's why he's trying his best to bring more people down with him. God loves everyone, and He blesses those who try their best to serve Him. He also keeps His promises. Just like when you see a rainbow, it is a reminder that God will keep His promise that He won't destroy the world with a flood again. God is the one who stops a hurricane from destroying your house. Why do I say God is mighty? Of all the evil things that go on in this world, it takes a mighty force to hold it up, but beware, all of you evildoers, because that mighty force is going to destroy you.

GOD IS WORTHY

Children of God, our Father is worthy to be praised. If it weren't for Him, we wouldn't exist. God is the one who has all the power. He created heaven and the earth. To Him we should give all glory and honor. His throne is in heaven where His Son Jesus Christ sits on the right-hand side of Him. God is able to conquer all things. He gave His children the power to conquer all things. He is always there to meet His children's needs. He is a great Father. If the people would only forget about themselves and stay focused on God the world would be a peaceful place. Our Father dwells in peace. He is peace. That's what He wants all of us to have. People, stop being selfish and bless the Lord. When you need a blessing, He blesses you, so why can't you bless Him? It's so sad the way people get caught up on themselves as if they run things. Everything belongs to God, and not man. God blessed you to be the boss at your job. He blessed you to be the CEO at a company, so don't forget about Him. God has the richest kingdom in the universe, and He loves all of us; therefore, you should worship Him for He is worthy.

GOD KNOWS HOW YOU ARE FEELING

How are you doing, my friends? I'm here to tell you that God knows how you are feeling. God is the searcher of hearts. He knows when you are happy or sad. He knows how you feel when you lose a loved one. He knows how you feel when you get a car. God knows how you feel when you graduate. He knows everything. Whatever you do, my friends, don't let anything drive you crazy. Give all of your worries to God. You can't do everything by yourself. God is a Father who is willing to help you. He will never neglect you. When you are down, He will be there to lift you up. When you are crying, He will be there to dry your tears. When you are lonely, He will be there to keep you company. Never think that God is not present because He is the first one, and the main source, that always knows how you are feeling.

GOD KNOWS WHAT'S BEST

Many people try to do things on their own. They just don't know that God will bless them with anything that their heart desires. God knows what's best for you. He was the one who created you, and if He created you, common sense should tell you that He knows what's best for you. God knows what kind of car your heart desires. He knows what kind of house your heart desires. He knows how much money your heart desires. God even knows what kind of spouse your heart desires. He knows everything about you. Just wait on God and He will provide you with all of those things. You have to work hard for everything that you want. You have to earn it. There are going to be trials and tribulations. It is up to you to stand tall doing the hard times. Everything is not going to be easy because Satan is going to ease his way on in, but you can't let him get the best of you. Once you keep your faith in God and hold on to Him he is going to bless you with everything according to His will. He is going to bless you to be successful and prosperous because He knows what's best for you.

GOD SEES THE LIGHT IN YOU

I know something that you don't know. God sees the light in you. Do you know why God sees the light in you? God sees the light in you because He is that light. God knows Himself and He loves Himself, and in God there is no darkness. Even if the sun never shines and the moon never rises, in God there still will be no darkness. Knowing that God's light shines, and it does shine, means that your light shines too because He lives in you. Do you understand where I'm coming from? God loves you so much that He is willing to live in you. Now *that* is something to shout about. Nothing can put out that light, and nothing can overtake that light which shines in you. That dynamic light feeds off of the Word of God. That dynamic light feeds off of love. That dynamic light feeds off of doing good. Everywhere you go, that light shines in you. Even when you die, that light is going to shine in you. Just like when Moses died the light was still shining in him. Rise up and know that God sees the light in you, and be happy for that light is greater than darkness.

GOD UNDERSTANDS

My brothers and sisters, don't be depressed about what you are going through and don't be down about your circumstances or situations because God is with you. He hasn't left you. God understands what you are going through. Just because you may not be at the place that you want to be at doesn't mean that God is angry with you. Don't get frustrated and don't be weary. God has a plan set out for you. I have felt the same way that you are feeling. God knows how you are feeling. He's saying your life is not over. He's not done with you. He understands how you feel. At this very moment, God is saying stop crying and complaining. He's saying that he has to prepare you. He understands that you may not be feeling good about yourself. He understands that you may feel guilty over what you have done. God does not hate you. He wants the best for you. Stop being hard on yourself. Love yourself and start back taking care of yourself. Open your heart to Christ and invite him in. I know you may feel that you disappointed Him and are afraid that you may do it again, but don't worry for He will be there to pick you up. I was in the same position that you are in. I felt like I let God down. I wouldn't forgive myself because I felt in my heart that I disappointed God. I felt as though I didn't deserve to be forgiven by God. Just know this that God understands what you are going through. He loves you, and He wants the best for you. He has not forgotten about you so what you need to do is talk to Christ Jesus, asking Him for His help so He can help you reach your destiny. Last but not least, stop feeling guilty and being hard on yourself. Don't speak negatively about yourself and get in a relationship with the Holy Trinity and remember that God always understands what you are going through.

HOLD YOUR HEAD UP

How are you doing, my wonderful saints and friends? It feels so good to serve the Almighty God. He is the one who uplifts our spirits. The Lord is good to all. I just want to tell you all to hold your head up. There should be no saint holding his or her head down. God loves all of us. His grace is upon all of His children. Whenever we slip, He will be there to pick us up. Whenever we fall into a pit, God will be there to get us out. Love God with your whole heart. Don't put anyone before Him. God will never leave or forsake you. He is with you even when you think He's not. Continue to walk boldly in faith. Remember that God is right by your side. Have faith in the Lord and know that you can't be brought down. Don't let the enemy come and take your joy. Don't let the enemy come and take your confidence. "No weapon that is formed against thee shall prosper" (Isaiah 54:17). God has given us the power to tread over the enemy. It is up to you to use it. Hold your head up high and let people know that you are more than a conqueror.

IT'S ALL ABOUT GOD

My friends, talk to yourselves and say it's all about God. God is the great one. He created you from the dust of the earth. He knows everything about you. God is the greatest craftsman in the universe. Look at the trees, the sky, the oceans, and the solar system. God created them all. When it comes to His children, He nurtures them. God doesn't leave His children weak. He gives them strength, knowledge, wisdom, love, joy, and peace. He blesses His children daily. He feeds the earth with His unique rain. God is an unselfish God. The earth cries out to God, and He shields it. He is the protector of us all. His blessings are everlasting. His love for us is everlasting. Whenever you get noticed by doing something marvelous, just remember, it's not about you; it's all about the Almighty and trustworthy God.

KEY TO SUCCESS

Everyone has a goal that they desire to accomplish. Sometimes we may refer to that goal as a dream and hope that someday it will come true. Every day we work hard to reach that goal. We all have the power to be successful. I'm writing to tell you that with God you can become successful because He is the key to success. God will be there to guide you through your struggles. "For this God is our God for ever and ever: he will be our guide even unto death" (Psalm 48:14). God will not lead you astray. He will be with you every step of the way for "The steps of a good man are ordered by the Lord: and he delighteth in his way" (Psalm 37:23). When you study for a test, He will be there to help you. When you train, He will be your coach. When you are at a job interview, He will be your confidence. God will be anything that you ask Him to be except evil. He just wants you to have faith in Him with your whole heart. God will open the door of opportunity for you to become successful, and that's why I say He is the key to success.

LET GOD DIRECT YOUR MIND

It's a beautiful day that Almighty God has created. He is a unique God. Always remember that God cares about you. My friends, let God direct your mind. All God wants to do is lead you the right way. He is making a way for you to get closer to Him. He doesn't make things hard for you. God makes things easier for you. God doesn't give you too much that you can't handle. It is up to you to stand tall in your tribulations. God is mightier than anything or anybody. The Greek gods don't stand a chance against Almighty God. "I will instruct thee and teach thee in the way which thou shalt go: I will guide thee with mine eye" (Psalm 32:8). God will be your favorite teacher if you would just pay attention to Him. Give God your full attention. In class you won't get bored because He will keep you smiling. God will shower you with joy. He will shower you with blessings. He is a great motivational speaker. God will show you things that you've never seen before. Keep pressing in the direction of God and you will become successful. Everywhere that you go, God will shine His light upon you. Others will recognize that there is something special about you. When God directs your mind, you will make the right decisions. When God directs your mind, you will make great decisions. He is a great guidance counselor, and that's why I say you should let Him direct your mind.

LIFT UP YOUR HANDS

We should all give praises to God for being in our lives. Look at all of the wonderful things that He does for us. He blessed us to be healthy and have clothes on our backs. He blessed us with shelter and transportation. God deserves all of the praises and blessings from us; therefore, we need to lift up our hands to Him. When it comes to His children, God does not hesitate to meet our every need. He knows what our hearts desire. As long as you bless God, He is going to continue to bless you. He is a loving God. Sometimes words can't describe how great He is. God is that tree that gives you shade when it's too hot outside. He is that friend who helps you study. God is that star that shines the brightest. He is that map that gives you guidance so you can head in the right direction. Don't take God for granted because He doesn't play any games. He is real, and a force that will blow you away. In everything that you do, acknowledge Him because He loves being the center of attention. He is the one that is going to help you make it to the top of the ladder, so lift up your hands unto the Alpha and Omega.

LIVE TO BLESS GOD

It's an awesome day that the Almighty God has created. It's takes an awesome king to create such an awesome day. My brothers and sisters, live to bless God. Why do I say live to bless God? Because He was kind enough to create you. He spent His precious time planning out how wonderful He wants you to be, and you know what a good job He did in creating you. He did not make any flaws creating you. The beautiful earth that you are living in He created it (Genesis 1). The beach that you are surfing at God created it. The solar system that you gaze at God created it. If I were you, I would be praising God. If I were you, I would be honoring Him. Look how beautiful God made your wife to be. Look how handsome God made your husband to be. Look how precious He made your children to be. Must I go on to tell you to live to bless God? He was the one who sent His beloved Son to die for you. He was the one who cured you from all of your infirmities. It would not hurt you to open your Bible and read it. Get closer to God and adore Him. Live to bless God all of you creatures here below and bless the Lord at all times for He is the one who smiles down upon you with joy.

LOVE ONE ANOTHER

Hello, everyone that's on this great planet that God created. God did a great job creating this planet. He has everything set in a remarkable way. I love God, and I thank God for creating such a beautiful planet. My friends, everything that God created on this planet He created out of love, so we should love one another. He created us out of love. God wants us to love each other and not hate. Forgive those who trespass against you. Love your enemies. It lets God know that you have a caring heart. It lets God know that you don't let hate control your heart. Those who have hate in your heart or an angry spirit take it to Jesus Christ and He will take it out of you. Jesus Christ doesn't want anyone walking around with hate in his or her heart. He searches everyone's hearts to make sure that they have love in it. Like I always say, I love Almighty God, and I thank Him for Jesus Christ for He is real, and His love is real. Where you find Jesus Christ you find love. Where there is a close family there is Jesus Christ. My brothers and sisters, show love toward each other for we are joint heirs of Christ, one big happy family. You might as well get used to loving one another and show love down here on earth because when you go to heaven you're not going to have a problem doing it. Love one another, my brothers and sisters, for it makes your Heavenly Father proud of creating you. It makes Jesus Christ smile because you are one of His joint heirs, and it fills Abraham with joy that you were one of the stars that God told him to look upon. Amen.

LOVE WHAT YOU DO FOR GOD

Please hear me, my brothers and sisters, love what you do for God. Loving what you do for God lets Him know that you appreciate Him. It lets Him know that you care about serving Him. It also lets God know that you are not ashamed of what you do. I don't care if it's mopping the floor, vacuuming the rugs, cleaning the windows, or painting; love what you do for God. When God sees that you love what you do for Him, He will increase your talent. He will let people see the great works that you do for Him. I know God just loves the ministers that do the works that He tells them to do. It lets God know that they are not disobedient. It lets God know that they love Him. The best part about it is that the ministers will tell you that they don't do it for the money and cars, but they do it because they love God. When God rewards those who love what they do for Him, don't hate because you see the sweat, tears, and the hard work that they put into it. Love what you do for God, embrace it, and be proud of what you do, for it lets God know that the works that you do for Him are remarkable in His and His Son's eyes. P.S. God does not hate what He does for you; He loves it.

LOVE YOURSELF

Let me ask you a question. How could you love someone if you don't love yourself? You've got to have love to give it. Many people today look for man to give them love instead of looking for love from the true source. When you love God, you love yourself for He is in you. Before you look to others to give you love, look to God. God loves you more than anybody. God loves you more than you love yourself. Treat yourself with kindness. Take a look at yourself in the mirror and say that you love yourself. If there is no one around to give you love, what are you going to do? That's why you've got to love yourself. It's not a guarantee that people are going to love you. Keep your eyes on God, and all His love will shine upon you. God loves you with a passion. No matter how many times you do wrong, He still loves you. Even when you put Him on a shelf He still loves you. God loves you regardless of what you do. Don't be selfish, people, put God first in your life. You came into this world by yourself, and you are going to leave by yourself. Shower yourself with love. Be happy about yourself. Be willing to love yourself. Always remember that Jesus loves you, and, yes, you know for the Bible tells all of us so. And on that note, my dear friends, as you wake up each day, give yourself a big hug and say that you love yourself.

MASTER OF THE UNIVERSE

Read this very carefully. Some people go from place to place not knowing who God is. Some people don't have God on their minds. There are people who've heard of Him, but refuse to get to know Him. There are people who know Him, but refuse to praise Him because they are upset with Him. I'm here to tell you all that God is the master of the universe. God created all things. He created the entire solar system. Man did not create anything. Satan did not create anything. These other gods that you all serve don't have any power to create anything. God is so magnificent. All He did was open His mouth and the earth was created. His throne is in heaven where He and His Son dwell. God keeps His eyes on the earth. He watches everyone's coming and going. God is the most powerful force in the universe. He can't be destroyed. When He speaks, mountains tremble. God doesn't want you to run away from Him. He wants you to praise and worship Him. God is not a monster. He is a loving and caring Father. It is amazing the way the stars, sun, moon, and the clouds obey Him. How many people that you know can control the universe? No one can control the universe, but Almighty God can, because He is the master of it.

MOVE SWIFTLY

Hurry, get up, and move before you miss your blessings! My brothers and sisters, you have to move swiftly for God. When God tells you to feed the poor, go do it. It pleases God when His children do something for the poor. God is not a slow mover, and He doesn't want His children to be slow movers. As soon as you blink your eyes, God has blessed you with a car, a spouse, a house, children, and riches. It just sickens me when people say that God is slow. The truth is that they are not patient to wait on Him. Just like you want your blessings to be fast, God wants you to move fast for Him. God has all of your blessings in His hands. When it comes to blessing you, He is not going to close His hands because you are obedient to Him. Prove to God that you are willing to serve Him. Show God that you are a faithful servant and believe me, He is going to test you. He is going to challenge you to see if you truly love Him. Move swiftly for God. Honor, trust, and adore Him for He is the holy king. When you stand firm for God, it impresses Him. It makes Him feel good when you praise Him. I love God because of the many praises that He receives. He doesn't brag, boast, or get arrogant. He is a force that is worthy to be honored, so move swiftly for God so He can cherish you.

OBEY THE LORD

It's true the Lord is good to all. He is an amazing force. God is the epitome of perfection, and that's why you need to obey Him. If you are hearing that God is perfect, you should be willing to serve Him. God wants you to obey Him so you can live eternally with Him. He is not trying to take your fun away. He just wants you to abide with Him. When you obey the Lord, your spirit is free. When you obey the Lord, He will grant you anything that you need. Just ask Him, and you will receive it. God is not selfish. Believe me, He will bless you. Let your mind and heart dwell with God. That is the best feeling that you can ever have. God is your guide to eternal happiness. I know that you are getting sick and tired of worrying about paying bills, feeling pain, and getting hurt. Put your life in God's hands. Trust me, you won't be disappointed. That would be the best decision that you will make in your life. You would not only be successful on earth, but you would also be successful in heaven, and that is the greatest reward that you can ever receive, so obey the Lord for He is the top God.

PLEASE GOD

How are you doing, my brothers and sisters? I'm doing great. I just want to recommend that you live to please God. God is the one who watches everything. He watches your every going. God knows that it's hard trying not to sin because we are living in a world of sin. That's why through Jesus Christ He has given us grace and mercy. God is a merciful king. He is a God of comfort. Please God by trusting in Him. He won't mislead you. He won't break your heart. He is a force that does marvelous works. Please God by opening your heart to others. It lets Him know that you care about your neighbors. The more you open your heart to others the more your blessings come down. Love God with your whole heart. Let God take full control of your life. When God is in control, nothing can stop you from reaching your destiny. Live to please God for it shows that you are willing to go and stay on the right path.

PUT GOD FIRST

Let me ask you a question. Does God come first in your life? If He doesn't, it's time for you to put Him first. God doesn't like being second, third, fourth, or fifth. He likes being first. God is a jealous God. He said don't put anything before Him. He has the right to be jealous because He created you, and you have the nerve to put something, anything, before Him. You put your house before God, your car, and your job before Him. He is the one who made the way for you to get those things. When you put God first, watch how many blessings pour down on you. Whatever you do, acknowledge the Lord. Let Him know that you appreciate Him. Don't take Him for granted. Keep your mind focused on Him. Open up your heart to Him. God is the richest source in the universe. He can provide you with anything that you want. All you have to do is obey His commandments. God is not a monster. He won't do anything to hurt or harm you. My friends, just put God first in your life, and keep Him first.

RECOGNIZE GOD

It's pathetic how people cry when they don't receive any attention. Some people actually think that the world revolves around them. Well, I'm going to give you all a reality check. The world doesn't revolve around you. It revolves around the Almighty God. Everyone needs to recognize God. How do you think the solar system operates? How do you think it rains? How do you think the days change? It all happens because of Almighty God. "Be still, and know that I am God" (Psalm 46:10). It was God who created the earth. It was God who created the solar system. God is perfect in everything that He does. God doesn't make any mistakes. Many try to figure Him out but don't get anywhere. He can't be figured out. Just continue to ask God for more wisdom and understanding. Anything that you want to know, God will tell you. He is a faithful and just Father. God will leave you amazed by the works that He does. He is an awesome God. Who helped you get out of tough situations? Who helped you pass that class that was giving you problems? Almighty God did. People, just recognize God and may peace be with you.

REFUSE TO BE ABUSED

Listen to me very carefully, my brothers and sisters, refuse to be abused. I'm speaking to you with an open heart. Refuse to let anyone mentally abuse you or physically abuse you. When someone does this, it's not love. You hear women say, "He beat me because he loves me." That is a lie. Don't let any man lay his hand upon you. True love is godly love. If someone loves you, he or she will not abuse you, physically or mentally. There are many people who are in bondage over someone mentally abusing him or her. They are afraid to step out in faith due to this abuse. Someone may have told them that they are not going to amount to anything. Someone may have constantly cursed them out. I don't care if it's your parents, schoolteacher, or spouse; don't let anyone mentally abuse you. Moreover, don't let anyone spiritually abuse you. I hate when people get spiritually abused. Don't let any one steal your peace, joy, happiness, kindness, hope, patience, and love from you. They are spiritually robbing you. My brothers and sisters, stick to Jesus Christ. He will never do those things to you. He will not mentally, physically, or spiritually abuse you. He gives you that real-deal love, the type of love that you don't have to beg for. My brothers and sisters, refuse to be abused for abuse is the fuse of lifelong fear and bondage.

SHARE YOUR GIFT

It's wonderful when you have good health. When you have the ability to move around. The strength to endure things. Almighty God anoints you to have those things. As your brother, I'm asking you to share your gifts that God granted you. If Almighty God granted you the gift to sing, you should sing. If He granted you the gift to write, you should write. If He granted you the gift to preach, you should preach. You will be surprised about how many lives you will touch with your gift. When God grants you something, He wants you to use it. When God grants you something, He doesn't make any mistakes. He is sharing His power with you. Now if God can share His power with you, you can share your gift with others. It's not like your gift can't be taken away from you. God granted you that gift, and He expects you to share it. It's not all about you. It's all about God. God does not want you to be selfish. He wants you to be like Him, so be generous and share your gift.

SHOW GOD LOVE

What's going on, my brothers and sisters? How are you all doing? I'm doing just fine. I just want to tell you all to show God love. He shows you love. God takes great care of those who show Him love. He preserves those who love Him. When you feel like nothing is going to happen for you, just hold on and know that God is going to make a way for you. All God wants you to do is keep believing in Him. It is for your own good. God will bless you with anything that your heart desires. He will help you climb that mountain all the way to the top. Pursue His kingdom and everything shall be added unto you. God doesn't deal with unbelievers; He deals with believers. Give God the glory each day when you are awake. Praise God for blessing you to be a beautiful creature. Everything that God created is beautiful. He doesn't dwell with ugliness. He is a God of great kindness. He is a God with everlasting love. Show God love; besides, He shows you love.

SPEAK POSITIVELY

The journey of life would be much easier if we spoke positively to each other and ourselves. There are many people today speaking negatively to each other. Why do we speak negatively? Is the God that created us negative? He is nowhere near negative. I recall that in Genesis chapter one God Almighty said everything that He created was good. God did not speak negatively about what He created. Why can't we be the same way? Why can't we speak positively like God does? He wants us to speak positively. The journey is hard enough for us, but we make it even harder when we speak negatively toward each other. Don't pour negative in your sisters' and brothers' spirits; pour positively. God wants each and every last one of us to speak positively to each other. With all the evil that's going on in this world we all need to fight against it. Nothing is going to change unless we change. Speak positively, live positively, and be positive, for the world that God created is awesome, but it can be even more spectacular if everyone dwelling in it would just love one another.

STAY HAPPY

Some people think just because they are unhappy that you are supposed to be unhappy. They will try their best to make you feel the same way. My brothers and sisters, don't feed into that. Continue to stay happy. God blessed you with your happiness. Don't let anything or anyone take it away from you. He is an awesome God. Every place that you go, let your light shine. Don't worry about what people might say to you. You have something that they don't understand. You have something that they are searching for. They just don't know what trials and tribulations that you go through. People are always quick to judge and assume things for the worst, but don't let that get you down. You just keep seeking after God's righteousness. No one has a place to put you at when you die. Serve God with hope. Serve God for He is worthy to be praised. If God blesses you with happiness, why should you worry about what people say about you? If they don't care about being happy, so what? You just continue to stay happy, for your Heavenly Father granted you your happiness.

STAY IN TOUCH WITH GOD

It is so tremendous to have the great and Almighty God in your life. There is nothing better than to have Him in your life. My brothers and sisters, if you have God in your life, make sure you stay in touch with Him. You stay in touch with Him by reading your Bible. You stay in touch with Him by praying. You stay in touch with Him by going to church, Bible class, and by watching Gospel shows on television. For those of you who don't have God in your life, get Him into your life. He is not hard to find. Believe me or not, He is right there with you. He is a God that loves you and will love you better than anyone or anything else. He is a God that is full of compassion. He is a God that is right there with you when you are hurt. He is a God that is right there with you when you fall. Once you get Him into your life stay in touch with Him. My brothers and sisters, you can't breathe without God, and you can't survive without Him so be glad that you accepted Him into your life and make sure you stay in touch with Him.

THE GENERATOR OF MOTIVATION

God is the generator of motivation. He blesses all of His children with confidence. If we are weak, He blesses us to be strong. A strong mind is more powerful than a strong body. God gives us the willpower to make it through any trial or tribulation. He gives us the extra push to make it to the top. "In my distress I cried unto the Lord, and he heard me" (Psalm 120:1). God will hear your every cry. He will never forsake you. He loves all of us. Never lose sight of God. You can't make it through life without Him. God is not here to put harm on you. He just wants you to serve Him. When you start serving God watch how all your blessings come in. God will protect you from any hurt, harm, or danger. Look at the way that God gave Samson the motivation to defeat the Philistines (Judges 15:9–15). Look at the way that God gave David the motivation to defeat Goliath (1 Samuel 17). God will help you pass any test. He will help you triumph over anything, and that's why I say He is the generator of motivation.

THE REAL DEAL

Please let me have your attention. I just have to tell you who the real deal is. The real deal is the Almighty God. He is a mighty force that doesn't leave evil standing. He doesn't play any games. When God tells you to do something, do it because He doesn't like slow movers. The more you obey God, the more blessings you are going to receive. He is a God that gives you hope. He is a God that makes your dreams come true. God causes the sun and the stars to shine. He causes your car to keep moving when you are about to run out of gas. When a storm approaches, He causes it to pass over your home. God can do everything. All you have to do is believe in Him. He drives away evil like a hurricane rushes through a city. God is the one who blesses you to be healthy. He is the one who helps you move around.

Take heed of what I'm saying because God is the real deal, the creator of Evander Holyfield.

THE TRUE VISIONARY

Who is the true visionary? Almighty God is the true visionary. He sees and knows what's going to happen in the future. God knows what you are going to do before you do it. He knows what you are going to say. That's why you have to be careful of what you do or say. God has a vision for all of us. His vision is a great vision. God has the best things waiting for us. We have to seek after His kingdom to receive those things. God has high hopes for all of us. He has a place for each of us in His kingdom. Those who serve the Lord continue to serve Him. He is going to especially bless you. For all of the other people, turn aside from those false gods that you serve and get to know the true Almighty God. He has so many blessings in store for you. "Trust in the Lord with all thine heart; and lean not unto thine own understanding" (Proverbs 3:5). Once you do that watch how God shows you His vision, for He is the true visionary who sees everything.

THERE IS A GOD

I know that things get hard for you sometimes. I know that things get bad for you, but don't worry, for there is a God. This God who I'm talking about is not a small God. He is a huge God. He is there with you during your good times and bad times. He lives inside of you. He is with you as you are reading this book. Whatever you do, don't stop reading the Bible. The Bible is your guide to life and through life. The Bible guides you to life, which is Jesus Christ. The Bible guides you through life that is on earth. It also tells you about more life, which is living eternally with God. Understand this, my brothers and sisters, the Bible is good for you. Don't be afraid to open it. Don't be afraid to believe in God. As you read the Bible, you will hear God's voice. God will speak to you. He will guide you through each situation that you face. He will make your life easier for you. God will tell you who to hang around and who not to hang around. God is all about your safety and well-being. He will open doors for you that no man can. All God is asking you to do is seek after His kingdom. Now don't get me wrong, seeking after His kingdom is not easy because you have a coward out there that is trying to destroy you, and his name is Satan, a fallen angel. God doesn't want you to fear Him for He gave you the power to defeat Satan. Live your life with God. He will reveal His Son Jesus Christ to you and the Holy Spirit. They are the Holy Trinity, the best relationship to have. Just follow the lead of God and you will not only have a prosperous future in this lifetime, but also in the afterlife, where there will be no more pain and suffering.

YOU ARE NOTHING WITHOUT GOD

Dear brothers and sisters, I just want to remind you that you are nothing without God Almighty. God Almighty was the one who created you (Genesis 1:26–27). God Almighty created you in His image and His Son's. God Almighty is the reason for your existence. You walk around this earth like you are God. You think just because you are rich that you are better than everyone else. That money that you are flaunting God created it. That car you are driving God made. What gives you the right to turn your nose up at people? You are nothing without God. God put that breath in your body. God blessed you to have a good reputation. How would you feel if God allowed all that to be taken away from you? Because of your arrogance you fall. Because of your pride you forgot who the one was who helped you reach the top. Ask God for His forgiveness. Thank Him for finding you. Thank Him for understanding you when nobody else could. Last, but not least, tell God that you are nothing without Him, and by you acknowledging that, watch how the great and mighty God increases every area in your life, for you just came back to your senses and realized that God is the truth.

YOU ARE SOMEBODY

Just to remind you, my wonderful saints and friends, God shows up whenever He decides too. When He shows up, it is amazing. He is awesome in everything that He does. My friends, don't put God on a shelf for anything. When someone tries to bring you down, just know you are somebody. You are somebody because God is your Father. Don't let anyone walk all over you. Don't let anyone control your life. You women are queens, and you men are kings. We all know who the ultimate King is and that's Almighty God. My friends, "Ye are the light of the world" (Matthew 5:14). Don't let anyone put your light out. Pray for those who are jealous of you. Continue to love God and watch how many moves He makes for you. Keep your head up and walk toward the King. As you walk toward the holy King, there will be some interference, but keep moving on because the Lord is a strong tower. "Let your light so shine before men, that they may see your good works, and glorify your Father which is in heaven" (Matthew 5:16). And on that note, my spiritual friends, you are all somebody.

YOU CAN'T LIVE TWO WAYS

Open up your mind to these pages that you are about to read. It is important that you take it in. There is only one God, and He dwells in heaven. You have to serve Him willfully, and remember, you can't live two ways. You can't serve God and Satan at the same time. You have to love one and hate the other, or despise one and serve the other. I want you all to serve God and hate Satan. I want you all to love God and despise Satan. You can't go to the strip club and the next day attend church. Going to the strip club is not serving God. You can't preach the Word of God and have curse words coming out of your mouth the minute you stop talking about God. God's words are pure not filthy. Don't think that you are going to make it to the kingdom of heaven by serving both of them; you would be fooling yourself. God is going to be in heaven, not Satan. Be careful about the music that you listen to. You can't listen to Gospel, and the next minute you listen to gangster rap music or sex music. That is being unequally yoked. There is only one way to make it to God, and that is through Jesus Christ. Jesus didn't live two ways. Jesus didn't serve two masters; He served one, and that was the Almighty God, so get your life together and know that you can't live two ways.

YOU CAN'T OUTPOWER GOD

How are you doing, my brothers and sisters? God is a righteous force. One thing you can't do is outpower Him. How are you going to outpower a force that created you? He knows everything about you. God knows your next move in life. You can't figure God out, but He can figure you out. He is smooth in everything that He does. The heavens praise Him, and hell fears Him. I'm talking about the God who shakes the whole world when He speaks. I'm talking about the God who makes demons tremble. He doesn't play any games. God is a smooth operator. Remember the way that He eased His way into the fiery furnace to protect the Hebrew boys? I mean He is awesome. He outpowers everything and everybody. He is the Lord of Hosts. I love Him and will do anything for Him. "God, you are a mighty force. We know that you have all the power to conquer over our enemies. God, you are our Father, and we know that nothing can outpower you, for you are the creator of power."

YOU CAN'T USE GOD

What's up, my brothers and sisters? What's going on? God is a trustworthy God. When you need Him, He is always there. He is there even when you think He's not. You are not the only person in the world. Just like you need help from God, other people also need His help. I'm just here to remind you that you can't use God. Many people try to use God to get what they want. They say they love God, but don't really mean it. In church, they put on an act as if they are praising God. "Wherefore the Lord said, Forasmuch this people draw near me with their mouth, and with their lips do honour me, but have removed their heart far from me, and their fear toward me is taught by the precept of men" (Isaiah 29:13). Do these people think God is stupid? God knows everyone's intention. He knows if you are doing things from your heart, or doing things to uplift yourself. God knows what you are going to do before you do it. Instead of trying to use God, have faith and believe in Him. God always keeps His promises. You think God is not going to bless you? What do you take God as? He owns everything. He is the richest force in the universe. He is not selfish as you all are. Everything He does is for good. "And it shall come to pass, if thou shalt hearken diligently unto the voice of the Lord thy God, to observe and to do all his commandments which I command thee this day, that the Lord thy God will set thee on high above all nations of the earth" (Deuteronomy 28:1). Hearken unto the Lord's commandments and remember, you can't use Him.

YOU DON'T GIVE GOD ORDERS

First of all, who do you think you are to try to give God orders or try to tell Him what to do? God is not your servant; you are His servant. He called you to serve Him, and not Him to serve you. If you don't want to serve God, fine. God has plenty of people that desire to serve Him. You are the one that will be missing out on the riches of God. Do you think God is going to cry if you stop serving Him? God is full of joy and happiness. Surely, God loves you and surely God cares for you, but He's not going to stop living because you stop serving Him. God doesn't need to be delivered. God doesn't need to be healed. God doesn't need Jesus Christ to make it to heaven. *You* need those wonderful things. You need Jesus Christ. You need deliverance. You need healing. You ask God to work things out for you, and help you, and you ask God to bless you, but don't tell Him what to do, and don't give Him orders. He is the one that is sitting on the throne of heaven. He is the one that has wonderful and majestic angels worshipping Him. He is the one that appointed you to serve Him. So what you need to do is relax, serve God with joy, and get ready to receive your inheritance when you depart from this wonderful place.

YOU JUST DON'T KNOW

Every day you should give thanks to God for He blesses you to see another day. He is the most loving spirit in the universe. You just don't know how special you are to God. He talks about you all the time. God tells His holy heavenly angels how faithful you are. He also tells His Son who sits on the right-hand side on the throne how unique you are. You just don't know that God has already prepared a place for you, and it is so tremendous. God loves you in a special way. He loves you more than you love yourself. He appreciates the way that you share your gifts. It lets Him know that you are using your gifts. You just don't know how precious you are to God. He shields and protects you every day from your enemies. He comforts you every day. Tell God how much you love Him. He loves to hear it. Shower God with love. Spread His name with joyfulness. Our Father is so gentle. Even when we act like a fool, He nourishes us because He knows how we are. He knew how we were before He placed us on this planet. You just don't realize that God is a true provider so continue to stay focused on Him because He is a great Father.

CHAPTER **2**

ALLOW HIM TO SPEAK

A TRUE COACH

God is a true coach. He is a magnificent coach. He is training His people to fight against Satan and his demonic followers. He is coaching His people to stay motivated in the Bible. All they have to do is follow His teachings and stick to His teachings. God is a winner, and He is coaching His people to be winners. He does not train them to be losers. He trains them to be winners. God tells His people that they are more than conquerors. He tells His people that they can move mountains. He tells them that they can overcome obstacles, that they can do all things through Christ which strengthens them (Philippians 4:13).

God is the supreme coach. He is who Jesus Christ looks up to. He coached Jesus Christ to defeat Satan and the kingdom of darkness. He coached Jesus Christ to defeat death. He coached Jesus Christ on up to His heavenly victory. God also coached Moses to lead the Israelites out of the land of Egypt. He coached David to defeat Goliath. Should I go on? God coached His heavenly angels to cast the fallen angels (the angels that rebelled against God) out of heaven into hell.

Do you see what I'm talking about? Do you know what I'm talking about? God is a coach that always has a plan. He is a coach that never loses. He is a coach that always prevails. He never fails. Continue to listen to Him and follow His teachings and I assure you that you will come out on top. God is a true coach that empowers His team to success.

A TRUE INSPIRATION

In life we have things that inspire us. The one who inspires me is God because He is a true inspiration. Everything that God does is positive. Everything that He does is good. Everything that He does is righteous. God inspires me to do the right things in life. He inspires me to do what is good. God is the definition of good. He is the God of goodness.

God never belittles me. He never calls me a loser. He never says that I would not be successful. He always pushes me to the next level. He helps me climb the ladder to success. God never hates on me. He never pushes me down. He always tells me that I'm going to make it.

When I'm down, God is there to uplift me. He knows when I am down. He knows when I am feeling happy or feeling sad. God is always there to motivate me. He is always there to encourage me. He lets me know that I am somebody. He lets me know that I am doing good and He's proud of me. Every day God tells me that He loves me. He showers me with His love. I love Him, and I am going to continue to love Him because He is a true inspiration.

BE CAUGHT UP

If you can be caught up on everything else, why can't you be caught up on God? You be caught up on watching television, playing sports, and going to work. Be caught up on God. He cares about you more than anyone or anything. He is the one who truly cares about you. He gave you those eyes that you are watching television with. He gave you those limbs that you are using to play sports and go to work with. It is selfish that you are not acknowledging Him.

What would happen if those things would be taken away from you? You would be trying to get in touch with Him then. God does not want anything to happen to you. He created you for His pleasure. He wants to spend time with you, but you have to be willing to spend time with Him. God is not going to beg you to spend time with Him. He loves you, but He's not going to beg you. You should be eager to be caught up in Him.

Be caught up on God to be cool with Him. Be caught up on God to be spiritual like Him. If you lack wisdom, He will grant it to you (James 1:5). Anything that you ask, according to His will He will grant it to you. Love God, my brothers and sisters. Admire Him. Be caught up on Him and He will never forget about you.

BE THANKFUL

Sometimes some of us complain too much. God blesses us with whatever our hearts desire, and we still complain. God loves us, and He will do anything for us according to His will.

First of all, we need to be thankful that God created us. God did not have to do it, but He did. He saw fit to put His living breath in us to make us exist. God put us on this beautiful planet which He created. He put us on this planet to enjoy His creation. He did not put us on this planet to fight among ourselves, but to enjoy ourselves.

Moreover, be thankful that God loves you. He loves you more than anybody does. He created you to love you. He created you for Himself. God will not do anything to corrupt you. He will not do anything to hinder you. That is not His doing. Why would He want to do anything to hurt you when He loves you? It is impossible for God to hate you. He will never hate you, so stop lying to yourself saying that God hates you.

My brothers and sisters, God loves you with all of His heart. There is nothing that will make God stop loving you. Be thankful to God for He loves you. Be thankful to God for creating you. He could have spent His precious time doing something else, but instead, He thought about you. Most of all, be thankful to God because He sent His only begotten Son down here on earth to die for your sins and set you free.

BE TRUTHFUL

Here is something I know that you would agree with me, that in this world there are too many liars. If you are a liar, stop being one. God does not want you to be a liar. He wants you to be honest. He wants you to be truthful.

First of all, you have to be truthful to yourself. If you are not going to be truthful to yourself, you are not going to be truthful to others, including God. God does not communicate with liars. I know that I don't. How are you going to be truthful to others when you are not truthful to yourself? You can't. It's impossible. That is why you have to be truthful to yourself, and then you can be truthful to others.

"God is a Spirit: and they that worship him must worship him in spirit and in truth" (John 4:24). Notice Jesus Christ did not say in spirit and in lies. He said in spirit and in truth. Jesus Christ is telling you to be truthful. That is the way you communicate with God, in spirit and in truth. That is the source of being truthful. When you pray, you are in the spirit, and you must tell the truth. You have to be honest with yourself and God. Notice I did not say honest just to God. I also said you have to be honest with yourself. It takes two to be under agreement.

Let the truth be told. Many people are in the grave and behind bars for telling lies. A lie can not cover up a lie and be successful. It takes truth to deliver you from lying. God does not want you to end up in jail, in the grave, or worse—going to hell due to lying. Don't let the spirit of lying and deception control or overtake you. Be truthful to God, yourself, and others, because no one likes a liar.

BE WHAT GOD CREATED YOU TO BE

If God created you to be a man, be a man. If God created you to be a woman, be a woman. God did not create a man to be a woman. God did not create a woman to be a man. You have men walking around like they're women. And you have women walking around like they're men. I'm proud to be who I am, and that is a man. If God would have created me to be a woman, I'd be proud. Anything that God would have created me to be I'd be proud. God did not make any mistakes when He created us. Everything that He made is good (Genesis 1:31).

God made man for woman and woman for man (Genesis 2:22–25). He did not make man for man, and woman for woman. The world and sin are trying to make man for man, and woman for woman, but that is wrong. Anything that is ungodly is wrong.

Pray and ask God to help you to be the man or woman that you need to be. Tell God that you do not want to be like the world. The world is sinful. The world will try to set you in a trap. Don't allow the world to set you in a trap. Be who you are, and be proud of who you are because that is what God created you to be.

BELONG

Let me straighten you out. You belong to God. You don't belong to anyone but God. You don't belong to yourself. You don't even belong to your parents. Your parents may have brought you into this world. Your parents may have done a great job raising you, but you still belong to God. It is your parents' duty to raise you. That is the commandment that God gave to your parents.

What did Jesus tell Joseph and Mary? He told Joseph and Mary that He belongs to God. He told them that He was about His Father's (God) business (Luke 2:49). He knows whom He belongs to. He knows that God created Him. God created you, so what makes you think that you don't belong to Him? God knew you before He put you in your mother's womb (Jeremiah 1:5). He knows everything about you (Psalm 139).

God created you for Himself. He created you for His pleasure. He did not create you to walk after your own lust. What does it say in Psalm 37:23? It says that the Lord orders the steps of a good man: and he delighted in His way. He or she is delighted not in his or her way, but in God's way. God is the one who delights. He is the one who guides and empowers you. God gives you the power to empower yourself. That power that you have belongs to God.

My brothers and sisters, believe what I'm telling you. It is a good thing that you belong to God. I'd rather belong to God than to belong to anyone or anything else. God does not abuse people. He doesn't make people look bad on the inside. He beautifies the inside. I'd rather belong to God than to belong to drugs. Most of all, I'd rather belong to God than to belong to Satan. Satan doesn't care about you. He hates you, so be glad that you belong to God because He made no mistake when He created a beautiful human being like you. Remember that you are made in God's image (Genesis 1:27).

BUILD YOUR SPIRIT

Build your spirit. And how do you build your spirit? You build your spirit by reading the Bible, praying, and going to church. When you read the Bible, God speaks to you. His words come inside of you. His words strengthen you and your spirit. Without reading God's Word, the Bible, your spirit is not going to get build up. You have to read the Bible. The Bible is what wakens your spirit. The Bible is what enlightens your spirit. It gives your spirit life.

Praying is very important. It shows that you care about yourself. Praying shows that you care about your spirit. You communicate with God through prayer. And as you communicate with God through prayer, it builds your spirit because His spirit is connecting with your spirit. And when your spirit connects with the Spirit of God, it has no choice but to get strengthened. God's Spirit does not weaken your spirit; it builds and strengthens it. God's Spirit is not weak but powerful. That is the power of prayer, and it will build your spirit.

Moreover, going to church builds your spirit because it is a place where the presence of the Lord is felt. God wants you to go to church so He can work on and build your spirit. It is a place where your spirit gets revived. Going to church is what keeps your spirit alive. It helps you endure through your trials and tribulations. It keeps your spirit built. During the week, someone may upset or anger you. The church is where you go to praise and shake it off. And as your spirit gets built by going to church, that person that angered you can't get to you anymore, because your spirit is built up and has matured.

People, you have to build your spirit. If you don't build your spirit, what will happen to it? It will die. It is your duty to keep your spirit alive. It is your duty to keep your spirit running and going, so read the Bible, pray, and go to church.

CLEAVE

My brothers, cleave unto your own wives. My sisters, cleave unto your own husbands. There are too many men trying to take other men's wives. There are too many women trying to take other women's husbands. God is saying stick to your own. If you are not satisfied with your spouse, get a divorce. Don't try to take another person's spouse simply because you are not satisfied with yours. That is why you can not be quick to get married. Get to know someone before you marry him or her.

When you get married, there are commandments you have to follow. You have to cleave unto your own husband or wife. You can not commit adultery. Committing adultery is breaking one of God's commandments (Exodus 20:14). God does not want you to do that.

Marriage is honorable to God (Hebrews 13:4). God respects marriage. That is why He gave us the gift of sex for marriage. He does not want us to have sex until marriage. That is why it's not a sin to have sex when you are married. He gives you the freedom to have sex when you are married.

Learn to love your spouse and to respect your spouse. Don't try to take someone's spouse. It is not good. It is not right to try to take another person's spouse. Husbands, cleave unto your own wives, and wives, cleave unto your own husbands because God respects and honors that (Colossians 3:18–19).

COME INTO THE LIGHT

My friends, come into the light. Don't be afraid to come into the light. The light is beautiful. The light is powerful, and better yet, God is the light.

People always refer to the light as death. They always say when you see the light you are on your way to death. They always say if you see the light, avoid it. Don't go into it. Well, I'm here to tell you the light is where you *want* to be. The light is where you want to spend your life, for it is life. There is nothing fearful about the light. There is nothing horrific about the light. It is where your protection lies. It is where your blessings lie. It is where your prosperity and success lie. Everything you need and desire is in the light.

God wants you to come into the light. He wants you to relax and chill in the light, for there is peace. In the light there is freedom. Your spirit is free. Your spirit is alive. There is nothing dull about the light. There is nothing dead about the light, for God is not dead. He is surely and positively alive. My brothers and sisters, come into the light and take pleasure in the joy it gives.

P.S. God's light never blows out.

COME OUT OF YOUR SHELL

Knock. Knock. Knock. It's me, Demetrice, telling you to come out of your shell. How long are you going to remain in there? Are you enjoying yourself in there? Are you having fun in there? Why are you closing yourself in? There is a big world out there, so come out of the shell and enjoy it.

God did not create the world just so you would stay in a shell. He created the world for you to enjoy. God wants you to enjoy His creation, but you can not enjoy it if you remain in a shell. There is nothing in a shell but darkness. Ask a turtle, and if he or she could talk, he would tell you. What happens when a turtle comes out of the shell? It crawls; it walks; travels; and lives freely. That is the way the Heavenly Father wants you to be. He wants you to live freely. He wants you to travel and go to places.

You could not stop Jesus Christ from traveling and enjoying Himself. He traveled 24/7. On land and water He traveled. Jesus Christ was not in a shell. He did not put Himself in a shell, and He does not want you to put yourself in a shell. He wants you to smell the fresh air. He wants you to smell the lilies of the valley. He does not want you to be in darkness.

My cool brothers and sisters, God does not want you just to work and not play. He wants you to work *and* play. He wants you to reward yourself by doing such a wonderful job. Don't you deserve to reward yourself? Yes, you do. You can not reward yourself in a shell. God has so many blessings for you, but you want to remain in a shell. Come out of the shell and get your party on. Let me ask you this. How can you tell people about God if you are in a shell? You can't. Hear the heavenly bells and come out of the shell where freedom and light prevail.

CONTINUE IN PRAYER

People of God, continue in prayer. You can not survive in this world without it. I know that I can't survive without prayer. I get on my knees or lie in my bed and pray every day.

Prayer is a remarkable thing. When you pray you get closer to God. When you pray, you get strength and power from God. Through prayer you communicate with Him. Prayer is your spiritual passageway to God. It invites you to be in His presence. Prayer is powerful and awesome.

Prayer also shows that you have a relationship with God. It shows that you respect and acknowledge Him. It shows that you go to Him for strength and guidance. It shows that you need His help. Prayer shows that you are committing and humbling yourself unto God. It also shows that you are making peace with Him.

My brothers and sisters, I remember how Daniel continued in prayer. I remember how David continued in prayer. I remember how Jesus Christ continued in prayer. They did not let anything stop them from praying, and you can do the same, so "continue in prayer, and watch in the same with thanksgiving" (Colossians 4:2).

DO NOT CARE ABOUT WHAT SOME PEOPLE SAY

Do not care about what some people say about you. Notice that I said some people, because all people are not against you. The world is full of many liars and hypocrites, but it doesn't mean that you are one. I'm telling you to not worry about what some people say about you because some people are negative. They would say anything to bring you down. They would say anything to make you feel bad about yourself.

Always know that God loves you. Always know that God is on your side. You have to continue to serve Him. When people say something negative to you, you say something positive back. Do not respond with a negative response but with a positive one. Be like your Father God, and that's speaking positively.

The only one you should care about saying something to you is God. God is positive not negative. He is not a liar. He is not a hypocrite. God tells you the truth. He speaks to you to encourage you, not to hurt you or bring you down.

You see some people will say things to discourage you because they see God in you. They know that you are something special, and they are jealous about that. You just continue to live your godly life and don't care what they say about you, for you are rich in Jesus.

DON'T BE A HELL-RAISER

Don't be a hell-raiser. Be a peace-raiser. God does not want you to be a hell-raiser. He wants you to be a peace-raiser. He does not want you walking around raising hell. He wants you walking around raising peace because He is peace. He is the founder of it.

There are too many people in the world raising hell instead of raising peace. They hate and despise peace. They are murdering others. They are kidnapping, brutalizing, and torturing others. These things ought not so to be. God did not create us to be evil. He created us to be lovers.

God loves His creation. You have people in the world that are trying to make God's creation look bad. God did a marvelous job creating earth and human beings. You have individuals out there trying to destroy both earth and human beings. They are being hell-raisers. God did not create us to be hell-raisers.

God did not create hell for earth. He created hell for Satan and his demonic followers. You have people that are trying to make hell on earth. They think that they are gods. They think that they can just walk around and do whatever they please. Instead of being kind to others, they are violent to others. I'm going to give all of you hell-raisers a warning: if you continue to raise hell, God is going to destroy you.

P.S. I'd rather be destroyed by man than to be destroyed by God. With man, you are destroyed just on earth, but with God, you are destroyed on earth and in hell for all eternity. So don't be a hell-raiser.

DON'T BE AGAINST WOMEN PREACHERS

My brothers, don't be against women preachers. Support women preachers because they are serving our Father the Almighty God.

They are bringing His Word. Don't hate on them. Don't down them. And don't throw stones at them. You can learn a lot from them.

God wants you to support His women preachers. He does not want you to hate or be against them. They are doing His work. Don't hinder them from doing His work. The Bible that you read is what they preach. So what's the problem? They are preaching the Bible that you read, so there is no problem. There is no deception. I'm not trying to cause division between men and women preachers, but women can preach just as good as men. They can bring the Word just as good as men. They have the Holy Spirit in them just as well as men do.

I refuse to be against women preachers. I refuse to hate on them. I would be a fool if I hate on the women of God. If I hate on them, I will hate on God because He was the one that raised them to preach. My brothers, continue to go to church. Continue to read your Bible, but please don't be against the women preachers because they are called by our Heavenly Father the Almighty God.

DON'T PUT GOD ASIDE

Don't put God aside, put Him on the inside. Keep Him on the inside. Many people get what they want to get from God, and then they put Him aside. They put God aside until they are ready to get something else from Him. They try to use and manipulate Him for their personal pleasure and benefit.

God is sick and tired of people trying to use Him. He is sick and tired of people trying to make Him out a flunky. God is not a flunky. He is the holy and omnipotent King. He is not our servant. We are His servants. He never puts us aside. He carries us everywhere He goes. He blesses and takes care of us.

Many of us are selfish. We don't think about God's feelings, we just think about our feelings. For example, some of us don't care that God is a jealous God. Some of us don't care about His commandments. Some of us don't care about obeying Him. We walk in arrogance thinking that we are God's gift to the world. Jesus Christ is God's gift to the world, not us. We walk in arrogance not giving God the glory, but giving ourselves the glory.

God does not like that type of attitude. He created us. We did not create Him. God is an awesome God. He is a powerful God. He is the ruler of the universe, so acknowledge Him and don't put Him aside because it would not be a good thing if He put all of us aside. Be courteous to God.

DON'T TALK BAD ABOUT PEOPLE

Don't talk bad about people. How would you feel if someone talked bad about you? You would not like that, would you? People have feelings. It's not good to hurt their feelings. It's not right to hurt their feelings. That is the problem with the world today. People want to talk bad about each other. People want to down each other. And people want to hurt each other. That is not right. That is not of Christ. And it is surely not of God.

God did not create us to talk bad about each other. He did not create us to hate or hurt each other. He created us to talk good about each other. He created us to love and to enjoy each other. God wants us to be kind to each other.

Talking bad about people is cruel. Talking bad about people is harsh. It is insensitive. I refuse to do it. I refuse to talk bad about people. I refuse to hurt people's feelings, because I don't want people to talk bad about me. I don't want people to hurt me. My brothers and sisters, don't talk bad about people because talking bad about people is evil.

GOD DOES NOT HATE YOU

Listen up! Listen up! People, God does not hate you. If He hated you, He would have never created you. God did not create you to hate you; He created you to love you. You are the one that hates God because you don't know Him. Once you get to know Him you will see that He loves you.

You can't get mad at God because the world is not perfect. It is not God's fault that the world is not perfect. It is sin's fault. God did not bring sin into the world. God brought love into the world. He created you out of love.

God does not make you hate Him; sin makes you hate Him. Sin is your enemy, and not God. Sin hates you. God was the one who provided you with shelter. God is the one who provides you with food on your table. He is the one who keeps you in good health.

Saying that God hates you is an insult. Saying that God hates you is ridiculous. Saying that God hates you is ignorant. There is no hate in God. There is love in God. He is love and the definition of love. And if you still think that God hates you, open your Bible and read John 3:16 and you will see that God truly loves you for He sent His only begotten Son to die for your sins. Praise God for His wonderful kindness and remember, He does not hate you.

GOD DOES NOT LIE

God does not lie. There is no reason for Him to lie. And if there were a reason for Him to lie, He still wouldn't lie. He is God. He does not have to lie. He does not have to lie to get what He wants. What does God look like telling a lie? Come on, my brothers and sisters, I'm talking about God. He never told a lie, and He's not about to start now.

Many people lose hope because they think that God is not going to come through for them. God always comes through for His people. Those who lose hope must learn how to be patient and wait on God. He does not come when you want Him to come. He comes when He wants to come. He comes when He is ready to come.

Who are you to tell God what to do? Who are you to give God orders? Who are you to hurry God? You are nothing but flesh. Who are you to call God a liar? Did God lie to Abraham? No! Did God lie to Joseph? No! Did God lie to Jesus? No! So, who are you? You are no greater than those men that I just mentioned.

Believe what God tells you. Have faith in Him. Trust in Him. Keep acknowledging Him and you will see that everything that your heart desires will come to pass. God does not lie.

GOD IS A GENIUS

God is a genius. He created this beautiful earth in seven days. God is a mastermind. Check out the solar system. Look how beautiful

He made men. Look how beautiful He made women. Look how beautiful He made the fowls of the air and the creatures in the seas, the forest, and the jungles. Only a genius can do that.

God is a master planner. He made a plan how His Son was going to come down on earth and die for our sins. He made a plan how Jesus was going to defeat death and Satan. He made a plan how His Son was going to resurrect from His grave and prepare a place for you and me. God set it all up. And His plan was a success. God's plans never fail.

When you look in the mirror, see God in you. Know that God is in you. His living breath and Spirit is in you. His love is in you. My brothers and sisters, you were created by a genius. And if God is a genius, you are a genius because you are made in His image. You are made in His likeness. God has nothing but love for you. I have nothing but love for you. God is a genius, so please don't forget it.

GOD IS NOT AGAINST YOU

God is not against you, so stop saying that He is. God loves you, and He will do all that He can to bless you. Having God in your life is a blessing. We all go through trials and tribulations. That is life. Just because you go through trials and tribulations doesn't mean that God is against you.

When you are going through your trials and tribulations, God is with you. He is telling you to hold on. He is telling you to be strong. If He was against you, He would say forget you. He would say you are nothing, but He's right there by your side cheering you on to victory. God does not want you to suffer. He does not want you to be depressed.

Living in this world you may struggle because that is life. Struggling makes you tough. Struggling teaches you how to survive and how to be strong. Stop complaining and weeping about your situations. Stop complaining and weeping about your problems. Stop saying that God is against you for "neither death, nor life, nor angels, nor principalities, nor powers, nor things present, nor things to come, Nor height, nor depth, nor any other creature, shall be able to separate us from the love of God, which is in Christ Jesus our Lord" (Romans 8:38–39).

GOD IS SERIOUS ABOUT YOU

Let me tell you something: God is serious about you. He is serious about blessing you, so you need to be serious about blessing Him. God is not selfish when it comes to blessing you. And He will never be selfish. Being selfish is not part of His nature. Being selfish is not part of His character. And He does not want it to be part of your character. He is serious about blessing you.

When it comes to preserving you, God is serious. He is serious about your well-being. He doesn't want you to end up with the wrong mate. That is why He is preserving you for the right mate. God does not want you to be unequally yoked. Being unequally yoked interferes with the Spirit that He has placed within you, the Holy Spirit. He is preserving you for the right mate, a mate that has the Holy Spirit like you. He is not preserving you for an unrighteous mate. He is preserving you for a righteous mate. He is serious about preserving you.

Moreover, God is serious about protecting you. He does not want anyone or anything to hurt you. He does not want anyone or anything to harm you. He does not want anyone or anything to be destroyed. You belong to Him. And anyone or anything that tries to harm you, He will punish. God loves you, and He is going to do all that He can to protect you. When God says He gives life more abundantly, He gives it. He does not want you to die before your time. He does not want the thief to steal, take, or destroy your life. He is serious about protecting you.

My brother and my sister, God is serious about you. He is not like man that plays with your emotions. God is better than man. He does not take you for granted. He does not take your heart for granted. He does not want to destroy your heart. He is serious about your heart. Never think that God doesn't care about you because He does. And He is serious about doing it. He is serious about His relationship with you.

P.S. If you don't have a relationship with God, get one!

GOD IS VERY IMPORTANT

God is very important, so get to know Him. He is very important for everything. He is very important for your health, body, and soul. God wants you to be healthy. He wants your body to be in great shape. He wants you to be clean inside and outside. He wants your soul to be saved.

God cares about you. He cares about your spirit and soul. He does not want you to go to hell. He does not want you to live a sinful life. He wants every aspect of your life to be spectacular. God is here to make your life spectacular. If you invite Him into your heart, you will not lose a step. The only thing that He would take away from you is sin.

God is not here to take away your joy and fun. He is here to take all the pollution that is inside of you away. Getting clean from all of your sin is where the fun begins. He created you to have fun. He created you to enjoy His creation. He just wants you to enjoy His creation in a godly and respectful manner. Sinning is not a godly manner. Polluting the earth is not a respectful manner. God does not want His earth to be dirty and filthy. He wants His earth to be clean. Without God we would be nothing. God is very important to all of us. He is the source of our lives. I'm glad that He is God. I'm glad that He is a God of cleanliness. He saw fit to put us on His beautiful planet. He saw fit to blow His living breath in us. God deserves our undivided attention. He deserves to be worshipped. He deserves to be honored. God is very important, and you better believe it.

GOD KNOWS YOU

How are you doing, my brother? And how are you doing, my sister? I just would like to tell you that God knows you. He knows everything about you. He knows your strengths. And He knows your weaknesses. God knows when you are happy. And He knows when you are sad. He knows the things that anger you. And He knows the things that make you glad.

There is not one single individual or creature in this world that God does not know. There is not one area or place in this world that

God does not know about. He knows everything. You can not keep anything away from Him. You can not keep secrets away from Him. He knows everyone's secrets. He knows the sins that we committed, but it's okay because He will forgive us. I'm not saying that it's okay to sin. It is not okay to sin. God does not want you to sin, but if you do, He will forgive you.

God knows that you are not perfect, and He knows that you are going to make mistakes. My brother and my sister, I hope that you are doing well. Please do not think that God does not know you. Please do not think that God does not care about you because if you do think those things, it is a lie. God knows you and cares about you.

GOD LOVES ALL COLORS

Many people think that God doesn't like them. I'm here to tell them that God not only likes them, but also *loves* them. As a matter of fact, God loves all colors. He loves all colors equally. God is not prejudiced. He is not biased. He has no respect of persons. God is going to judge everyone by the same book.

Take the blinders from your eyes and see that God loves you. Know that God loves you. Know that God loves all races equally. He created all of us from the same dust. He blew the same breath in all of us. He gave the same commandments to all of us. He is the ruler of all of us.

It is a lie when someone says that God doesn't love him or her. God sent His Spirit down to comfort us. He sent His Spirit down to be the spiritual intercessor for us. God does not leave us comfortless. He will not leave us comfortless.

I dare you to say that God hates you. I dare you to say that God is against you. I dare you to say that He doesn't love all colors because that is a lie, and you are a liar. God created all colors, and He loves all colors equally as He loves His Son Jesus Christ.

GOD'S SIDE

What's going on? How are you doing? I just would like to tell you that God's side is the best side. On His side there is no confusion. On His side there is no catastrophe. God does not war with Himself, and

He does not war with His people for there is kindness on His side. There is love and peace on His side.

God's side is filled with goodness and greatness. His side is filled with protection. God surrounds and protects you with His love. There is no evil on God's side. There is no hate or sin on His side. He will not allow evil, hate, or sin be on His side. He is too holy and righteous for that.

God does not have time to fool with unrighteousness. He is not going to put up with it. His side is clean. His side is pure. All of the blessings are on His side. All of the riches and glory are on His side. Guess who else is on His side. Jesus Christ is on His side, and it can't get any better than that. If you choose to be on God's side, you will be there with Jesus Christ. God's side has it going on. Come on, join the party, because it is everlasting being on His side. And a great side it is.

IN GOD'S EYES

In God's eyes you are beautiful not ugly, so stop calling yourself ugly. God didn't create anything ugly, so He doesn't want you calling yourself ugly. He doesn't want you cursing yourself by calling yourself ugly. God said you are good after He made you (Genesis 1:31). He didn't say you are ugly.

In God's eyes you are special. Of course, you are special because you are made in His image (Genesis 1:27). He loves you that much to have made you in His image. For God to even think of creating you in His image should make you feel special. He loves you that much to think about you. You are special to Him, so know that you are special to Him.

My friend, know that in God's eyes you are beautiful. And know that in God's eyes you are special. Don't walk around with low self-esteem. Don't walk around with your head down. Don't walk around in defeat. And don't abuse yourself. Treat yourself with love and kindness. Love yourself. Speak positively about yourself. And think about this: If God says I'm beautiful I must be beautiful. In God's eyes you are beautiful. In God's eyes you are special. Now it is up to you, and time for you to believe it.

IT IS GOOD

People, it is good to have a relationship with God. Better yet, it's magnificent having a relationship with Him. It is good to have a relationship with God because He will take care of you. He will love you.

My friends, God will not leave you comfortless (John 14:18). He will not leave you hungry. He will feed you spiritually and physically. God will provide you with everything that you need, for He is the King of providing. He is the King with all the goods. He is the King that takes care of His people and kingdom.

Moreover, having a relationship with God is real for God is real. He does not play with your emotions, and He will not play with your emotions. He will not neglect you. He will not break your heart. He will not abuse you because He is not a fool that plays games. He is not a fool that will play you. He is not a fool, period. God will always be there to spend time with you.

My friends, God knows the importance of a relationship. He is the one that you should have a relationship with. He is the King of beautiful relationships. He is the King of successful relationships. He has all the tools of having a beautiful and successful relationship. And God wants to have a relationship with you, so open your heart and invite Him in, for it is good having a relationship with God.

IT'S NOT GOOD TO CURSE

My brothers and sisters, it's not good to curse, so why are we doing it? Each day we are cursing each other. Cursing someone doesn't prove that you are tough. Cursing someone doesn't prove that you are strong. Let me also add, cursing doesn't make you cool. It only proves that you are ignorant. How do I know? I know because I used to do it. I used to have cursed words coming out of my mouth. Cursing only made me a fool and ignorant.

In the Word of God, James said, "Therewith bless we God, even the Father; and therewith curse we men, which are made after the similitude of God. Out of the same mouth proceedeth blessing and cursing. My brethren, these things ought not so to be" (James 3:9–10). James said that we are made in the likeness of God, so we should not be cursing each other. He said don't bless God and curse men, but bless God and bless men. Men are made in the image of God. Men are made in God's creation, so don't curse them. Let blessings come out of your mouths, not curses.

Love your brothers and sisters. Speak kindly to them and about them. Don't speak negatively about them. That is why the world is filled with so much hatred because people are speaking negatively about each other. People are cursing each other. You don't hear people speaking positively about you often; you hear them speaking negatively. They speak negative more than they speak positive. They curse people more than they bless them.

God wants us to speak positively. He does not want us to speak negatively. God wants us to bless people. He does not want us to curse them. Many people have died because of their poisonous tongue. Some people's tongues are filled with too much toxins. They need Jesus to clean their tongues. They need Jesus to wash their tongues. Bless people with your tongue and don't curse them because it's not good to curse.

LIVE FOR GOD

It is so wonderful to have a master like the Almighty God. It is so wonderful to have a King like the Almighty God. It's a privilege to honor the Almighty God. That's why I'm encouraging you to live for Him.

Living for God is not easy because you have Satan trailing you. Satan is full of evil, but don't worry about him because God's remarkable Son Jesus Christ has triumphed over him. When you live for God, He will take care of you. When you live for God, He will comfort you. He is a great Father whose love surpasses the love of man. There is no love greater than His love.

Living for God is remarkable. You will not be in bondage living for Him. God will not slap you around or beat on you. He will not verbally abuse you. He will not pimp you. He will not hinder you from going after your goals.

Living for God you are free. You are not held captive. God does not put you in a box. God gave us commandments so we can be in control. Without rules or commandments, we will be out of control. We will be savages, meaning, not civilized. We would be bastards without His discipline. Live for God so you can be free. Live for God to please Him. Most of all, live for God so you can have eternal life.

STAY AWAY FROM

Christians, stay away from a heretic. When it comes to God, a heretic is no good. A heretic rejects God. A heretic rejects the truth of God. It is no good being around one. If you come across one, separate yourself. A heretic is a false teacher, a deceiver. He or she would try to influence you into believing his or her doctrine, a false doctrine. You don't need to be encamped around false doctrine. You need to be encamped around true doctrine.

Christians, the doctrine of God is true, but the doctrine of a heretic is false. Encamping around true teaching leads you to God. Encamping around false teaching leads you to destruction. God is about true teaching. A heretic is about false teaching. A heretic is a liar and a deceiver, just like his or her father Satan, the father of lies and deception.

A heretic is an antichrist. A heretic will try to take you off the good and righteous pathway. That is why Paul told Titus to reject a heretic (Titus 3:10). It is no use being associated with a heretic. You gain nothing by being with one. Continue to pursue God. Continue to serve God. Continue to gain knowledge and truth from God, but stay away from a heretic because heretics are on the path of eternal destruction.

STAY STRONG

My brothers and sisters, stay strong in God. Don't let anyone or anything break you or shake you. Only allow God to mold you. Don't let no man or woman mold; you let God mold you. When man or woman molds you, he or she makes mistakes. When God molds you, there are no mistakes. God will mold you into the man or woman that you need to be. He will mature you. Discipline you. Don't forget that God was the one who created you, and when He created you, He said it was good, meaning, that there are no mistakes. I just wanted to remind you about that.

To make it in life you have to stay strong in God because it is not easy living in this world. You have many types of demonic spirits in this world, such as lust, greed, hatred, envy, jealousy, betrayal, lying, and depression. For those spirits not to get attached to you, you have to stay strong in God. You have to put on and keep on the armor of God so those spirits won't get in you.

Living in this world is not a game. It is not a joke. The only spirit that I want in me is the Spirit of God, that is, the Holy Spirit. I don't need anything else but the Spirit of God. That is how I stay strong. You have to stay strong in God to survive. You have to stay strong in God to worship and praise Him.

Like I told you earlier, if you are not careful, those demonic spirits will get attached to you and stop you from worshipping and praising God. Those spirits are not weak, they are strong. They stopped King Saul from praising God. The spirit of jealousy came upon Saul, and he sought to kill David (1 Samuel 18:5, 19:8-24. They stopped Judas from following Jesus. The spirit of betrayal came upon Judas, and he betrayed Jesus (Matthew 26:47–56). My brothers and sisters, stay strong in God and I assure you that you will not only reap an earthly harvest, but also a heavenly eternal harvest. Don't be moved. Stay strong in God.

TAKE GOD SERIOUSLY

My brothers and sisters, take God seriously. God is the real deal. He is the truth. He is not a joke. He is not a toy or game to be played with. Do not be slack when it comes to Him. Do not take His words as a joke. Do not take His commandments as a joke. His words and commandments are real. His words are going to be what keeps you alive. His words will keep you from being deceived, so take Him seriously.

When a prophet of God speaks, listen and take heed. Do not disregard what a prophet says. He or she is giving you a message from God. It is for your own good. The prophecy may be a life-or-death situation. You have to hearken unto it and take it seriously. I remember when a prophet of God came to Abraham and told him that Sarah was going to bear a child. And who did you hear laughing in the background about it? Sarah was in the background laughing about it (Genesis 18:9–15). She thought it was a joke. She did not take it seriously. And what came to pass? Sarah bore a child (Genesis 21:1–8).

When God says He is going to do something, He does it. He is not slack concerning His promise (2 Peter 3:9). He does not lie. He does not talk just to get your hopes up, and once He gets your hopes up He forsakes you. God is not a God like that. He will not leave or forsake you. He will not give you empty or false promises. He never told a lie, and He is not going to tell a lie. He is the same God that He was yesterday, and throughout the beginning of time.

What makes you think that you should not take Him seriously? Do not let the fact that you don't see Him be a reason to not take Him seriously because if you do, you are pathetic. Regardless of whether I see God or not, I'm going to take Him seriously. I will still believe in Him and know that He's real. I don't have to see God to know that He's real. I don't have to see God to believe in Him because I feel Him. I feel God on the inside of me. God does not have to give or show me a sign to let me know that He's real or that He exists. I know God is real and believe that He's real. My brothers and sisters, take God seriously and know that He's serious because He is serious.

THE COOLEST BOOK TO READ

What's the coolest book to read? The Bible is the coolest book to read. It excites you. It encourages you. It teaches you the correct way to live. It guides you through life. It teaches you how to handle tough situations. It helps you make it through your trials and tribulations.

The Bible is also powerful. From the Old Testament to the New Testament it is powerful. From the New Testament to the end of Revelation it is powerful. There is no other book like it. The Bible is not a book of fairy tales. It is not a book of fantasies. Everything in the Bible is real. The people in the Bible are real. They are not characters. They are not actors.

God's people in the Bible felt the hardships of life. They experienced trials and tribulations. They have been through the wilderness. It was God's Word that kept them alive. It was God's Word that kept them moving in faith. It was God's Word that kept them getting blessed. And that is why the Bible is the coolest book to read, for it is the Word of God.

WALK IN LOVE

People on earth, walk in love. Walking in love is a wonderful thing to do. It is something that we all should desire to do. Walking in love is better than walking in anger. It is better than walking in hate. It is better than walking in hurt.

When you walk in love, it shows that you have the Holy Spirit within you. It shows that you have God inside of you, and in God there is no darkness. When you walk in love, you treat your brothers and sisters with kindness. You greet them with kindness. You speak positively to them and show them that you love them.

Moreover, when you walk in love, hatred does not come out of your mouth. You do not speak hatred to people. Anger does not come out of your mouth. You do not speak negative to people. You do not curse people. Speaking negatively and cursing people is not walking in love. It is not of God. It is evil and polluted. Speaking negatively is toxic waste coming out of your mouth. And how toxic it is.

My brothers and sisters, I love you. And I want you to love me. I do not want you to walk in hate. I do not want you to walk in anger. I do not want you to walk in hurt. And most of all, God does not want you to walk in those things. "Be ye therefore followers of God, as dear children; And walk in love, as Christ also hath loved us, and hath given himself for us an offering and a sacrifice to God for a sweetsmelling savour" (Ephesians 5:1–2).

YOU CAN NOT DESTROY GOD'S WORD

Men and women, you can not destroy God's Word. God's Word is powerful. His Word is going to stand. His Word is not going to perish. Many people have tried to destroy God's Word, and they failed

(Jeremiah 36:11–32). The Bible is not going anywhere. God's Word is not going anywhere. His Word is here to stay.

You must be out of your mind thinking that you can destroy God's Word. His Word created you. His Word created this entire solar system. His Word crafted each and every last one of us. His Word is the beginning and the end. Heaven and earth are going to pass away, but guess what's not going to pass away? God's Word (Luke 21:33).

What is wrong with these people that are setting God's churches on fire? What are their problems? All I know is that they are going to have a big problem dealing with God. He is not going to let them get away with burning His churches. They are going to face His wrath big time. You can not stop the movement of God. You can not slow His spirit down. And remember, you can not destroy His Word.

YOU DO NOT KNOW EVERYTHING

There are many people out there in the world that think that they know everything. They think no one can tell them a thing. They think that they have the answers to everything. I'm here to tell them that they don't know everything. God is the only one who knows everything. He knows your every thought.

God did not create us to know everything. If He created us to know everything, He would have never created wisdom. He would not tell us to get knowledge and understanding because we know everything. My ear is always open for knowledge. I don't walk around like I know everything.

People who think that they know everything will never grow in life. People who think that they know everything don't have many friends. I don't want to associate with someone who thinks that he or she knows everything. That person would never listen. What you say to him or her would go into one ear and out the next.

My brothers and sisters, learn how to listen to others. Gain wisdom, knowledge, and understanding. Last, but not least, realize that you don't know everything because you are not God, the only one who knows everything.

YOU HAVE GOD ALL WRONG

Some of us have God all wrong. God is not hateful. God is not evil. Many of us walk around claiming that God is those things. God does not hate anyone. He does not wish anything bad to happen to someone.

If you would open your Bible and read it, you will clearly see that God does not hate anyone. You will see that you are born into a world of sin. You will see that the world is wicked. It's not God's fault that the world is wicked. It's not God's fault that you think those bad things about Him.

Who made you think those bad things about God? Who is the cause of you being hurt? Many people say things due to them being hurt. Many people say things due to them being confused and frustrated. God is not the reason of you being hurt. He is not the reason of you being confused and frustrated. He does not hurt people. He loves and comforts them.

I'm praying for those who don't have any knowledge of God. I'm praying for those who don't have a relationship with Him. I'm praying for those who are walking around in hurt. I'm praying for those who are walking around in anger. As long as you walk around in those things, you will never experience the joy of God. It takes you to come to know the truth of God. It takes you to get a relationship with Him. And when He delivers you from hurt or anger, you will see that you had Him all wrong. God has love for you, and it is eternal.

A CARING FATHER

God is a caring Father. He cares about all of His children. He doesn't love one more than He loves the next. He loves His children equally. There is nothing biased about Him. And there is nothing prejudiced about Him. God cares about all of His children no matter what color, creed, or race they are. He watches over all of them. He protects all of them. His children are safe with Him. When one gets lost, He keeps searching until He finds him or her. He is a Father of commitment. He is a Father that takes care of His responsibility. His people are His children, which are His responsibility. He keeps His children fed with the Holy Spirit. And He adores them with the Holy Spirit. God is a caring Father. And I'm proud that He's my Father because He cares about me.

BE LOYAL

My friends, God is a kind God. Through His kindness He blesses us each day. He is an unselfish God, and that is why I'm asking you to be loyal to Him. God doesn't have to do anything for us, but He does. He spends His valuable time shielding and protecting us from evil. He spends His precious time blessing us. We should be blessing Him. We should be honoring Him, for it is He who made us. It is He who granted us His goods. We should recognize God for His wonderful creativity. We should acknowledge Him for His goodness. Even those who do evil works should acknowledge Him because God gives them mercy. He is withholding His wrath from them. He is giving them time to repent and ask Him for forgiveness. They need to repent and ask Him for forgiveness as soon as possible because the kingdom of heaven is at hand, and Jesus Christ is about to return. And God's wrath is going to pour out like a hurricane after His Son gets His bride. Be loyal to God. Admire and adore Him. Praise and worship Him for it is He who loves you more than life itself.

BE RESPECTABLE

Let me ask you a question and don't get offended by it. Are you respectable? If you are not, you need to be. When you are respectable, it shows that you are a great human being. When you are respectable, it shows that you have respect for others. It shows that you have manners. And that you are disciplined and well trained. People remember a respectable person. They reflect on how a person treated them with respect. And it makes others feel good that you are respectable to them. It makes them feel honored that someone showed them respect. It makes them feel good on the inside. I have to be a respectable person. I don't want anyone telling me off. I don't want anyone saying I don't have home training. My mother did a great job raising me. God did a great job raising me. Be respectable, my brothers and sisters, because that is the way God wants you to be. And it shows that you love and respect your neighbors.

BE SUPPORTIVE

My brothers and sisters, God is getting sick and tired of us fighting among ourselves. He is getting sick and tired of us being against each other. God does not want us to fight and be against each other, He wants us to be supportive of each other. Being supportive shows unity. Being supportive shows that you care about each other. Being supportive shows that you are in each other's corner. It feels good to be supported. It feels good to know that you have a cheering section. Therefore, don't throw sticks and stones at each other. Don't throw jealousy at each other. And don't throw hate at each other. But throw love, peace, and support at each other. When you throw love, it puts a smile on God's face. When you throw peace, it fills Jesus with joy. When you throw support, it fires up the Holy Spirit. My brothers and sisters, stop fighting and hating on each other. And begin to support each other for it brings love, happiness, peace, unity, and success.

BE TRUE TO GOD

My brothers and sisters, be true to God. Be honest to God. Don't make any promises that you are not going to keep. Don't make any vows that you are not going to keep. You would be only deceiving yourselves. All God wants you to be is honest and true to Him. That is all He asks for. How is He going to have a relationship with you if you are not true to Him? He can't. And He will not. God is not going to have a relationship or trust in anyone that He can not trust. He would be only wasting His time, which is precious. God honors those who are true to Him. He blesses and acknowledges those who are true to Him. He loves those who are true to Him. A truthful person is a faithful person, and that is what God appreciates. God appreciates a truthful person for He knows a truthful person is faithful. Be true to God, my brothers and sisters, because He will be true to you.

BE UNITED

My brothers and sisters in Christ, be united. There is strength in unity. There is power in unity. There is love and compassion in unity. There is too much evil in this world for us not to be united. There is too much wickedness in this world. We as the body of Christ have to stand together against the wiles of the devil. We have to be ready for his attacks. We can not defeat evil individually. We have to stick together. We have to stand together. We have to pray together. We have to pray for each other. If Satan and his followers can be united, we too can be united. His kingdom is not stronger than God's kingdom. His kingdom is not mightier than God's kingdom. Be united, my brothers and sisters. And stay united.

CONTINUE TO SMILE

How are you doing, my sister? Is it okay for me to tell you that you have a beautiful smile? You do have a beautiful smile, my sister. I will not lie to you. As a matter of fact, you have an excellent smile. Don't let anyone or anything take it away from you. Don't let depression, anger, or stress take it away from you. Continue to smile. Love to smile. God gave you that beautiful smile. He blessed you with it, so don't be ashamed to show it off. Let others see your beautiful smile. Let others see how happy you are. When others see your beautiful smile, it brightens their day. It influences them to be happy. Continue to smile, my sister, because it shows how beautiful God blessed you to be.

CUT IT LOOSE

My friend, cut it loose. Cut those negative things that people said to you loose. Cut loose those painful things that people did to you. What's the use of holding on to it? There is no use. Those negative and painful things do nothing but hinder you from moving forward. Cut them loose. Cut those things loose that depress you. Cut those derogatory things loose. You have a bright future ahead of you. You have a blessed future ahead of you. Satan knows that God has an excellent future for you. He knows that God has a prosperous future for you. That is why he is trying his best to bring you down. That is why he is trying his best to keep you down. He is trying to destroy your mind, body, and spirit, but don't allow him to do it. Rebuke him and cut those wicked things loose so you can press toward the wonderful future God has planned for you.

DON'T BE A COWARD

Don't be a coward. God did not raise you to be a coward. He raised you to be bold. God does not want you to be a coward. He wants you to be bold as a lion. Confront your enemies just like David confronted Goliath. Confront your enemies just like Samson confronted the Philistines. They were not cowards. They were bold soldiers in God. They know that God is bold, so they had to be bold as well. The same power that David and Samson had, you have it. You have the power of God. You have more power than your enemies do. You have the power to stand up and defeat your enemies, so use it. With the power that you have, the enemy can't defeat you. Don't let the enemy punk you out. Don't let the enemy trample all over you. Don't let the enemy stump all over you. Don't let the enemy beat you down. God did not raise you to be weak. He raised you to be bold, so don't be a coward.

DON'T BE EVIL

Don't be evil. What do you gain by being evil? Do you feel good being evil? Are you proud of being evil? Do you find pleasure in it? I tell you this, if you continue to be evil, you are going to face the wrath of God. The wrath of God is something that you should not want to face. God hates evil. He despises evil. With one command, God can have His angels destroy this planet. Do you think I'm joking? God's wrath was poured upon Egypt (Exodus 7–12). His wrath was poured upon Sodom and Gomorrah (Genesis 19:24–25). God flooded the earth for forty days (Genesis 7:17). If God did that to a city and earth, what do you think He can do to an evil individual like you? Lot's wife was turned into a pillar of salt for being disobedient, and she was not evil (Genesis 19:26). For her not being evil, look what happened to her. You should be afraid, very afraid. It is not too late for you to stop being evil. Repent and turn from your evil ways. Apologize to God for your wickedness and make a promise to yourself that you are not going back to living evil. God loves you, and I love you.

DON'T BE THE CAUSE OF STRIFE

My friend, don't be the cause of strife. Continue to walk in peace. Though people try to get under your skin, you still walk in peace. You still show love and kindness. Don't be the one that starts up strife. You see, many people are bitter, and due to their bitterness they want to start up strife. They want to give others trouble because they are so bitter, but you don't have to be like them. You have God in your life, so act like you have God in your life. God's people walk in love not hate. God's people walk in peace not conflict. When someone starts up strife with you, kindly walk away in peace or hold yourself in silence. Though it may be hard, still do it. I know that you may want to curse others out. I know that you may want to ball up your fists and knock the crap out of somebody. If you do that, you are showing the enemy that he succeeded in getting you upset. And if you do that, you are playing right into the enemy's hand. The enemy wants you to get upset. He wants you to lose it. Continue to go out in public in peace. Continue to go to work in peace, and don't be the cause of strife because you are a child of God.

DON'T RESIST THE POWER OF GOD

Whatever you do, don't resist the power of God. The power of God is what you should want. The power of God is what you need. It is for your own good. It is for your survival. You have to want it. You have to desire it. You have to pray for it, for God is not going to force His power on you. He is not going to give you something that you don't want. God does not need your power. You need His power and without God's power you have no chance in defeating Satan. Satan will chew you up and spit you out. He wants you to resist the power of God for he knows if you resist the power of God, he has a better chance of destroying your soul. When you resist the power of God,

Satan is going to call you a fool. And when he destroys your soul, it is not going to be God's fault, but your fault because you chose to resist the power of God. The power of God is mighty. The power of God is unique. With His power, you will surely survive. With His power, you will surely overcome Satan. Don't resist the power of God for He loves you so much to offer it to you.

DON'T STOP LOVING GOD

Sometimes I know you feel like giving up. Sometimes I do. And I know that sometimes you want to go out into the world and live like the rest of them. You want to forget what you are doing for God and stop serving Him. My friend, I'm here to tell you, don't stop loving God. Continue to love Him. Continue to serve Him. Don't give in to the flesh. Don't submit yourself to the flesh. I know that it gets hard sometimes, but still don't give in to it. You look at other individuals and see what they've got and you don't have it. You desire to get married. You desire to have a car, a big house, and money. And there is nothing wrong with desiring to have those things. Just don't let them be your main focus. Let God be your main focus. Continue to wait on Him and be patient, and He will provide you with those things. Who doesn't want sex? We all want it, but don't lose your mind over it. God is going to take good care of you. Don't stop loving God because He is surely not going to stop loving you.

DON'T TALK BAD ABOUT GOD

Don't talk bad about God. Talk good about Him. There is no reason to talk bad about God. There is no reason to talk negative about Him. So why do you choose to do it? He doesn't say anything bad about you. He doesn't say anything negative about you. He loves you. He adores you. And He speaks positively about you. Why would He speak badly about you? He was the one that created you. His living breath is in you. His living spirit is in you. It is ridiculous to tell others that He hates you. It is ridiculous to tell others that He is evil. God loves you because if He didn't, He would not have sent His only begotten Son Jesus Christ on earth to be sacrificed for your sins (John 3:16). And God is surely far from evil. He could never be evil. Being evil is not His type of party. Walk in the light of God and not in the shadow of darkness. And remember, don't talk bad about Him.

DON'T TURN AWAY FROM GOD

In all that you do, or whatever you may do, please don't turn away from God. I recommend that you don't do that. I don't care how hard it may get, don't turn away from Him. He is the one who is going to help you through your difficult times. He is the one who is going to help you through your obstacles. And it would be foolish to turn away from Him. Don't let money turn you away from God. Don't let material things turn you away from God. Don't let any relationships turn you away from God. He is more important than those things. He is more valuable than those things. He is all that matters. And if you turn away from God, things are not going to get better for you, but harder for you. God is the one that keeps things at ease. He is the one that keeps things calm and smooth. It will be ignorant to turn away from Him. So before you think about turning away from Him, think twice because you will not be improving yourself, but lowering yourself. Please don't turn away from God. It is for your own good.

DON'T TURN BACK

My friend, don't turn back to the way that you used to be. Don't go back to living the life that you used to live. Stay in God. Stay on the righteous path. The path that you used to walk was the path of sin, which leads to death. Sin does not care about you, neither does death. It would not be good to go back to it. While you were on the path of sin, you had fun. Don't get me wrong, there is nothing wrong with having fun. All I'm saying is that I'd rather have fun on the path of righteousness than to have fun on the path of sin. Like I said earlier, the path of sin leads to death, but the path of righteousness leads to the everlasting and living God. In God there is no death, only life. So why would you want to turn back to the way you were living? That would be foolish. Surely the path you used to live on had pleasures, but what felt good to you was not always good. That is the deception of sin. Don't get tired in well doing. Enjoy your life in God. He wants you to have fun. God does not want you to be in a box. He does not want you to be in a shell. Don't turn back to the life that you used to live because Jesus Christ does not want you to be cast into outer darkness, but you are not going to give Him any choice but to cast you to into outer darkness if you do go back to living a sinful life.

DON'T WALK IN BITTERNESS

My brothers and sisters, don't walk in bitterness. Walk in love, joy, and peace. No one likes to be around a bitter person. A bitter person is always angry or depressed. A bitter person is no fun to be around. A bitter person is a party pooper. A bitter person takes the fun out of things. A bitter person has no sense of humor. All he or she does is spoil things. It's not cute walking in bitterness. It's not cool walking in it. Have you ever been around a person who has nothing good or positive to say? If you have, know that that person is bitter. I've been around plenty of bitter people, and I tried to spread my joy and happiness, but you know what? They remained bitter. So I stopped hanging around individuals like that because if I'm not careful their bitterness can rub off on me and that is something I don't want to happen. I don't want to be bitter. I want to remain joyful. And I want the same for you, so don't walk in bitterness because there is nothing good about it.

EXPRESS YOUR LOVE FOR GOD

Express your love for God. Don't be afraid or ashamed to do it. God is not afraid to express His love for you, neither is He ashamed. He does not care what people have to say about Him. He cares less what people have to say about Him. He knows how poisonous people's tongues are. Some of them are quick to speak negatively. Some of them are quick to throw stones. For example, I told this female that I am married to God, and she called me crazy. She laughed at me. I don't care what you say about me. I am going to express my love for God. I love Him. God means everything to me. He is my faith, hope, and salvation. He is my deliverer. He is the smile on my face. He is my light in darkness. Many people are afraid to express their love for God. They fear what people are going to say about them. I'm here to tell them to express their love for God because there is no height, principality, nor death that is going to stop Him from expressing His love for them (Romans 8:38–39).

GIVE THE CHILDREN HOPE

Give the children hope. Don't give them abuse, but give them hope. Many children are growing up in homes where the parents abuse them. I'm not talking about physical abuse, I'm talking about verbal and mental abuse. There is no hope in mental and verbal abuse, only hurt. In Colossians 3:21, it says fathers, provoke not your children to anger, lest they be discouraged. When you yell at your children, you are provoking them to anger. When you yell at your children, you discourage them. And when they get out in the world, they will have no confidence in themselves due to the abusive home that they live in. When they get out in the world, they feel that they have no hope for if their parents are constantly speaking negatively to them they fear that others are going to do so as well. The spirit of fear comes upon them. And when the spirit of fear comes upon you, it is hard to succeed, especially when you are a young child. That is why you must speak positively to children, so they won't grow up in fear. Give the children confidence. Speak kindly to them. God is watching your every move. And He is holding you accountable. He does not want you to verbally abuse the children. Let me ask you a question. How would you feel if God verbally abused you? You would not like that, would you? The way you feel about God verbally abusing you is the same way that child feels when you abuse him or her. God does not abuse His children. He gives them hope, so follow in His footsteps so the children can have hope in themselves and make something out of their lives.

GLORIFY GOD

Listen up, my brothers and sisters, it's time for us to glorify God. Forget about your problems and situations. Forget about what you are going through and just glorify God. Glorifying God helps you make it through your struggles. Glorifying God conquers the issues that you are having. Are you sick and tired of worrying? Are you sick and tired of beating your head against the wall? Are you tired of being confused and frustrated? I know you are because I am. I want my whole life to be dedicated to God. I live for God, and I love Him. I don't care what the adversary says about me. I don't care how people look at me. No one is going to stop me from glorifying God, and I mean no one. God saved me from my sins. He lifted me up when I was down. He brought me out of bondage, and He will do the same for you. Begin to glorify God and continue to glorify Him for He is awesome.

GO ALL OUT FOR GOD

My brothers and sisters, go all out for God. Why not? He goes all out for you. For example, He went all out for you when He gave up His only begotten Son to be sacrificed for your sins. He went all out for you when He prepared a place for you. God loves you and will always be there for you. All you have to do is call upon Him. It's that simple. Why would He not be there for you? You belong to Him, and He will do all that He can to keep you. And in return for His grace and mercy, acknowledge Him. Tell others about Him. Bring more people to Him, and He will appreciate it. He appreciates those that work hard for His kingdom. He blesses those that work hard for His kingdom. Go all out for God and watch how high He will bring you.

GOD CAN DEFEND HIMSELF

God can defend Himself. He does not need you to defend Him because He can defend Himself. God is not weak. He is strong, mighty, and powerful. He is the most powerful being in the universe. He can defeat anyone. He is not a wimp. He is not a coward. He is not a punk. He is not a chump. God is the one that defends you. He is the one that protects you from your evil enemies. He is your God. He is your shield and protector, so why would He need you to defend Him? All God wants you to do is serve Him and let Him do the defending. The armor you wear belongs to God. It is the armor of God.

God does the defending, not you. He does the protecting, not you. He is the one that equips you with power. He is the source of power. He is the creator of power, so don't ever think that God needs you to defend Him for He is bold, powerful, and courageous enough to defend Himself. He is God, strong and mighty.

GOD DOES NOT WANT YOU TO PERISH

God does not want anyone to perish. If someone perishes, it is his or her fault. God gives everyone an equal opportunity to get saved. God gives everyone the time to get knowledge of Him. It is up to each individual to gain knowledge of God. It is up to each individual to get in a relationship with Him. God is not going to throw Himself on anyone. You have to throw yourself on God. God is the one that will never perish. He is the one that has eternal life. You've got to be willing to have eternal life. You have to be willing to get knowledge of God. You have to be willing to live and not to perish. God has His place in heaven. You've got to get your place in heaven. If you don't have a relationship with God, the only place that is going to be available to you is hell, where you will perish eternally. If you get a relationship with God, He will keep you from perishing. Like I said, it's up to you. Like I said, it's your decision to get a relationship with God. I choose to have life. I choose not to perish, and you can choose the same, so get a relationship with God and get to know Him, because He does not want you to perish.

GOD HAS FORGIVEN YOU

My friend, God has forgiven you. Why are you still mourning? Why are you still talking about what you have done? God has forgiven you, so get over it. When God forgives you, you are forgiven. Stop lingering in the past. Stop dwelling on the sin that you committed. You are not perfect. You are not the only individual that has sinned. We all have sinned, so don't be too hard on yourself. Get over your sin and move on. Knowing that God has forgiven you for your sin you should be happy not sad. You should be joyful not down on yourself for you have another chance to prove yourself faithful to God. God knows that you are not perfect. He knows that you are going to sin. And when you sin, He is going to forgive you. You are human. You are not God. God is the only one who is not going to sin. Just let God know that you are truly sorry for sinning. And when He forgives you, move on. God wants you to move on. He wants you to press on. As long as you dwell on the sin that you committed, you are not going to reach the destiny that God has for you on earth. God has forgiven you, my brother. God has forgiven you, my sister, so hold your head up high and move on.

GOD HAS THE BEST FOR YOU

God has the best for you. He has all that is good for you. You are His child, so why should He not have all that is good for you? He loves you, and His purpose is to have the best for you. He is not going to give you anything that's ruined. He is not going to give you anything that's torn apart. God is a Father that supplies good things which means all the things that He has are in good condition. They are in excellent condition. And they are for you. They are yours for the giving and offering. Continue to move forward toward God. Continue to pursue His kingdom and righteousness and you will see that God has the best for you.

GOD HAS YOUR BACK

God has your back. So what are you afraid of? There is no need for you to be afraid. The enemy doesn't stand a chance against you. When the enemy sees that God has your back, he is going to flee. The enemy knows how tough God is. He knows that God's wrath is lethal. He knows that God is the most powerful being in the universe. The enemy is not stupid. He may be evil, but he's not stupid. The enemy also has wisdom. Do you think that I'll try to get up in God's face and try to battle with Him? Oh no! Hell no! You must be a fool if you get up in God's face. God has your back, so don't be afraid of the enemy. And don't be afraid to face the challenges that life brings.

P.S. Satan is the enemy.

GOD IS ABOUT YOUR WELL-BEING

God is about your well-being. Why do you think He sticks around you? He sticks around you because He cares about your well-being. He sticks around you because He loves you and wants to keep you safe. God does not want you to get hurt. He stays concerned about you. He cares for you. He wants to keep you safe from danger. God knows that evil is present. He knows that Satan is seeking to destroy you. It is His job to protect you from Satan. It is His job to protect you from those who follow Satan. Who do you think protected you from those guys who were out to jump on you? Who do you think protected you from those girls who were out to jump on you? Who do you think protected you from those vicious dogs that were trying to attack you? It was God that protected you. Thank God for being there for you. Acknowledge Him for being with you because He cares about your well-being.

GOD IS GOING TO REWARD YOU

God is going to reward you, so stop bickering. And stop complaining. Continue to work hard for His kingdom. He is not going to leave you high and dry. He is not going to neglect you. God sees and knows the hard work that you are doing. He sees and knows the sacrifices that you make for His kingdom. He knows that your heart is in the right place. He knows that your intentions are good. Be merry in well doing. Have no strife or grudge in your heart. Fill your heart with the Word of God. Continue to work hard for Him. Wait on Him and trust Him, and believe me, He is going to reward you. "And we know that all things work together for good to them that love God, to them who are the called according to his purpose" (Romans 8:28).

GOD IS NOT A FOOL

God is not a fool, so you better not take Him for one. Many people try to take Him for a fool, but they are the ones that are fools. God is far from stupid. He is nowhere near stupid. Many people try to outsmart Him. How are you going to outsmart someone who created you? And how are you going to outsmart someone who knows everything about you? I don't care about how many times you've been to school. I don't care about how many degrees you have or how many years you've been in school. I don't care how smart or intelligent you may be. I don't care how spiritual you may be. You can never outsmart God. You are not smarter than He is. God is the wisest being in the universe. He is the smartest and most intellectual being in the universe. No one can match the intelligence of God. His intelligence is beyond the universe. His intelligence is beyond any book that you read. His intelligence is beyond your mind. God is not ignorant. God is not naive. God is not a fool, so when it comes to Him, you better be cool.

GOD IS NOT AN EVIL GOD

Many people are confused about God. They think that God is evil. Well, I'm here to tell them that God is not evil. God does not mix Himself with evil. He is too good to be evil. God does not murder people. He does not rape or abuse people. That is of Satan's doing. Satan is the evil one. Many people forget that they are born into a world of sin. God did not bring sin into the world. Satan brought sin into the world. He is the cause of all the chaos that we see. God is a caring God. He is a loving and peaceful God. I dare you to say or think that He is evil. He created you with His love and kindness. What made you think or say that God is evil? Get to know God. Get a relationship with Him. Then you will find out the truth that He is not evil.

GOD IS NOT FAKE

God is not fake. He will not be fake. And He's not going to be fake. God has too much going on for Himself to be fake. He is an honest and true God. He is a real God. He is the living God. God has too many souls to save to try to be fake. Saying that God is fake is ridiculous. Saying that God is fake is foolish and ignorant. He is too real to be fake. God is not comforting people, and then later He abuses them. He is just comforting them. God is not blessing people, and then later He curses them. He is just blessing them. God is not an unbalanced God; He is a balanced God. God is not two-faced. He is one-faced. God wants people to serve Him not abandon Him. He wants people to trust Him. If God were fake, no one would trust or follow Him. No one likes a fake person. And knowing that no one likes a fake person, no one is going to associate him or herself with a fake person. A fake person can not be trusted, but God can for He is not fake and will never be fake.

GOD IS NOT GREEDY

God is not greedy. Don't compare Him to the tax collectors and billing agencies that want what is due to them. God wants what is due to Him and that is tithes and offerings. Besides, God gave you everything that you have. He blessed you with everything that you have. He is the reason why you have what you've got. Don't be selfish; give Him His cut. All He's asking for is 10 percent. He should be asking for everything, but He's not greedy. Whose planet are you living on? Whose air are you breathing? Whose spirit and body do you have? All of those things are God's. It was His pleasure to grant you blessings. It was His pleasure to grant you with riches. All He is asking for is a gift in return. Let Him know that you appreciate Him. Glorify Him. He is not asking for everything in your wallet. He is not asking for everything in your purse. And He is not asking for everything in your bank account. He is not greedy like humans. You should be glad that He's not greedy. You should be glad that He's not selfish because if He were, you would not have anything. My brothers and sisters, God is not greedy. I dare anyone to say that He is.

GOD IS NOT WEAK

God is not weak. Why do you think that He is? God is stronger than anyone or anything. He is tougher than anyone or anything. He is mightier than anyone or anything. There is no weakness in Him. He is too strong to be weak. He is too tough to be weak. Let me also add, He is too powerful to be weak. God has never backed down from a fight. He has never backed down from a battle. God has never run from anyone. He never hid from anyone. Do you still think that He's weak? God is the master of the universe. He is the King of heaven and earth. God's heavenly seat is strong. The beings that are encamped around Him are strong. His attributes are strong, and none of them contains weakness. God's love for you is not weak. It is strong. His love conquers all the evil that is against you. Now, if you still think that God is weak, something is truly wrong with you. I tell you what, try praying to God, and He will take away that stronghold that is hindering you. Then you will stop saying and thinking that God is weak.

GOD IS WITH YOU

Many people think that God is not with them. I'm here to correct them because God *is* with them. Every move that you make and every step that you take He is with you. He is not going to leave you. He does not want to leave you. He does not want to forsake you. When you get into trouble, He's with you. When you achieve a reward, He's with you. When you are birthing a child, He's with you. God loves you. He created you so He can be with you. He created you to walk with you. God desires to be your best friend and protector. When you got into that car accident, God protected you from getting seriously hurt. He was the one that gave you a warning not to drink that beverage because someone slipped poison inside of it. My friends, always remember that you are never lonely because God is with you.

GOD WANTS YOU TO HAVE A LIFE

God wants you to have a life, so you need to stop lying, saying that He doesn't. God wants you to have a life. He created you to have a life. So what's your problem? What are you complaining about? Enjoy yourself. He doesn't just want you to go to church, read the Bible, and pray. He wants you to get out and enjoy life. I'm not saying that going to church, reading the Bible, and praying is not enjoyable because they are enjoyable. I enjoy doing those things, and I have fun doing those things, but there is nothing wrong with going out and enjoying life in other ways. God created the earth, so you can enjoy it. He made wonderful things on earth for you to enjoy. Stepping out of the house is not a sin. It is certain things that you do or think that are a sin. Don't have any wrong impressions about God. God does want you to have a life, for He is the creator of it.

P.S. God gives you abundant life. He does not put you in bondage. You are free in God.

GOD WILL NEVER DO ANYTHING TO HARM YOU

Stop listening to those lies that the enemy is telling you. I'm here to tell you that God will never do anything to harm you. God was the one that helped plan a way of escape for you. The enemy is Satan, and he is feeding negative thoughts into your mind to make you turn against God. He also has evil followers. My brothers and sisters, Satan hates God, and he wants you to hate God. He is going to do all that he can to make you hate and turn against God. He asks, why do you serve God, and why do you wait on and love Him? He also says, go ahead and sin. Don't listen to Satan. He is a con artist. He does not care who he deceives. God is the one that does not lie. God is not the thief that seeks to destroy your life. He is the provider of life. He gives life more abundantly. He loves you. So whenever the enemy brings thoughts into your mind, rebuke him and then say God will never do anything to harm me.

GOD'S HEART IS BEAUTIFUL

My brothers and sisters, God's heart is beautiful. His heart is full of love. There is no evil in His heart. There is no hate in His heart. Peace, joy, love, and happiness take up all the space in His heart. And what's in His heart is for you. He wants your heart to be beautiful as well. He wants your heart to be labeled with His love. Don't reject it; accept it. If you want your heart to be like God, pray for it to be like His. I'm telling you His heart is beautiful. God will take away the sin from your heart and bless you with a clean, beautiful heart. He will flush all that sin out of you. And when God blesses you with that beautiful heart, you are going to fill good on the inside. You are going to see how it feels to be loved by God. He loves you that much to bless you with a beautiful heart like His. God's heart is clean. God's heart is sinless. Sin has never and will never be in His heart. Sin can't get close to His heart. God's heart is beautiful, and beautiful forever it will be.

GOD'S TIMING

God's timing is great. It is not pathetic. It is not slow. God picks and chooses when He wants to arrive. He does not take orders from anyone. He does not come when you want Him to come. He comes when He decides to come. When He says that He is going to bless you, count on it. Do not look at your clock because God does not operate by clocks. He does not operate by man's time. He operates by His own appointed time. God's timing is not poor. He knows when He wants to work things out. The time that He works things out is the right time. His time is always the right time. Your time may not be the right time for God, and that is why He appears when He decides to appear. Your time is not greater than His time. No one's time is greater than God's time. His level and appointed time is more advanced than your level and time. Wait on God and lean not to your own understanding. And I love what Elder Christine Gates says. She said, "When God shows up, He shows out," because His timing is awesome.

HAVE TENDER CARE

Have tender care for your neighbor. You never know what your neighbor may be going through. By you showing your neighbor tender care, he or she knows that you are concerned. He or she knows that you care. It lets your neighbor know that someone in the world does care about him or her. God appreciates those who show others tender care. He admires those that show others tender care. He lets His light shine on those who show others tender care. By you showing others tender care, it lets Him know that you are doing your job. It lets Him know that His people are following His commandment, "love thy neighbour as thyself" (Matthew 22:39). Have tender care for your neighbor because God has it for you.

I CARE ABOUT YOU

My friend, I care about you. I don't want anything bad to happen to you because I care about you. Be careful of your surroundings. Pray before you leave your house, asking God for His protection, for protection from God is what you need. The world is dangerous. There are many wicked spirits and people living in this world. And due to the wickedness in the world you need God. There is no surviving without Him. My friend, you are a beautiful person, and don't let anyone tell you otherwise. Make sure you have the breastplate of righteousness on because the enemy is out to damage your heart. The breastplate of righteousness guards against the enemy from damaging your heart. And make sure you have the helmet of salvation on so you won't get deceived by the enemy. The enemy doesn't care about you. He is out to kill, steal, and destroy all those that he can. I don't want you to be among that number. My friend, I care about you, so please don't forget it.

HE IS AS BRIGHT AS THE SUNLIGHT

God is as bright as the sunlight. As a matter of fact, He does not need the sunlight. His glory shines brighter than the sunlight. Where God is at, there is no sun. There is no need for it. His glory lights up heaven. God does not need the sun to light up heaven for His glory is brighter than the sun. God is the one that created the sun. And He did not create it for Himself. He created it for you and me. He created it for the creatures on earth because the creatures on earth are the ones that need it. He does not need it; we need it. We are the ones that need light to see. God will never live in darkness. He will never be in darkness. He will never worry about being in darkness. God is as bright as the sunlight, a powerful light is He. "And the city had no need of the sun, neither of the moon, to shine in it: for the glory of God did lighten it, and the Lamb is the light thereof" (Revelation 21:23).

IS

God is a true light. With Him in your life, you will surely shine bright. God is a God with power and might, and at His presence, evil knights flee in fright. God is a God that is bold, whose heart will never turn cold. He is a God with grace that is filled with love, not hate. God is a God with good and high standards. When you're with Him, nothing else matters. God is a God with high hopes that doesn't fool with foolishness, no joke. He is a God that will ease your pain, and living in Him, your life will not be in vain. Also, living in God, you will surely dig because when the blessings come, they come big. God will take away all of your sins. In Him you can truly depend, my friend.

IT IS NOT RIDICULOUS

My brothers and sisters, it is not ridiculous serving God, so serve Him. He is the greatest master to serve. God is real. He does exist. Do not have any doubts in your mind about it because He does exist. Many people say that those who serve God are ridiculous. They also say that God does not exist. What I'm telling you is, don't listen to those individuals. You see those individuals are in denial. They deny the power of God. They want to continue to live their worldly lives. They are caught up in the pleasures of this world. They are caught up in the lust of this world. They are just like the young rich ruler who did not want to give up his riches to follow Christ. Those who serve God know that He's real. We know that God exists. And we know that we are not wasting our time serving Him. God has a great reward for those who serve Him. And when we receive our reward, there is going to be nothing ridiculous about it because it is not ridiculous serving God, and He is not ridiculous.

KEEP UP THE GOOD WORK

Children of God, keep up the good work. You are doing a wonderful job serving God. God appreciates you. He appreciates your hard work. He appreciates the hard work that you are putting into serving Him. He appreciates the choir practice that you have. He appreciates the way that you are studying His Word and reaching out to others, so continue to do it. God is going to wonderfully bless you. He knows that you get tired sometimes. He knows that you get weary, but hang on in there. God is going to renew your spirit. According to His will, He is going to bless you with all that you ask for. He did not forget about the promise that He made to Abraham. He is not going to forsake that promise. You are Abraham's seed, and God is going to take care of you. He made a promise to Abraham, and He is going to keep it. God is not a liar. He is not a hypocrite. He says what He is going to do, and He does it, so keep up the good work because God is proud of you.

P.S. Stop being so hard on yourself. Learn how to reward yourself.

LOVE YOUR BODY

My friend, love your body. Honor your body. Your body is God's temple, so take care of it. Your body is important to God because His spirit lives in your body. Your body is the Spirit's home. God's uses your body to get His message across. If your body is healthy, your spirit is going to be healthy. If your body is out of shape, your spirit is going to be out of shape. That is why it is important to take care of your body. And how do you take care of your body? You take of your body by exercising and working out. Keeping it in shape. You also take care of your body by drinking water and eating the right meals. I don't want to be phony. I'm going to tell you the truth. I drink plenty of water. I work out and exercise. My body is in shape, but the one thing that I don't do enough is eat vegetables and fruits. I can eat. Sometimes I eat big. I have to eat the right meals and take care of my body. I have to love my body more. When you love your body, it shows that you love yourself. When you take care of your body, it shows that you love it and love yourself. My friend, love your body, but don't damage it for you are showing God that you are going to take care of what He had joyfully made for you.

LOVE YOUR HUSBANDS

Wives, love your husbands. Respect and honor them. They are your kings, so show them love. God made you to show them love. He made you to give them honor and respect. He didn't create you to give them hell. He didn't create you to verbally abuse them. He created you to respect them. Humble yourselves unto your husbands. Treat them with love and kindness. Just because men have hard bodies it doesn't mean that their hearts are hard. Some of them have soft hearts, so don't hurt their hearts. Women, men's hearts are precious as well as your hearts. They may be strong, but men do have feelings. Men have emotions. They hurt just like you hurt. Maybe they don't show it on the outside, but in the inside, they feel it. When your husbands come home from a hard day at work, don't give them drama. Give them peace. Ask them how their day was and uplift them. Solomon said, it is better to dwell in a corner of the housetop, than with a brawling woman in a wide house (Proverbs 21:9). Wives, respect your husbands. Make God proud by you honoring them. Give them love and affection and believe me, you will not hear any complaints.

LOVE YOUR WIVES

Husbands, love your wives. Respect your wives. Your wives are queens, so treat them as queens. Don't worry about what your homeboys will say about you. Forget what your homeboys say about you. All they do is run their mouths and half of the time they don't know what they are talking about. Treat your wives with respect. Love your wives. Live joyfully with them. Adore them. In Colossians 3:19, it says, husbands, love your wives and be not bitter against them. It does not say mistreat your wives. It does not say abuse your wives. It does not say treat your wives like trash. It says love your wives. Treat your wives with love and affection. Spend time with your wives. Don't neglect your wives. Even when your wives nag you, still show them love. You have to understand that women are emotional human beings. That is what God created them to be. They are precious and very lovable. Husbands, love your wives for it shows that you are being obedient to God, and you are great men that love and appreciate the virtuous woman that He brought into your lives.

PUT AWAY AND SERVE

Put away those idols and serve the true and living God. God is the real deal. He is a true God. He is more powerful than those idols that

I told you to put away. Those idols don't have any power, and if they did, they still can't match or outpower God. Look what happened to Dagon, an idol that the Philistines worshipped (1 Samuel 5). God ripped that statue into pieces. He does not want you to worship anyone or anything but Him. He wants all the glory. No statue created you. No human being created you. God created you. We all need to serve Him. God does not want to pour His wrath upon us, but He has no choice if we continue to worship and serve other things. Pour out your heart to God. Ask God to save you from His wrath. Put away those idols and serve God because, believe me, if they could talk, they would tell you to.

SHOW GRATITUDE

My brothers and sisters, it is important to show gratitude. It is important to show gratitude to those who do nice things for you. You have to let them know that you appreciate them. The more you show gratitude, the nicer people are going to treat you. Everyone wants to be appreciated. Everyone wants to be thanked. It is what motivates us to continue to love our neighbor as ourselves. It is what motivates us to continue to give love and respect. No one likes an unappreciative person. No one likes an unthankful person. The world can do without a person like that. The world has enough problems as it is. Showing gratitude lets an individual know that you care. Showing gratitude lets an individual know that you appreciate his or her hard work. It lets an individual know that you are thankful for his or her efforts. God shows His gratitude daily toward His children. He shows it by keeping them healthy, peaceful, joyful, and safe. And if God can show His gratitude, we too can show our gratitude, for we are made in His likeness. Show gratitude toward others, and I guarantee that they will not forget about you, for no one forgets a thankful person.

STAND AGAINST THE WILES OF THE DEVIL

People of God, stand against the wiles of the devil. Look out for the wiles of the devil. Be on guard. The devil is very sneaky. He will try to lure you into one of his traps. Do not fall for his tricks. He has many. And he is ready to shoot his tricks at you. The devil is a master deceiver. He is a master manipulator. He doesn't care who he deceives. He doesn't care who falls into his trap. The Word of God says, "see then that ye walk circumspectly, not as fools, but as wise, Redeeming the time, because the days are evil" (Ephesians 5:15–16). The Word of God also says, "Be sober, be vigilant; because your adversary the devil, as a roaring lion, walketh about, seeking whom he may devour" (1 Peter 5:8). My brothers and sisters, I don't want him to devour you so be ready to stand against his evil attacks.

STOP ARGUING SO MUCH

Husbands and wives, mothers and daughters, fathers and sons, mothers and sons, fathers and daughters, brothers and sisters, please stop arguing so much. What are you going to gain by arguing? The only thing that you are going to gain by arguing is drama and more drama. The only thing that you are going to gain by arguing is separation from each other, which is not good because a family is supposed to stick together. Families are supposed to love one another. You are not going to get anywhere by arguing. Your relationship will drop if you continue to argue. There is no love in arguing, only chaos. Be civilized and learn how to compromise. Be civilized and respect each other. You are beautiful people, so act like it. Don't let the Satan take your home captive. He will if you allow him to. All he needs is an open invitation. Live peacefully among each other. Learn how to speak nicely to each other because constantly arguing is not going to solve a thing. Husbands and wives, mothers and daughters, fathers and sons, mothers and sons, fathers and daughters, brothers and sisters, learn how to respect each other and stop arguing so much so you can have a peaceful and loving home and relationship.

STOP BEING PREJUDICED

Stop being prejudiced. Love the opposite race. And love the opposite sex. You have men that hate women, and you have women that hate men. That is so ridiculous. God made men for women and women for men. He didn't create men to hate women and women to hate men. He created men and women to love each other. On jobs there are women plotting against men and men plotting against women. That is evil and unprofessional. Cut that foolishness out. Now back to the race issue. Each race that God created is unique. Each race that God created is gifted, talented, and intelligent. We need to pull together and work as one. Use the gifts and abilities God has given to us for good, not evil. No one should be prejudiced. That person you hate is made just like you. The only thing that is different is the color. People, don't be prejudiced because prejudice is evil.

STOP BEING SO HARD ON YOURSELF

Stop being so hard on yourself. Take it easy on yourself. You are not perfect. You are going to make mistakes until the day you die. God knows that you are not perfect. And He doesn't expect you to be perfect. If you were perfect, you would not need Him because there would be no use for Him. God knows that you are going to make mistakes. Making a mistake is not a sin. It is not a crime. So you need to chill, relax, and cool yourself down. Realize that you are human. And realize that it's not the end of the world if you make a mistake. Continue to work hard and don't give up. And please stop being so hard on yourself, because being too hard on yourself can and will destroy you.

THE EARTH IS BEAUTIFUL

The earth is beautiful. And it is because of God that it is beautiful. God, with His majestic and wise self, made this beautiful planet. With His wonderful creativity, He created this beautiful planet. He laid down the foundations of the earth, and how beautiful are they. The creatures that He made are beautiful. The trees and the flowers are beautiful. The rivers, oceans, streams, and lakes are beautiful. The mountains and the valleys are beautiful. And if the earth is beautiful, that ought to let you know that God is beautiful because He was the one that created it. If anyone wants to question if God is beautiful, tell him or her to look at earth, His creation. And then they will see that God is beautiful. I'm glad that God created the earth. I'm glad that

God created every living thing in it because it lets me know that the earth is beautiful and He is beautiful.

THE GOD OF LOVE

I know a God who loves you more than life itself. And no matter what you do, He stills loves you. He is compassionate about you. He cares about you. This God who I know is God Almighty, and He is the God of love. He is not the God of hate, but the God of love. He loves you so much that He sent His Son on earth to be sacrificed for you. He put His Son up for sacrifice. That is how much He loves you. The God of love also blessed you to be a beautiful human being. He blessed you to be a unique human being for He poured His breath of life inside of you. Satan will not do anything good for you because he is full of crap. He is full of hate. God is the one that keeps you warm in cold weather. God is the one that keeps you from entering into danger. He is the one that delivers you from bondage. God is the God of love. He is the God of eternal love. He prepared a wonderful place for you to live for all eternity. You are going to feel His eternal love because you are going to be with Him for all eternity. God is the God of love, so don't forget that.

THE TRUE GOD

Who is the true God? God Almighty is the true God. He is the one and only true God. There is no one or nothing else true like Him. There is no one or anything on His level. There is no one or anything near His level. He is the greatest of the greatest. He is the best of the best. He is the most famous creator in the universe. He is the greatest being in the universe. How many times did you hear Him tell a lie? You never heard Him tell a lie because He doesn't tell lies. God is majestic. He is rich in wisdom. He is rich in love. His throne is up above all creation. God is the true God, and there is nothing anti about Him.

THE WAY MAKER

I understand now. I understand what people before my generation said about God. God is the way maker. He makes ways out of no way for you. There is nothing too impossible for God. There is nothing too difficult for Him. There is nothing that He can not do. God can do anything. He made a way for me to graduate from high school with honors. He made a way for me to get my high school diploma. He makes ways for people to get healed from cancer. He makes ways for people to get healed from deadly and serious diseases. I'm telling you God is powerful. All you have to do is pray and God will make a way out of no way for you. You may be broke. You may not have enough money in your pocket or bank account to get a house or a car. If you pray, have faith, and work hard; God will make a way out of no way for you to get that car or house. Remember, my brothers and sisters, faith without works is dead. You do the possible, and God will do the impossible. Come on, my brothers and sisters, He is God. He made a way for you to build buildings and fly in the sky. He made a way for you to predict the weather. He made a way for you to be wealthy. But most of all, the enemy thought this couldn't be done, but God made a way for you to go to heaven. God is, and truly is, the way maker because with Him, all things are possible.

WALK IN FAITH

My brothers and sisters, walk in faith. Do not walk in fear. Do not walk in doubt, but walk in faith. By walking in faith you please God. And if I know that I can please God by walking in faith, I am going to walk in it. I am not going to let anyone or anything stop me from doing it. Walking in faith gives you the strength to endure hard times. Walking in faith pushes you to the next level. It pushes you toward greatness. It is a key to being complete in Christ. Walking in faith also brings you many blessings from God because you believe in Him. You believe that God can do anything. You have faith that God can do any impossible thing. And if you believe that God can do any impossible thing, you are believing right because He can do any impossible thing. He is God. There is nothing too impossible for Him to do. There is nothing too hard for Him to do. It may be hard to us, but to God, it is easy. If you believe that God can not do anything, you would be insulting Him and hindering yourself from receiving anything from

Him. Trust in God and walk in faith so you can receive the blessings that He has stored for you.

YOU ARE A WARRIOR

You are a warrior, so act like it. Stop allowing people to walk all over you. Stop allowing people to abuse you. Be a warrior and stand up for yourself. Fight for yourself. Defend yourself. Guard yourself. As long as you allow people to abuse you, they are going to do it. You have to love yourself enough to not allow them to abuse you. Some people are wicked. Some people are evil. They don't care about you or your expectations. My brother, you are a warrior. My sister, you are a warrior, so stand up for yourself because you are mighty.

YOU ARE NOT ABOVE GOD

You are not above God, so you better check yourself. You better wake up out of your dream. No one is above God. No one is higher than He. Whosoever thinks that he or she is higher than God, that person needs counseling. He or she needs to come into reality. Stop living in fantasyland. God is above all creations. He is greater than all creations, so you should not think that you are above Him. You shouldn't have the nerve to think that you are above Him. It is God's breath that is in you. It is God's vessel that is in you. Everything that is within you belongs to Him. The planet that you live on belongs to God. The heavens belong to Him. As a matter of fact, God is above the heavens. He is above the solar system. The only place you may be above is your household, and the reason that you may be above your household is if God allowed you to be above your household. Get on your knees and ask God for forgiveness, saying that you repent for thinking that you are above Him. And please don't think that you are above God because I don't want Him to embarrass you.

YOU ARE NOT GOD

You are not God, so why are you trying to be Him? There is only one God, and He's in heaven sitting on His throne. He is the one and only God. He is the one and only true God. He is the only one that has the right and power to judge. So how are you going to judge someone when you have sinned? How are you going to be God when you have sinned? God never sinned. And how are you going to be God when He's the one you have to answer to? You can not answer to yourself. You are not going to answer to yourself. You are going to answer to God. And God is who you are not. When God sees you judge someone, He gets upset. When God sees you throw stones at someone, He gets upset. Why does He get upset? He gets upset because you are no better than that individual you are judging. He gets upset because He did not give you the permission to judge. When you leave earth, you're not going to yourself, you're going to God. When people die, they are not going to face you, they are going to face God. Don't walk around pointing your fingers at others. Don't walk around condemning others because that's not right. Let God do the judging. Let God do the condemning. Just be what He called you to be, and that is a servant, because you are not God, and God certainly did not call you to be Him.

YOU ARE NOT TRASH

My friend, you are not trash, so don't allow anyone to treat you like trash. You are not garbage. Refuse to let anyone treat you like garbage. You are a beautiful human being made in God's image. You are precious in His sight. You are His child, which means you are not trash. You are royalty. You are joint heirs with His Son Jesus Christ. Heaven is your eternal home. I dare you to let anyone treat you like trash. Sin is the only thing that is trash. And sin is not what you are. Sin is trash, and that is why Jesus defeated sin and cast it in hell where it belongs because hell is the place where trash belongs. Know that you are a wonderful person. Know that you are unique. Know that you are special. Love yourself and don't let anyone treat you like trash because trash is not what you are.

CHAPTER 3

TAKE HEED

ANSWER PRAYERS

My brothers and sisters, God does answer prayers, so continue to pray. Don't listen to the devil and your enemies when they say that He doesn't. And don't listen to them when they say you are only wasting your time because they are nothing but liars. But I'm not lying when I tell you that God answers prayers.

God hears your prayers, and He will surely answer them. He is not going to ignore them. He is a God that wants, and commands, you to pray. He is a God that anticipates it. Don't be like those nonbelievers that don't have any faith. Continue to keep your faith and trust in God.

God knows that there are going to be days that you are going to get weary. He knows that there are going to be days that you are not going to see anything, but believe me, God remembers your prayers, and He is going to answer them. Your prayers are important to Him. He doesn't take them lightly.

Sometimes you are going to have to understand what it means to be patient. When you start to lose patience, that's when the devil and your enemies start to ask where is the God you've been praying to? You respond by saying, the same place He has always been, and that's inside of me!

Consider this, when you think that God is taking too long to answer your prayer, maybe He is preparing something big for you. You have to use your imagination. Forget what the devil and your enemies are saying. The devil is just upset because he got the boot. And your enemies are just jealous because they don't have the Spirit of God like you. The Spirit of God is the richest gift to have. And remember, God does answer prayers, and you can most definitely count on His amazing results.

BE SECURE

The problem that many people have is that they are insecure. If they'd stop being insecure, things would run smoothly in their lives. I'm here to tell you, my brothers and sisters, be secure about yourself.

Insecurity doesn't do anything but bring stress and worry in your lives. Insecurity robs you of your peace, but when you are secure about yourself, it brings peace. When you are secure about yourself, you know yourself. You know who you are and are sure of yourself. When you are secure, you have amazing confidence in yourself.

Being a spiritual person of God you can spot a person that's insecure a mile away. It's in their body language and speech. You say to yourself, if only that person were secure in himself or herself they could move any mountain and break any barrier.

Insecurity brings low self-esteem. You don't trust in anyone or anything. I refuse to be insecure. I refuse not to have peace. I know who I am and am quite sure of myself. If a person is not interested in you, so be it! Don't let it bother you. Know who you are. Be secure about yourself, my brothers and sisters, and experience the joy, life, peace, and confidence it brings.

BREASTPLATE OF RIGHTEOUSNESS

I thank God for the breastplate of righteousness. The breastplate of righteousness protects your heart and spirit from all evil. It protects your heart and spirit from negativity, such as people's bitterness, anger, depression, frustration, and stress. Because, believe me, people are going to try to throw those things at you. Just because they are miserable, they want you to be miserable.

Misery loves company. Have you ever been around a group of

people that spoke negatively? I have, and I fled because if you are not careful, their spirit can get on you. That's why you have to pray and ask God for the breastplate of righteousness, so you will not get affected by those negative spirits.

When you have the breastplate of righteousness, you can not be moved by the things that people say. The breastplate of righteousness keeps you standing strong. You are on solid foundation with it. When someone lashes out at you, you will not be fazed by it because you are equipped by the breastplate of righteousness. The breastplate of righteousness is powerful. Nothing can destroy it. Nothing can get through it. "Stand therefore, having your loins girt about with truth, and having on the breastplate of righteousness" (Ephesians 6:14).

CLEARED CONSCIENCE

My brothers and sisters, having a cleared conscience is beautiful. It's when you know that God has forgiven you for all your sins. It's when you know that you are not burdened by any guilt. It's when you know that you didn't disrespect or hurt anyone's feelings. I feel bad when I hurt someone's feelings because it doesn't feel good hurting someone's feelings.

Nevertheless, having a cleared conscience also lets you know that the Holy Spirit has no problems with you. Because if the Holy Spirit did have any problems with you, He would let you know. He would tell you what you did to a person wasn't right. And you have to apologize to that person and repent to God for the wrong you've done. Believe me, my brothers and sisters, I've been through that experience millions of times. Every time I do something wrong, the Holy Spirit knocks on my door, and I know what time it is. It's time for me to get my conscience cleared for the wrong that I done.

Now back to me telling you how beautiful it is having a cleared conscience. When you have a cleared conscience, you have excellent peace. You have excellent joy, and you know that you have good standing with God, Jesus Christ, and the Holy Spirit. God is well pleased with you because you are following His orders. You are walking in no condemnation. You are walking free from guilt. I'm telling you, my brothers and sisters, having a cleared conscience makes you feel like you are flowing in the clouds. And yes, it feels that good. That's the peace I was telling you about.

P.S. The Holy Spirit is going to knock on your door until you get your conscience cleared.

COMBAT

Body of Christ, it is time for combat. We have to go to war with the enemy. It is time to stop putting up with his crap. He is not our friend, but our enemy. Let us stand tall and defeat him with the power of God.

The enemy is having a field day in our homes, jobs, school systems, churches, and country. It is time for us to kick his tail. I'm sick and tired of hearing husbands and wives fighting against each other. I'm sick and tired of hearing children disrespecting their parents and teachers. It is time for this bull to stop. Husbands and wives are supposed to be getting along. Children are supposed to be respecting their elders. That is why you are seeing people (young people) dying so early.

We as the body of Christ have to discern what's going on and see who the real enemy behind this is, and his name is Satan. Our homes are supposed to be a place of peace and rest, not chaos. Our schools are supposed to be institutes of learning and places to have fun. Now what do you see? You see husbands and wives murdering each other. You see children bringing weapons to school. I'm telling you these things ought not to be.

Body of Christ, the world needs us. God has called us to save this dying world. Without us, this world is not going to make it for long, so let's do our duty and destroy Satan and his evil followers for good.

GET SOME UNDERSTANDING

My brothers and sisters, some of us need to get some understanding. When it comes to understanding, some of us are ridiculous. The only way for us to get free from foolish and ignorant bondages is to get some understanding.

Where do we get it from? We get it from God's Word, the Holy Bible. The Holy Bible has all the information we need. It will help us understand why the world is the way it is. It will show us how to get through tough situations. That is why many people ask questions, like "Why did that happen to me? And what did I do? Is it that I'm living wrong? And why is the world the way it is?" If you get some understanding you will see why things happen and why the world is the way it is.

People, we are not living in a perfect world. There are many evil spirits in the world. You hear many people say, "That person is evil." I'm writing to tell you that it's not the person that's evil, it's the spirit inside the person. See, having understanding will let you know why that person is the way he or she is. Having understanding will tell you that person needs to be delivered from that evil spirit.

"For we wrestle not against flesh and blood, but against principalities, against powers, against the rulers of the darkness of this world, against spiritual wickedness in high places" (Ephesians 6:12). Spiritual wickedness in high places use people as puppets to do their dirty work, and until those people are delivered by Jesus, they are going to continue to be puppets for those evil spirits. That is why Ephesians 6:13 tells you to put on the whole armor of God, so you can be protected from those evil spirits. You are not fighting against your fellow man, but those evil spirits that have them captivated, so get some understanding by reading the Word of God, so you won't get captured as well. May peace be with you, and God bless you.

GOD DOES NOT HOLD ANYTHING AGAINST YOU

God does not hold anything against you, so what are you worried about? All the ungodly things you have done, He forgave you for doing them. What you need to do is let them go. Once you asked God to forgive you, He forgave you right then and there. And then he remembers your sins no more. You are the one that keeps on thinking about them. And if Satan keeps bringing them up, just simply rebuke him.

You see, God does not bring up your past; the enemy does. God tells you to press forward. He says forget about those things that are behind. Stop letting them hold you back from your great future. You have nothing to worry about. God knows you are not perfect. He knows you are going to sin for you are a human born into a world of sin. Receive your wonderful blessings from God. He knows you didn't know what you were doing. It is just the result of being part of the world. That is why God gives us grace and mercy, for He knows we are going to do things we do not supposed to be doing.

Like I told you earlier, we are born into a world of sin. Your flesh is going to battle with your spirit. Now that you are saved and delivered, it is time to release your past, and don't be afraid because God loves you and does not hold anything against you.

P.S. It is God's will and desire to bless you. Not to hold anything against you. He is the God of forgiveness. Just ask Him; you'll see.

GOD WANTS YOU TO BE SAFE

You know some people are actually out of their minds. And that's not even funny. Some people believe that God wants them to get hurt. I'm here to tell you that is a bold-faced lie. God wants you to be safe.

Why do you think He wants you to serve Him? He wants you to serve Him, so you can be safe. As long as you are in His presence, you are going to be safe. God is a mighty shield, and with Him shielding you, nothing is going to harm you. No one is going to destroy you. Why? Because you are protected by the Almighty God. He is going to keep you in His safety. He is not going to lose sight of you.

God protects His children just like a lion protects its cubs. Bad weather can blow by your house, and you along with the house, and it will still be standing. A bullet can fly past you, and you will not get hit for you are in the safety of God. Satan can't harm or touch you. He knows what would happen if he tries. He knows that God has got your back. There is no need for you to be shaky. There is no need for you to quiver for you are safe in the mighty hands of God, a God of safety.

GROW UP

My friend, it is time for you to grow up. I mean, you cry about every little thing. Don't you think it is time for you to grow up? Of course it is. It is time for you to get off the milk and get on the meat. It is time for you to be a true soldier of the Lord. It is time for you to be a true worshipper of the Lord. You can not be those things if you cry all the time. You have to push yourself to maturity. You have to train yourself to be mature.

Don't let negative things that people say move or shake you. You have to be strong. You have to understand that everybody is not going to be for you. There are haters in the world. There are people filled with jealousy and anger. And believe me, they are going to direct it toward you. That is why it is important for you to grow up, so your enemies won't affect you.

God does not want complainers, He wants appreciators. He wants those that are going to be able to handle the battlefield with no problems. If you don't grow, you are not going to be any use to Him. Believe me, you are not going to be sent on the battlefield unprepared. To be on the battlefield you have to be mature. And I'm telling you, my friend, the battlefield is where you want to be. Because when the smoke has cleared and the battle is over, all the blessings are going to come your way. I'm not lying. I'm telling the truth. Grow up so you can proceed to the glorious level God has for you. "For every one that useth milk is unskilful in the word of righteousness: for he is a babe" (Hebrews 5:13).

I BRING GOOD NEWS

The problem with most people today is that they always want things for free; they never are willing to pay or work hard for things. They just want everything handed to them on a silver platter. They even refuse to get their nails dirty.

The only way they will support you is if they are going to get something out of it. But when it comes to them, they want you to pay. Even if it costs a pretty penny, they are going to want that penny. It's sad, but true.

People like them are selfish. They don't want to support you, but they want you to support them. They are the people that smile in your face, but behind your back they hope you will fail. They wish bad on your business, your book, and your music, saying that you're going to flop. They are the world's biggest haters, always so full of negativity. Outside they look like sheep, but inwardly, they are ravenous wolves (Matthew 7:15).

But I bring you good news, my brothers and sisters, don't worry about them. Though they wish bad on you, God has good for you. Nothing they do or say will stop you from being successful. You are a child of the Most High God, and that means a lot. You have to know the power that you contain and how powerful you are. Keep pushing and striving. And don't worry because you have the biggest support group in the universe, and that is God and His holy kingdom.

IT IS SO BEAUTIFUL

People, I just want to tell you that it is so beautiful being with God. It is so beautiful being with Him because He does not mistreat you. His love for people is just so amazing. I'm telling you God will do anything for you; all you have to do is just ask. God speaks with love and sincerity. He doesn't speak to hurt or bring you down. He cares about the way you feel. He truly is a comforter.

Many people try to portray Him as a monster. They try to portray Him as a dragon. They tell others when God speaks, you better run. I'm writing to tell you when God speaks, don't run, but listen. Running is not going to get you delivered. Running is not going to set you free. God does not want you to run away from Him. He wants you to hearken unto Him. He does not want to destroy you. He wants to love you. He wants to hold you in His arms. He wants to feed you with His compassion.

Being with Him, there are no worries. He is going to handle all the things that burden you. All God wants you to do is relax, and He will take care of everything for you. It is so beautiful being with God, and once you are with Him, I guarantee you are not going to want to leave. Experience His wonderful splendor.

LOOKS AFTER

Let's vibe. God always looks after His children. They never have to beg for bread for He is always there to provide their needs. He is a

God of giving. He is a God that cares. He always hears and answers His children's cries. He is the keeper of their souls. And an absolute keeper is He.

God protects His children from Satan. He will not let the evil one destroy them. God knows how nasty and evil Satan can be. That he would do whatever it takes to get his hands on one of God's children, but God, being the keeper that He is, won't allow it to happen. You see, God is the shepherd. He won't let the big bad wolf take one of His sheep. When He sees the big bad wolf, He chases him away with His powerful and mighty staff.

God means business when it comes to His sheep. His sheep mean so much to Him (John 10:27–30). He always saves and delivers His sheep out of trouble. If He didn't, He wouldn't be God. And I know that He is God, and a great God and Father is He. He is the greatest protector in the galaxies. He is Lord of the universe. No one can stand toe to toe with Him. No one is that powerful. God always gets the victory for He is the most powerful and bravest being in the universe.

MOVE ON WITH YOUR LIFE

Hear me, my brother. Hear me, my sister. It is time for you to move on with your life. Okay, I understand that you've been hurt. But how long are you going to stay hurt? How long are you going to stay down in the pit of depression? You have to encourage yourself and move on. Who hasn't been hurt? I've been hurt plenty of times, but I've got over the hurt and moved on.

My brother, God has a wife for you. My sister, God has a husband for you, but you are not going to receive your spouse until you get over your past relationships. And knowing that you have a spouse coming from God should motivate you to get over that person who hurt you. The spouse that God has for you is wonderful. The spouse that God has for you is unique, so receive your spouse in the name of Jesus.

I tell you the truth, my brother and sister, I don't want God to keep my spouse away from me. I want mine, and in the name of Jesus, I'm going to receive mine. Believe me, hurt will control your life if you allow it. Instead, allow God to use your hurt to strengthen you. He will turn your hurt into joy. Love yourself enough not to get hurt, used, or abused again, and you do that by waiting on God. If you look for a spouse without the help of God, you are bound to get hurt again. How do I know? By experience. God knows the right mate for you. And He has the right mate for you, so move on with your life and love yourself by enjoying life and you.

NEVER KICK A PERSON WHILE HE OR SHE IS DOWN

My friend, let me give you some excellent advice: never kick a person while he or she is down. Uplift that person. How would you feel if someone kicked you while you were down? I know you won't like it.

It is painful enough that the person is down, but you make it even more painful when you kick the person. It is your duty to encourage that person. It is your duty to motivate that person. God gave you the gift, ability, and spirit to uplift, encourage, and motivate. Don't upset Him by making the situation worse.

What do you gain by kicking a person while he or she is down? Personally, I never kicked a person when he or she was down. Even if that person was my enemy. I don't get a thrill out of doing it. Jesus says to love your enemies not hate them (Matthew 5:44).

We as the children of God are supposed to help others with their problems. That is a big part of our mission and purpose. I tell you, my friend, I am just like the good Samaritan (Luke 10:30–37). He helped that person that was down. We are all supposed to be like him for he showed the character of Jesus Christ. Never kick a person while he or she is down because that is absolutely cruel.

NEVER UNDERESTIMATE THE ENEMY

My brothers and sisters, never, and I mean never, underestimate the enemy, which is Satan. If you underestimate him, you will find yourself in deep trouble. Don't get it twisted. Satan has power as well as we do.

I know God and Jesus gave us the power to triumph over him, but some of us are taking that power for granted. Some of us don't know how to use it. Instead of using the power to fight Satan, some of us are using that power to put our own selves on pedestals. We let pride and arrogance kick in. The power is being used for the wrong reasons. Satan doesn't even have to try some of us because we are letting our own pride take us down.

God wants you to respect Satan's power. He doesn't want you to take his power as a joke. He doesn't want you to underestimate it. For if you do, you will be on the other side of the laughingstock. You see, Satan is real tricky and crafty, and if you are not careful, you will get lured into one of his traps.

Satan is powerful. I'm not giving him any credit. I'm just telling you the truth. You can see it for yourselves. Just watch the news and you will see what I'm talking about. The way that people are killing, raping, and harming each other is of the devil.

The Word of God says that the enemy is after God's very elect (Matthew 24:24). If you are not careful, he will deceive and hold you captive. That is why you must rebuke him in the name of Jesus. You must use God's Word against Satan. Not your own word or power, but God's power. Satan will triumph over you if you don't use God's power.

I'm getting sick and tired of seeing generations dying. I mean, people are not even putting up a fight. They are giving in to Satan and his schemes. Fight the good fight of faith. Be a good soldier of Jesus, and remember, never underestimate the enemy.

ONLY GOD CAN JUDGE YOU

My brothers and sisters, don't let what people say worry you because only God can judge you. The person that is judging you is not perfect, did not die for you, and did not resurrect for you. Jesus Christ had to die for that person's sins, so don't worry about what he or she says about you.

None of us are perfect. All men and women have sinned (Romans 3:23). There is only one that's righteous, and that is Jesus Christ. Jesus Christ and God should be the only ones you should be concerned about. Forget about everyone else. God and Jesus Christ are the ones that are blessing you. They are the ones that are shielding, protecting, and providing for you. Don't give anyone the power or the authority to judge you, but only God and Jesus. The power of life and death are in their hands not in man's hands.

Like Jesus Christ told the scribes and Pharisees, those without sin cast the first stone (John 8:7–11). And what did they do? They walked away because they knew they had sinned and were not perfect. I guarantee you if Jesus Christ says the same thing to the person who is judging you, he or she will walk away just like the scribes and Pharisees did. Why? Because only God is perfect and can judge you.

OWN UP TO YOUR SIN

Stop crying about your sin and own up to it. Ask God for forgiveness and stop blaming others, saying that they were the cause for you sinning. No one caused you to sin. You chose to sin, so be a soldier and own up to it.

Stop pointing fingers. You are your own person. No one put a pistol to your head and told you to sin. You chose to sin. It sickens me when people say, "The devil made me do it." The devil didn't make you do a thing. God gave you the power over the devil (Luke 10:19). Jesus Christ defeated the devil and put him to shame. And here you go saying the devil made you do it. Stop giving Satan credit.

Get over your sin. What makes you think that you never sinned? What makes you think you are better than everyone else? We all have sinned and fallen short of the grace and glory of God. Get off your high horse and face the fact that you are not perfect. Face the fact that you are not God.

There is only one God, and it is certainly not you. And if you are so intelligent as you boastfully claim, you would know that we all are born into a world of sin, meaning that we are capable of and are going to sin, so when you do sin don't look at anyone but yourself because you are the one that has to own up to it. Don't be stubborn and not ask God for forgiveness. Ask Him and He will forgive you. He knows the sin that this world contains.

REFRAIN FROM EVIL

Listen here, my buddy, refrain from evil. Evil is not good, so refrain from it. I'm telling you this for your own good, and I love you. I don't want you to end up in jail, six feet under, or worse of all, in hell. Get yourself right in the Lord, go to church, pray, and read your Bible.

Check this out. God is not here to take your life away. He is here to give you life, and a great life at that. But He is going to take something away from you, and that something is sin. He is going to clean out all that pollution that is in the inside of you. He is going to take away those things that are causing you to do evil. But for Him to do those things you have to refrain from evil, submit, and humble yourself unto Him.

Submitting and humbling yourself unto God will give you life, and life more abundantly. Submitting and humbling yourself unto God will clean you from all your sins. Best of all, submitting and humbling yourself unto God will give you eternal life which is through Jesus Christ, the Supreme Being. That sounds great! I know that you feel me, so refrain from evil so you can chill with God, Jesus Christ, the Holy Spirit, God's holy angels, and me in heaven.

STAND YOUR GROUND

My brothers and sisters, stand your ground. Don't let anyone move you. Don't let your enemies overtake you. Stand up to them. I don't care how they look or how they may sound, still stand up to them. Use the power that God has given to you to slay them just like He gave David the power to slay Goliath (1 Samuel 17:49–50).

Some of us are afraid of people whose power is useless. We have the power of God. We should not be afraid of those who don't have His power. We are more than conquerors. Just like Fred Hammond's song says, "We are more than able. With the Lord on our side we can do it." Goliath ran his mouth like he was big, and bad. And David overheard him (1 Samuel 17:23–31). Goliath defied the armies of the living God which means He didn't have the power of God, and means he didn't respect Him (1 Samuel 17:10). And in the name and power of God, David whipped him like he stole something.

We have to whip our enemies as well. Our enemies are nothing but a bunch of cowards. The only thing that comes out of their mouths is hot air. If you say boo, they will run. Why? Because you have the power of God, the power that would have them fleeing in seven ways. Stand your ground.

STOP BEING IN SUCH A HURRY

People, stop being in such a hurry. Have some patience. A lot of crazy things happen when you are impatient. Many people are dead due to impatience. How did they die? They died in car accidents, meaningless deaths. Some of them were in a hurry to get to work on time. Some of them were in a hurry to get to the mall before they missed out on the last pair of shoes or outfit. And some of them were in a hurry to get their hair fixed. That is not funny, but ridiculous.

One day I was trailing my brother home, and some driver felt like I was driving too slow, so he jumped in front of me. The sad part about it, he jumped in front of me just to make a left at the next street which was just five seconds ahead of us. The way he jumped in front of me I thought he had an emergency at the hospital. And then another driver jumped in front of me. The sad part about that is that we all ended up at the same place, a red traffic light, so the driver wasted his or her precious time jumping in front of me. And I laughed about it.

Furthermore, when you are in a hurry, mistakes happen. That is why you should take your time. Things are done right when you take your time. Things are smooth when you take your time. I'm not talking about moving like a turtle; I'm talking about moving at a reasonable steady pace.

Last, but not least, many of us are in a hurry to get a blessing. You can not hurry God. He is going to bless you whenever He's ready. You don't have the right to hurry God, or the authority. You did not create God. He created you. He tells you what to do. He put that breath inside of you. And here you are having the audacity to hurry Him. None of us have that power, and will never have that power. Live each second, minute, hour, and day one step at a time. Stop being in a hurry because your life is more precious than anxiety.

STOP BEING SO CONTROLLING

Stop it, stop it, stop it, stop it. Stop being so controlling. There are too many people in the world that are so controlling. They try to tell everybody what to do. They try to control everybody. The only one they need to focus on controlling is themselves. That is why so many marriages and relationships have failed, because one of the partners was so controlling. And the other one got sick and tired of putting up with it.

I'm telling you the truth, if you continue to be controlling, you are going to find yourself by yourself. No one likes to be encamped with a controlling person. No one likes to be associated or involved with a controlling person because a controlling person is a dictator. A controlling person thinks that he or she has the answers to everything, which means that he or she doesn't listen to anyone but him or herself.

God Almighty is not even controlling, and He is the only one that has the right to be for He is God. He does not force anyone to do a thing, but you have people out there in the world that do. You have people out there that try to play the role of God when they are nowhere near Him. They are not in His league.

We have to respect people like human beings are supposed to. There is only one God, and He is in heaven. His commandment tells us to love each other, not to control each other. God says to have self-control, not control over others, so please stop being so controlling! Let others choose their own path of living.

P.S. It's okay to help others and give them good advice, but it is up to them to take heed to it. Don't get upset if they refuse. And if they fall on their butts, so be it! You did your job, which was telling them good advice, and they did not take it in. So you don't have anything to feel guilty about. Just don't try to control people.

STOP TRYING TO CHANGE PEOPLE

Stop trying to change people and let God do the changing on them. Who do you think you are trying to change someone? You just got saved a couple of days or years ago. There are some things that

God has to change concerning you. There are some changes you have to make, so stop trying to change others.

Only God has the power to change others, not us. We have the power to help and pray for others, but not the power to change them. It is up to them whether they want to make that change. If you keep telling a person to stop drinking, he or she is going to continue to drink. And if you keep telling a person to stop smoking, he or she is going to continue to smoke. Sometimes you have to leave people alone because if you keep harassing and trying to tell them what to do, they are going to keep doing what they are doing. Just let them be, and let God do the changing.

The best thing you can do is lead and live by example. Set a standard, and believe me, others will be watching. Instead of trying to change others all the time, focus on yourself. You keep yourself on that narrow pathway. You keep yourself spiritually and morally fit.

That's the problem with most people today; they try to change others instead of seeing what changes they need to make within themselves. There's nothing wrong giving others advice. There's nothing wrong trying to help others, but only God can change others because if we try to do it, things are only going to get worse. Stop trying to change others. There is only one God, and it is not you.

WAKE UP

You know what, my brothers and sisters? Some of us need to wake up. We need to recognize who loves and blesses us. God is the one who loves and blesses us. He is the one that sent His Son to the world to be sacrificed for us (John 3:16). And some of us are still not appreciative.

We are walking around running our mouths, bickering and complaining as if God owes us something. God doesn't owe us a thing. He gave us something that is priceless, which is salvation. Salvation is our seal to spiritual freedom and eternal life, but some of us still want more because we are greedy. Just because society is greedy doesn't mean that we should be greedy.

We are living in a world that is full of greed and lust. God doesn't want His people seeking after the things of this world. He wants us seeking after the things that pertain to His kingdom. If you tell some of God's people that they are seeking after the wrong things, which are the things of the world, they will curse you out.

Don't get me wrong. God does want you to have things, but when some of us do get things, our heads get big. And we forget about the one who was the provider of the things. We begin smelling our tails as if we are big shots. God is the Big Shot, and there is no one bigger than He. We should have power over the material things, not the material things having power over us. Wake up, my brothers and sisters, don't let the world overtake you like it is doing others, but let God overtake you with His beautiful and wonderful love.

A TRUE PROVIDER

God is a true provider. He provides for His people every day. God's people never have to beg for bread for He is always there to provide them with everything they need. His people never hunger or thirst. They always have clothes on their backs. He never leaves or forsakes them, for He is a true Father. He provides His people with shelter. He provides them with transportation to get from point A to point B. He provides them with great finances, so they can live decently. Look what kind of Spirit He provided them with: The Holy Spirit who enriches our spirits in the universe. I'm telling you God is not selfish. He always thinks about His people. He doesn't just sit on His throne and think about Himself; He thinks about others. He thinks about providing for others. God is a true provider. He is the God of provision.

AIM FORWARD

Stop dwelling on the past and begin to aim forward. The past is over with, so aim forward. The hell with what happened to you in the past. We've all been through hard times. We've all been disappointed and hurt, and that is why aiming forward gives us the motivation to move on. Aiming forward means there are good things ahead. Aiming forward means life is not over with. What did Jesus do? Jesus aimed forward. Even when He died, He aimed forward. Why? Because He knew there are better things ahead. He didn't let His past hurts and disappointments stop Him from aiming forward. Where is He now? He's in heaven sitting on the right-hand side of God (Hebrews 12:2). He is second in command. And He achieved that by aiming forward. If Jesus would have kept His mind on the past, He would not have made it to the cross. He would have given up, but like the mighty soldier that He is, He didn't. You have the same power that Jesus has. God has given it to you, so come out of the past, and aim forward.

BEING COURTEOUS

I tell you, my brothers and sisters, it feels so good being courteous, and that is why I urge you to be that way. Being courteous shows that you have manners. Being courteous shows that you have class. It also shows that you respect others as well as yourself. There is nothing wrong with being courteous. That is what the world needs. It needs people that are polite instead of people that are rude, violent, disrespectful, and hateful. The world has enough of that nonsense. Be nice to others and show kindness. That is what God commands you to do (Matthew 19:19). He commands that because it is the right thing to do. What do you have to lose by being courteous? People will remember you by your kind actions. Are you getting sick and tired of dealing with other's rude and disrespectful attitudes? But just because their attitudes are rude and disrespectful doesn't mean that ours should be that way. We have to live by example. We have to be role models. Be courteous, my brothers and sisters, because it is the right and godly way to be.

BE FAITHFUL

My friends, don't be stubborn unto God; be faithful unto Him. Why not be faithful to Him? He is faithful to you. Anything you ask, He gives it to you. Anything you need, He provides it for you. When you were sick, who was there to nurse you back to health? When you were about to be evicted, who was there to make sure you didn't lose your shelter? God was there. He is always there for you. He means what He says that He won't ever leave or forsake you. God loves you. You belong to Him. Show God love. Be obedient unto Him. Let Him know that you appreciate Him. Every day acknowledge Him. He is your King. He is your Father and Provider. Be faithful unto God and be happy about it.

BE FORGIVERS

My brothers and sisters, be forgivers. If someone disrespects, hurts, or abuses you, forgive that person. Don't walk around with bitterness, anger, and hatred in your hearts. Don't let ignorant and foolish people stop you from receiving blessings from God. You have the right to be blessed, but the only way that God is going to bless you is if you forgive those that trespassed against you. Instead of holding grudges against them, show them love. Kill them with kindness. Never return evil for evil and hatred for hatred. You are better than that. You are much more mature than that. Just because a person hurt you doesn't mean that you hurt that person. It doesn't mean that you beat that person down or curse him or her out. God trained you better than that. He disciplined you better than that. And being taught by God, you know forgiveness is one of the main things He commands us to do, so be forgivers and not violators.

BE GOOD ABOUT JESUS

My brothers and sisters, be good about Jesus. Reason? Because He is good about you. He is always good about you, for He has never been bad about you. He refuses to be bad about you because He loves you, and always will. He is not negative, but positive. And being positive is what He wants you to be. Believe it or not, Jesus was the one that delivered you from your infirmities. He was the one that helped you make it through the storms. He has always been there for you, and will continue to be there for you. Right now He's in heaven praying on your behalf. When Jesus tells you to encourage someone, do it. When He tells you to pray, do it. Don't refuse to do it, but love to do it. He didn't refuse to die for you. He didn't refuse to bless you, so don't refuse to do what He tells you to do. Who do you think was the one that made you beautiful? It was Jesus that made you beautiful. And He didn't complain while doing it. He never complains. You should be joyful being good about Him. You should be glad for He is joyful and glad to be good to you.

BRING GOOD TIDINGS

My brothers and sisters, let us stop bringing bad tidings and begin bringing good tidings. I know that you are sick and tired of hearing negative things. Let us do something about it, and that is, bring good tidings. Every day people always bring bad news instead of bringing good news. God is sick and tired of hearing negative reports. He wants to hear positive reports. I mean, you hear negative reports coming from all angles. You hear them on televisions, radios, newspapers, magazines, on the streets, and even in grocery stores. I am sick and tired of hearing about crap. It is time for the people of God to speak up. I know we are living in a troubled world, but it doesn't mean that we should speak bad. Let us use our mouthpiece like God uses His. If you throw good, good will come back. And if you speak good, good will come back. How are we going to reach the Promised Land if we continue to bring bad tidings? The truth is, we won't. "Death and life are in the power of the tongue" (Proverbs 18:21). "How beautiful are the feet of them that preach the gospel of peace, and bring glad tidings of good things!" (Romans 10:15)

COMING BACK

People, Jesus Christ is coming back, so you might as well get that through your thick skulls. He is coming back to get what rightfully belongs to Him: His people. And He's coming back to rule the earth. You see, "The earth is the Lord's, and the fulness thereof" (Psalm 24:1). And sooner or later you are going to find that out. God gave Jesus Christ the power to reign. He gave Jesus Christ the power to come back, and there is nothing any of us can do to stop it. One thing I suggest we should do is get ourselves right with Jesus, meaning we should get to know Him and learn His ways. Those that do that are the ones that look forward to Him coming back, for He is coming back with great rewards to give out to them. And let me tell you this, Jesus' rewards are eternal not temporal. He is not going anywhere for He is everlasting, so get ready for His glorious return, and receive Him with gladness.

DON'T BE ASHAMED OF YOURSELF

My friend, don't be ashamed of yourself, but love yourself and love who God created you to be. He made you differently from everyone else. You are very unique. Use the gift that He has given you. As long as you are ashamed of yourself, you are not going to be able to operate that gift. There are millions of people that want to get to know you, but as long as you are ashamed of yourself, they are not going to encounter you. When you touch them, they are going to ask, "Why were you so ashamed of yourself?" My friend, you are a wonderful specimen. God sees that in you, but you have to see that in yourself. He does not want you to be ashamed of yourself. He wants the world to see His glory in you, but as long as you are ashamed of yourself it's not going to happen. God is not going to force you to come out of your shell. You have to be willing to come out, so don't be ashamed of yourself, my friend, for you are very awesome.

DON'T DROP GOD

Whatever you do, my friends, don't drop God. Don't let go of God for anyone or anything. Women, I don't care how handsome a man may be. Men, I don't care how beautiful a woman may be. I don't care how fancy a car may be. I don't care how much money you make. Don't drop God for any of those things. Don't even think about it. God is bigger and better than those things. God is greater than those things. Why should you want to drop God anyway? God is marvelous. He is awesome. He can bless you with those things and more. He is the one that created those things. And God loves you more than anyone or anything. Keep Him in your heart, mind, and soul. Take Him everywhere you go. Don't be ashamed of Him, and most definitely, don't drop Him. For if you do drop Him, things in your life are going to turn for the worse.

DON'T HARDEN YOUR HEART

My friend, I know you may not be feeling good right now, but please don't harden your heart toward God. God is the one that is going to make you feel better. If you harden your heart toward Him, you are not going to get better. He is the one that is going to uplift your spirit. He is the one that is going to brighten your day. God knows that there are many things that trouble you. He is the one that is going to deliver you from them. Living in this world you are not going to be excused from troubles, but know that there is a God that will deliver you from them, and He is surely mighty. Believe it or not, God is not your enemy. Satan and the lust of the world are. Satan is the one you should harden your heart toward, not God. It is not the time to harden your heart to God. It is never the time to harden your heart toward Him for He loves you more than anyone or anything, so open your heart and receive Him so He can overwhelm, overtake, fulfill, and consume you with His love, joy, peace, and happiness.

EMBRACE EACH DAY

My brothers and sisters, embrace each day. Why? Because God gave you the privilege to see the day. He created days for you to embrace them. I don't care if the day is rainy or sunny, still embrace it. God woke you up for you to embrace the day. He doesn't want you to curse the day, but to embrace it. Be thankful that you get to feel the gentle wind, smell the aroma of the fragrant flowers, and hear the birds sing. You also get to speak to and see the wonderful people whom God made in His image. With God, every day is beautiful for He is beautiful. It had to take a beautiful God to create such beautiful days, and because of His grace and mercy you were allowed to see the days. It is God's good pleasure for you to enjoy each day. I don't care what your circumstance is, still embrace the day. No circumstance is bigger than the wonderful day that God allowed you to see. If God blesses you to see the day, He will also help you make it through the circumstance. And when He does that, you have no choice but to embrace the day because every day is great when you serve a wonderful and awesome God, so embrace each one.

FORTUNATE

What's up, my brothers and sisters? What's going on? Come on, you know who this is. This is Demetrice reminding you that you are fortunate. You are fortunate because you serve the Almighty God. And you became fortunate when you made the decision to drop everything you had and begin to follow Him. God knew that it was a big sacrifice for you. And believe me, He is going to greatly reward you. God knows following Him is not easy because you have to deal with the ways of this world (temptations) and Satan, but don't worry because God's Son Jesus Christ overcame this world (John 16:33), and His power is within you. Those who have Him are very fortunate. You are talking about the Resurrection, and the Life (John 11:25), the King of kings, and Lord of lords (1 Timothy 6:14–15), and the Prince and Savior (Acts 5:31). You are most definitely fortunate having Him. He is not going to leave you broken and shattered. He is not going to leave you comfortless (John 14:18). He loves you with all of His heart. My brothers and sisters, you are fortunate not only in this life, but also the next because once you get hooked on God, Jesus Christ, and the Holy Spirit, you are hooked for all eternity.

GET BACK FOCUS

All right, all right, I understand that you made mistakes, but now it's time for you to get back your focus. It's time for you to get back your focus on God and your destiny. Don't feel bad about the mistakes you made for we all have made them. You have to bounce up from the mistakes you made. Don't keep abusing yourself for them. And don't forget, no one is perfect but Almighty God and His beloved Son Jesus Christ. You are human, meaning that you are going to make mistakes and get off track at times, but the key is getting back on track, and you do that by getting focused. God loves you. He is not going to punish you for making mistakes. As a matter of fact, He loves when you make mistakes because when you make them, you learn from them. Making mistakes matures you. Making mistakes grows you up. My friend, I love you and will always do my best to give you good advice. There is no need for you to keep downing yourself. It is not too late for you, so get back your focus and move toward your destiny.

GOD DOES NOT WANT YOU TO BE

God does not want you to be broke, busted down, and disgusted. Some of us choose to be that way. God wants you to be healthy spiritually, financially, and physically. "He is not the God of the dead, but the God of the living" (Mark 12:27). You can't put all the work on God. You have to do your part. If you want to be spiritually healthy, you have to pray, fast, read your Bible, and go to church. If you want to be financially healthy, you have to work. Get yourself a job, pay your bills on time, and put some money in savings. You have to build your credit and wealth. And if you want to be physically healthy, eat right, work out, and exercise. God is not going to do those things for you. You have to get off your lazy tails and do it for yourself. You have to be willing to be healthy. As long as you are lazy and not want to do things for yourself you are going to be broke, busted down, and disgusted. Stop feeling sorry for yourself! Stop crying and complaining. God is not lazy. Just look around and you will see He created everything that's surrounding you. He is not broke, busted down, and disgusted, nor does He want you to be.

GOD IS NOT A MONSTER

Hey, I know I just didn't hear you say God is a monster! What are you saying? God is not a monster. Where did you get that from? Who told you that lie? Who or what influenced you to say that? God is not a monster. I say that in love, truth, and honesty. God doesn't hate you, He loves you. He doesn't want to destroy you, He wants to give you life. Why are you in denial? The one you should be calling a monster is Satan. He is the one that doesn't care about you. He is the one that wants to destroy you, but God is preventing him from doing it. God wants to use you for His kingdom. He has mighty works for you to do. Go ahead and take Him up on His offer. You will not be disappointed. In God, there is love, peace, and joy. My friend, you must be told the truth. I can't have you going around telling vicious lies about God.

There is nothing evil about Him. I will not leave you in ignorance. I refuse to leave you in ignorance. God is not a monster. Try Him and you will see for yourself.

GOD IS NOT WEAK II

You must be out of your mind thinking that God is weak. God is not weak, He is strong. Don't get kindness and compassion confused with being weak because if you do, you are horribly mistaken. There is nothing weak about God. He is the strongest being in the universe. Just because He loves and forgives doesn't mean He is soft. Just because He's a God of peace doesn't mean He is soft. God is tough, so don't you forget that. As a matter of fact, He was the one that cast Satan and the fallen angels out of heaven. He was the one that had hell built for them, so tell me what is weak about that. There is nothing weak about that. It took a strong and mighty God to kick those no-good and inconsiderate beings out of heaven. God makes the rules. He holds all the power in His hands. And with His power, He gives to His children, so they too can be strong and tread upon the enemy. God is powerful and mighty. God is strong, and He is most definitely not weak.

GOD KNOWS WHAT YOUR BODY NEEDS

Hey! You need to relax and cool down because God knows what your body needs. He was the one that created it. Don't you think He knows what your body needs? Every vessel, vein, and artery that's inside of you He made. He wonderfully crafted your body. God knows your body needs food and water. He knows your body needs clothes. Certainly, He knows your body needs sex. Yes, I said it sex. He was the one that gave you the gift of sex. I'm not only talking to you, but also to myself. Sometimes I lose patience and want to go out and have sex, but I have to wait on God. Meaning, I've got to wait until I'm married. That's the only time God approves of sex is when you are married because He wants it to be holy. Yes, I had sex before, but I had to repent because it was outside of marriage, and thus, outside the will of God. God wants sex and your marriage to intertwine into something special. Believe me, I know how you feel, and God knows how you feel because He knows what your body needs.

GOD KNOWS YOUR HEART IS IN THE RIGHT PLACE

My friend, God knows your heart is in the right place, so take it easy on yourself. Stop stressing and pressuring yourself. God knows that you are willing to work for Him. He knows that you love and adore Him. He sees that you are motivating and encouraging others. He sees that you are preaching the Gospel. Believe me, there is not one day that you don't cross His mind for He knows that you are faithful. And He sees that you are diligent in following Him. God never overlooks you. He never forgets about you. He tells His angels about you. My friend, everyone in heaven knows about you. And they are looking forward to spending eternity with you. God knows your heart is in the right place, and that was the message He wanted me to deliver to you.

INFERIOR

My brothers and sisters, you are not inferior. You serve the Most High God, so there is nothing inferior about you. It was our God that created this planet. It was our God that created everything. The book of Genesis proves it. You have the right and authority from Almighty God to be down here. I dare you to let anyone put you down. I dare you to let anyone discourage you. And I dare you to let anyone say that you are inferior and get away with it. No one is greater than you but God, His Son Jesus Christ, and His Holy Spirit. You are not beneath anyone. Don't let tares tell you who you are. Don't let tares validate you for you were already validated through the blood of the Lamb Jesus Christ, and there is no validation greater than His. The power that you have is not from this world, but from Almighty God. The power of God is more powerful than silver and gold. God's power is something that you can not buy. And you have the nerve to think that you are not somebody! You are royalty, my brothers and sisters. You are great. You are not inferior to anyone, so take that to the bank and cash it!

KEEP DOING WHAT YOU ARE DOING FOR GOD

My brothers and sisters, keep doing what you are doing for God, and don't let anyone tell you otherwise. God is blessing you. He was the one that blessed you with that beautiful spirit. It wasn't anyone else but Him. When you need something, who do you call on? You know who you call on; you call on God. And you know I'm right. God loves you more than anyone or anything. He gave you that bold spirit. He gave you that nice-paying job, and that boat you are having gatherings on. Of course, you are going to keep doing what you are doing for Him because you've got sense. There is no one out there that can bless you as well as He can, so don't listen to those doubters. Let those haters and nonbelievers keep laughing. Let those haters and nonbelievers keep calling you crazy because when Jesus returns you shall have the last laugh. The rewards He has for you are plentiful. And together, we are going to stand and say, "I'm glad we kept doing what we were doing for God."

KEEP TRUSTING IN GOD

My friend, I know that life has not been easy for you. I know that you are going through rough times, and you may feel that everyone is against you. I'm here to tell you, my friend, in spite of how you feel, keep trusting in God. Don't lose your trust in Him. God loves you. He will never leave or forsake you. He sees and knows what you go through. He is there with you. And you know what, my friend? He is going to bring you out. He is not going to let you suffer for long. I know you may feel or think that God is not with you. I'm here to tell you that He is with you. He is always with you. There is not going to be a time that God is going to leave you. You mean the world to Him. You are His child. He loves you with all of His heart. Not part of His heart, but all of His heart. Walk with your head up high and keep trusting in Him, and you can rest assure that He will not fail you.

LISTEN TO THE GOOD

My friend, don't listen to the evil inside of you, listen to the good. Listening to the good is what's going to keep you upright. Listening to the good is what's going to keep you in good standing with God and society. What would have happened if Jesus would have listened to Satan? We'd all would be in big trouble. We'd all be in hell suffering. But I thank God that He didn't give in to Satan. You see, my friend, we all have to be like Jesus. Jesus didn't give in to evil. He overcame it. And He overcame it by listening to the good that was inside of Him because He knew listening to the evil would have destroyed us all. He is our example of listening to the good, and a great example is He. As long as you listen to the good, you are going to stay out of trouble. You are not going to dig yourself into a deep hole. I'm telling you, my friend, some holes are hard to get out of, so listen to the good inside of you and enjoy the freedom and life it brings.

NOT DAMAGED GOODS

Listen to me, my friend, you are not damaged goods. There is nothing wrong with you. The person that was in your life was not the one for you. God has someone better for you, so pick yourself back up and move on with your life. Get prepared for the individual that God has ready for you. When God sends you your mate, He does not want you to be depressed. He wants you to be happy. Having low self-esteem is not attractive, so get some confidence. There is nothing for you to feel bad about. You should be thanking God about the person that let you go, for it should let you know that God has someone specially prepared for you. You see, my friend, God wants you to have the best, and nothing less. As long as you are with God, there is still hope. You are not ugly. You are amazing. And the person that God has for you is amazing as well. You have a beautiful spirit. I can feel it. You are not damaged goods, only godly goods, so please believe it. I love you.

NOT DISAPPOINTED

My friend, God is not disappointed in you, so stop being hard on yourself. And stop putting yourself down. Why would God be disappointed in you when you have faith in Him? He is not a God that contradicts Himself. It pleases Him when you have faith in Him, not disappoints Him. God sees that you are working hard for Him. He sees that you are helping others reach His kingdom. He is in no way disappointed in you. As a matter of fact, He is proud of you. And believe me, He is going to wonderfully reward you. Never think that God has forgotten about you. Just like Tonéx's song says, "God has not forgot." Every day, God smiles at you, not frowns. You are doing great works for Him just like Jesus said that you were going to do. And coming from Jesus, that means a lot for He is King of kings, and Lord of lords, so pick yourself up and be happy because God is not disappointed in you, but joyful.

NOT FULL OF BULL

God is not full of bull. He is not full of lies. When He says He is going to do something, He does it. When His prophet speaks a word from the Lord, some people say in their minds that's bull. They don't believe the word. They think the blessing is not going to come. They let their circumstances overshadow God's Word. For example, "How am I going to get a house if I have poor credit?" "How am I going to get a job if I don't have a college degree?" With God, all things are possible (Matthew 19:26). There is nothing too hard for Him. This is His planet. He is the operator. Whatever He says, goes. Many of us have to realize that God is God. By word of mouth, He created the heavens and the earth. You must have some nerve saying that God is full of bull. The truth is that you don't have any faith. And by you not having any faith, you try to place the blame on God. God always comes through on His promises. His Word never comes back to Him void. Everything He says does come to pass. He is Alpha and Omega. He is the Author and Finisher of life. I dare you to say He is full of bull. There is nothing bull about Him, only truth.

OUT OF SIGHT

God is out of sight, meaning, amazing. It doesn't take God long to do anything. Those who say it takes God long are the ones who can't wait on the blessing. Those are the ones who are not patient. Those are the ones who don't want to earn it. They want a quickie. They want things on a silver platter. Now that I've got that off my chest, I'm going to get back to telling you God is out of sight. His ears are ready to hear from you day and night. I'm telling you He is out of sight. His glory is limitless. His blessings are limitless. God is contagious. Once you taste Him, you will get hooked on Him. You will be overwhelmed by His power, glory, and majesty. It doesn't take Him long to show you how marvelous He is. Just look in a mirror and see what He created, which is you. You've got that right. He created you. And what a great and excellent job He did. What a glorious job He did, for you are a marvelous creation. You are a great person because you were made by a God that is out sight, which is God Almighty.

OWN WORSE ENEMY

My brothers and sisters, please hear me. You know sometimes you can be your own worst enemy. The problem is not others, but you. You think that others are against you, which may be true, but check yourself because it can be you that are against yourself. It can be you that hates and despises yourself. Sometimes I'm my own worst enemy. When it comes to looking after others I'm great, but when it comes to myself, I'm dung. Others tell me that I'm great, and others tell me how good of a man I am, but if I don't believe it for myself, it is all vanity. My brothers and sisters, it is time for us to stop being our own worst enemy. We have to compliment ourselves. We have to have confidence in ourselves. And we have to love ourselves. It is bad enough that we have to deal with Satan and his demonic followers. We know that he and his demonic followers are the true enemy. They should be the ones that we despise, so honor yourselves, but don't be an enemy to yourselves.

PAVED THE WAY

Jesus Christ paved the way for you, so what are you down about? He paved the way for you to see the Holy King, the Almighty God. You should be happy, not sad. At first, you were on your way to hell due to the fall of man (Genesis 3:1–13), but then the second Adam came (Jesus Christ) and changed your direction from hell to heaven when

He died for all of your sins (Matthew 27:32–50). He gave you the chance to see God. You should be rejoicing because you are saved. Jesus paved the way for you to have eternal life. There is no life greater than eternal life. I'm talking about a life that you get to spend with God alongside with Jesus Christ in His holy kingdom, where God's glorious angels sing and rejoice. A place where there is no more suffering and no more wars. It is a place where there is no darkness. A place where Jesus prepared for you. And you think that He prepared that place for you to be depressed? No, He did not. Now, I will understand if you were on your way to hell, but you are on your way to see God. And knowing that, there should be nothing to be bitter about, so rejoice and be glad for Jesus paved the way for you to see and be with an awesome God for all eternity.

PERSONAL

My friend, stop taking everything so personal. Everyone is not against you. Sometimes when others criticize you, they criticize you for the best. Criticism makes you stronger and tougher. It also helps you to improve. Criticism is not always negative. Sometimes people are hard on you because they love you and see good in you. They see that you have potential to become someone great. You have to differentiate criticism from negativity. Everyone is not out to destroy you. And everyone is not hating. Do you feel me? Stop taking everything to heart because everything is not meant to be taken to heart. So get rid of that "me against the world" mentality because you do have support in your corner. Don't take everything so personal.

PLAY YOU?

Play you? Are you crazy? God will never play you. He loves you, so why would He do something like that? If you sow God some money, I guarantee He will double it and return it back to you. He will not play you like that person did you in your previous relationship. He is not like man that He would try to run money games on you. When you are in a relationship with God, He will not try to get you for every penny that you've got. He will not try to play you to get material possessions from you. God is not a gold digger. He is not a groupie. We are talking about a God who created everything. All God wants from you is time. He will not play with your emotions. You are a great person; you deserve to be treated like royalty, not played. God will always make time for you no matter what the situation is. His schedule is never too busy for you. He always has time for you. He will never run a scheme or scam on you. He loves and adores you, so go ahead and try Him. I guarantee that you will not get played because God does not play games.

PUT NO LIMITATIONS

My brothers and sisters, put no limitations on God. He can do anything. He will take you further than what you could ever imagine. You will say, "Man, I made it to my destination." And God will say, "No, you have not." He will take you further than what you thought appeared to be your destination for His thoughts are higher than our thoughts and His ways are higher than our ways (Isaiah 55:9). We think and say we reached our peak, but God thinks and says otherwise. You see, God holds the answers, not us. There is nothing too high for Him, and there is nothing too impossible for Him. God will take you up higher than what you thought you could ever be. You will be amazed by the wonderful works that He displays. God does not only want you to be amazed by Him, He also wants you to believe in Him. Put your trust in Him. Let Him take full control of your life and you will see and realize that with God there are no limitations.

RUINED

My brothers and sisters, don't let anyone ruin your day. Don't let anyone take your joy and peace away. Continue to live joyfully and peacefully. And forget about living bitter, angry, and depressed. If others choose to live those ways, so be it. You just don't choose to live those ways. Don't let anyone's bitterness, anger, or depression rub off on you. It would if you allowed it to. And if it does, you have to shake it off in the name of Jesus. Continue to smile and walk in cheerfulness. What does it profit you walking in anger? What does it profit you moaning and groaning? It doesn't profit you a thing. Every day that God makes is beautiful, so choose to wake up with a smile on your face and let that smile carry on throughout the day.

SINGING A SONG

You know, sometimes, my brothers and sisters, we need to sing a song to God. Sometimes a song is all He wants to hear. God wants to be praised and worshipped. He wants to be loved, honored, and adored. Singing a song expresses how we feel about Him. It shows Him that we appreciate Him for bringing us through, and out of trials and tribulations. Singing a song shows that we don't take Him for granted. God doesn't have to do anything for us, but He loves us so much to do things for us. He is always there. There was never a time that God left us high and dry. He is always there to fill our cup, even though some of us will not admit it. A day should not pass by without us singing Him a song. You know, singing a song keeps you happy. Singing a song keeps you joyful and glad. I know I can't sing like Donnie or Deitrick, but I do try my best. "Let the word of Christ dwell in you richly in all wisdom; teaching and admonishing one another in psalms and hymns and spiritual songs, singing with grace in your hearts to the Lord" (Colossians 3:16).

STOP ABUSING ONE ANOTHER

We as the people of God need to stop abusing one another. We need to stop gossiping and speaking negatively about one another. And instead, love, respect, and speak positively about each other. We are all sisters and brothers in God. We are His children. We are His sheep. It upsets Him when He sees His children dispute and fight among themselves. We're supposed to know better. We're supposed to follow in His footsteps. Disputing and fighting among ourselves is not following in His footsteps. Abusing each other is not following in His footsteps. We're supposed to live in the way of love. Don't tear down each other, but build and uplift each other. Encourage one another. Motivate one another. We should help each other feel good. We should bring each other good tidings. We shouldn't be acting like fools. We are trained and disciplined by Almighty God, meaning that we are obligated to maturity. There is no excuse for us abusing each other. We don't belong to Satan. We belong to God, so we need to get our acts together and stop abusing one another.

STOP DEGRADING YOURSELF

Stop degrading yourself. You have been degrading yourself long enough, so now it's time for it to stop. You are made in God's image. There is no need for you to degrade yourself because you are a remarkable being! There is nothing wrong with you. You are an intelligent individual. I know that you are, but you have to know it for yourself. God sees nothing but good in you, so why are you constantly degrading yourself? You have to encourage yourself. You have to love yourself. Degrading yourself is not encouraging or loving yourself. It is putting yourself down. It is being your own worst enemy. How are you going to encourage or love someone else when you don't do it for yourself? You have to do it for yourself first, and then do it for others. It all begins with you. You have to set the foundation. My friend, you are a beautiful being with an excellent spirit, so see what God sees in you and stop degrading yourself.

STOP PUNISHING YOURSELF

Hold on just a minute. I mean, hold on! Stop punishing yourself. What do you gain by doing it? Punishing yourself is not going to make you feel any better. It's not going to give you any improvements. If you did something wrong, don't punish yourself; forgive yourself. God forgives us when we do something wrong. Are you much better than He that you can't forgive yourself? If you think that you are, you are truly fooling yourself. He forgives, so He expects us to forgive. It is us that choose to lie in our mess. You have to get up out of your mess and move on. As long as you continue to punish yourself, you are going to be down in that mess. Love yourself enough to forgive yourself. Love yourself enough not to punish yourself. Half of the time it's not God punishing us. We ourselves do it. We are not living in a perfect world. Bad things are going to happen, but don't let the bad things dictate your character. Always remember, the good outweighs the bad. You have to keep pushing and pressing on, so stop punishing yourself.

STRONGHOLDS

Heavenly Father, God Almighty, I thank you for taking the strongholds away from me. Without you doing that for me, I would not have peace. You know and I know that strongholds keep you from having peace. They keep you from being free because they keep you in daily captivity. The only way to be released from them is with your power, Heavenly Father, God Almighty. Many people today are still held captive because they deny that they have them. As long as they don't acknowledge that they have them and don't come to God, their minds are going to continue to be bound. Your salvation, O Lord, will deliver them from their strongholds just like it did me. They have to believe it and receive it. God, there is nothing more power than you. The power of deliverance is in your hands. And I thank you for the power of deliverance because that is what got me detached from those strongholds.

TAKE IT EASY AND RELAX WITH GOD'S PEACE

My friend, take it easy and relax with God's peace, not worry with His peace, but relax with it. There is no need for you to be stiffed up because God is with you. Why do you think He gives us peace? He gives us peace so we can take it easy. He gives us peace so we can enjoy ourselves. And peace does not give you worries, it gives you relaxation, so when God offers it to you, take it. Peace does not make you uptight. It makes you calm and loose. It eases your heart, mind, and soul. When you have the peace of God, nothing should get to you. Nothing should shake, move, or faze you. You should not be worrying about the cares of this world, so take it easy and relax with God's peace.

THE TRUE LIVING GOD

God is the true living God. He is more alive than anyone or anything. He has more power, life, and light than anyone or anything.

No one shines brighter than He because compared to Him everything is in darkness. He is a God that doesn't need the sun, moon, and stars to shine. He carries His own light, and believe me, it is brighter and greater than those things, for He is the light, and what a glorious light is He. Anyone or anything He touches comes to life, for He is the giver of it. "God is not the God of the dead, but of the living" (Matthew 22:32). Which tells you He's not dead, but alive. And if you are hooked up to Him, you are alive as well. No idol can give you life. Neither can a statue because they are dead. They have no life (Isaiah 46:1–13). That's why many people don't have any power, because they worship idols and statues which are false. There is only one God, and He is the true living God whose throne is in heaven.

WIN SOULS

My brothers and sisters, I just want to motivate you to continue to win souls. Make winning souls your hobby and duty. Besides, God wants you to win souls. He was the one who ordained, consecrated, and commissioned you to win them. You are obligated to win them. And He wants you to continue to win them, for there is plenty of space available for them in heaven. It is up to you to help bring them in. It is up to you to lead and march them in. God is counting on you. He is trusting you. Continue to preach, teach, and shout, so those souls can join your soul with God in heavenly adorable love.

YOU ARE SOMETHING SPECIAL

Hey, my brother! Hey, my sister! I just want to tell you that you are something special. I thank God for you. And knowing that you are something special excites me for it brings joy to my heart. God gave me the privilege to honor you. And I'm glad that He did. You just don't know how good you've got it. You have a beautiful attitude and a beautiful spirit. That's why the enemy hates on you 24/7. He hates the fact that you are made in the image of God. You have the King of kings' qualities! Many people want what you have. Many people want to be like you, but they can't for you were chosen by God. That's what makes you special. It is good to be something special because God has you set aside from the rest. He is going to use you for His glory. What a blessed person you are! You should be glad. You should be shouting praises with joy. You are something special, so realize it.

CHAPTER 4

HEAR YE! HEAR YE!

BALL

Okay, you dropped the ball. So what? Pick it back up. I dropped the ball numerous times, but I kept picking it back up. You are not perfect. Sometimes in life you are going to fail. That is what you call life, but that doesn't mean you have to give up and give in.

What do you want me to do? You want me to feel sorry for you? Be a soldier and do what you've got to do. God is not going to pick the ball up for you; you have to do that for yourself. When you pick it up, He is going to be there to help you carry it, but you are the one that is responsible for it.

No one can live your life for you. No one can do your duty for you. You have to do it. God has you accountable for it. Moping around is not going to help you. Moping around is not going to get you anywhere. Stop feeling sorry for yourself. A soldier doesn't always win the battle, but the soldier has to keep persevering so he or she can win the war. Rambo (a movie character played by Sylvester Stallone) said to win a war you have to become war.

The world is a huge battlefield, and with the war of terror going on, everyone is in danger. It is spiritual warfare in this world. We as the children of God have to do what we have to do. We have to keep praying. We have to serve God without fear. We have to live without fear. No terrorist is more powerful than God, so pick the ball back up, my friend, and get back in the race. We need you.

BE MOVED BY THE SPIRIT

My brothers and sisters, be moved by the Spirit, the Holy Spirit, that is. Why? Because you can't go wrong when you are being moved by the Spirit. The Spirit is not going to lead you the wrong way. The Spirit is righteous, and it is of God, so it has no choice but to lead you the right way.

My brothers and sisters, you have to be wise enough to follow it. I didn't say be smart, but wise. There are many smart people in the world, but it doesn't mean that they are wise. Being smart and being wise are two different things. I know a lot of smart people that are foolish. Do you get what I'm saying? Do you understand what I'm saying?

"Enter ye in at the strait gate: for wide is the gate, and broad is the way, that leadeth to destruction, and many there be which go in thereat: Because strait is the gate, and narrow is the way, which leadeth unto life, and few there be that find it" (Matthew 7:13–14). If you follow the Spirit, you will be among the few whom Jesus was talking about that find life. Now do you want to be among that few? I know you do. Who doesn't want to have life? Who doesn't want to be with the King of kings, and Lord of lords for all eternity?

Don't let anyone, and I mean anyone, turn you away from entering in at the strait gate. Follow the Spirit, and you shall enter it. There is nothing sweeter than the strait gate, and there is nothing more beautiful than it. You heard what Jesus said. He said that all the other gates leadeth to destruction. Jesus Christ doesn't want destruction for you, He wants life for you. His Spirit is the Spirit of truth (John 16:13), so be moved by it and receive the joy of the Lord.

BE RIGHT ABOUT PEOPLE

My brothers and sisters, be right about people. Meaning, be good about them. Don't try to use anyone. If people are being good about you, be good about them. Don't take advantage of someone.

Everybody is not out to get you. Everybody is not out to destroy or bring you down. There are people who actually have good intentions about you. Just because someone is treating you right doesn't mean that the individual is trying to get something out of you. For example, a man maybe treating a woman like a queen, and in her heart she is thinking he is doing it because he wants to have sex. No, no, no, no, no. All men don't think that way. All men don't have those intentions. A woman is supposed to be treated right, not abused. What I'm basically saying is don't be insecure about every little thing.

I know that there are some bad people out there, but there are also some good people out there as well who are willing to help. If you owe someone money, pay that person back unless that person tells you it's okay not to pay him or her back. I mean, some of you just forget about paying the person back whom you owe. And that's not right.

God is watching each and every last one of us. He knows when we are being wicked. He knows when we are taking advantage of others' kindness. Don't do that. Be right about people, and if they are not being right about you, always remember, vengeance is of the Lord (Romans 12:19).

BONDAGE

My friend, God doesn't want you to be in bondage. If you are in bondage, He will deliver you. He is the God of deliverance. He always delivers His people from bondage. It is not God's fault that some of us are in bondage. Some of us choose to be in bondage. God's plan for His people is to be set free. That is why He sent His Son Jesus to earth so the captives will be set free (Luke 4:18–19).

God wants you to be free spiritually, mentally, and physically. He doesn't want you to be a slave to anyone or anything but Him. The slave He wants you to be to Him is a servant, so don't get what I'm saying twisted.

God is a loving and righteous God. He is a merciful God. He would never put you in spiritual, mental, and physical shackles. He wants you to love Him with all of your heart, soul, and mind (Matthew

22:37). So if someone tells you that God puts people in bondage, before you walk away from that individual, tell him or her that God loves people, and will never put them in bondage for He is the God of deliverance, not bondage. May peace be with you, my friend, and God bless you.

CARE FOR OTHERS

My brothers and sisters, why don't you care for others? You should care for others just like God cares for you. You are made in God's image, meaning you have ways like Him. God does not have hateful ways. He has loving and caring ways. God says to care for everyone, including your enemies. He said if your enemy hungers, feed him. He said if your enemy thirsts, give him something to drink (Romans 12:20).

God did not say to hate your enemy, but love your enemy. Just don't be a fool for him. Don't let your enemy abuse your kindness. Don't let your enemy treat you like dirt. By you being nice to people they can change. Everyone has a conscience. They will say to themselves, "I'm going to stop giving this person a hard time because she cares for me. She is looking out for me and being nice to me. She actually loves me."

My brothers and sisters, it is our duty to care for others. It is our duty to love others. Some people out there in the world are being abused. Some people out there in the world need counseling. God does not want us to just focus on ourselves. He wants us to focus on helping and caring for others as well, so you should write *care for others* on your agenda, and then apply it.

COME BACK

My friend, I urge you to come back to the Lord. It wasn't God who hurt you, it was man. You see, my friend, you can not compare man to God. God is not a sinner. God is not a liar or hypocrite. He didn't have anything to do with a certain preacher, teacher, usher, brother, or sister hurting you in church. That was the work of the devil.

All churches don't have the Spirit of God. Everyone doesn't go to church to serve God. Some go for their own selfish motives. The devil has some of his people set up in church just to turn you from the face of God. And that's what happens. Satan turns you away from God, but God has summoned me to tell you that He loves you, and He is calling upon you. He has some mighty works for you to do. Don't be afraid, my friend; come back to Him.

God is going to build you up. He is going to prepare you so nothing like that would happen to you again. He is going to give you the power to see who the enemy is. Everyone doesn't have your best interest at heart. They are out to destroy you. The devil sees your future. He knows that you have some great works to do for God. That is why he is going to do all that he can to stop you. Come back to God, my friend, because with Him is where you belong.

P.S. I'm not telling you to go back to the church that turned you away from the Lord. I'm telling you to go back to the Lord Himself. Then He will direct you to a church where His Spirit absolutely dwells. A place where your brothers and sisters in Christ will greet you with love.

DIFFERENT

Hold up just for one second. You are crying because no one wants to accept you? So what? There is nothing wrong with being different. You are always trying to please everyone. That's your biggest problem. You care about pleasing others more than you care about pleasing yourself.

Forget about pleasing others. You need to focus more on pleasing God, and then yourself. Accept yourself. It's okay being different. I personally love being different. I don't want to talk, walk, and laugh like everyone else. I want to have my own talk, walk, and laugh. I'm glad that God created me to be the way that I am, and you, my friend, should love the way that He created you to be. He didn't create you to be like everyone else. He created you to be you.

No, you are not a mistake. Many people want to be like everyone else. They are what you call followers, but you, my friend, are not a follower but a leader. Leaders are different. They can't be like everyone else, so stop being so ashamed of yourself.

My friend, you are different from everyone else, so thank God you are. The real truth about those people whom you are trying to please is that the majority of them don't know who they are and can't sleep at night due to not having peace of mind.

DOESN'T CARE ABOUT YOU

I'm telling you there was a need for me to write this one. People, Satan doesn't care about you. Many of you are serving, following, and worshipping him. I'm telling you he doesn't care about you.

Satan is leading you all straight to hell. He is not applauding you, but laughing at you. He is calling you all fools. Satan's sentence is hell, and if you continue to serve, follow, and worship him, it is going to be your sentence as well.

There is nothing pretty about hell. It is a place of wailing and gnashing of teeth (Matthew 13:42). It is a place of complete and everlasting suffering. Now does that sounds like a loving place? Does that sounds like a caring place? That is the place where you all are heading toward. A place where your lord is leading you all to.

Satan is not concerned about you. How is he going to be concerned about you when he is not concerned about himself? Satan hates himself. He doesn't love himself, so how is he going to love you? He doesn't know what the word means.

Those of you that are in Satanic cults, and those of you who live the way of the world, I love you. I even know someone who loves you more than I do, and that is God Almighty. God doesn't want you to suffer. He doesn't want you to go to hell. He has the best for you. He cares about you. Forget about living the way of the world, and forget about serving, following, and worshipping Satan, and begin to serve, follow, and worship God. I guarantee you God has a beautiful life for you on earth, and a beautiful afterlife for you which is eternal. Heaven.

DON'T BE DOWN

My friend, I know that you just got out of a tough relationship, but don't be down about it. Know that God will always be there for you.

He will never leave or forsake you. That person who lost you lost a good thing because you are royalty.

What you have to do, my friend, is move on with your life. I know it's going to be hard, but trust me, you can do it. You have a God that believes in you. You have a God that supports you, so I know you are going to prosper. He will never leave you alone. He is confident in you.

You are a good person. God has a wonderful mate for you, so smile and be glad. That person who you were in a relationship with is not on your level anyway, so thank God that you are no longer with that individual.

You see, my friend, you want to be with someone who you are compatible with. You want to be with someone who will meet you halfway, someone who is God-sent. A person who is not God-sent will be only wasting your time, heart, and money. A king belongs with a queen, and a queen belongs with a king. A queen doesn't belong with a peasant, and a king doesn't belong with a peasant. If you are hooked up with a peasant, the relationship is not going to last.

A person who is God-sent will be faithful to you. A person who is God-sent will not lie or cheat on you. That person is going to love you with everything within. I'm telling you, my friend, I just can't wait until God sends me my wife. I'm going to love her with all of my heart. She is not going to have to want for anything. And, my friend, the minute you get up, you are going to feel the same way about the mate God is going to send to you. Get up, my friend! Get up! There is no need for you to be down any longer.

DON'T DEPART FROM JESUS

My friend, don't depart from Jesus. Jesus loves and cares about you. No one or anything is going to love you the way that He does. No one or anything cares about you the way He does. Jesus was the one that healed you. Jesus was the one that saved and delivered you. And Jesus was the one that died for your sins. Your mother, father, sister, brother, or spouse didn't do it; Jesus did it.

Why would you want to leave someone that loves you? Why would you want to leave someone that cares about you? That doesn't make any sense. That is crazy, and may I also add, foolish. Jesus descended from heaven to give you true and pure love. He descended from heaven to give you a better lifestyle to live. That was unselfish of Him. What you need to be is thankful.

Jesus is the King of Glory. He is the Epitome of Righteousness. He is the Supreme Savior. He is the Good Shepherd. There is no one or anything greater than He. There is no one or anything that is going to give you greater love. Be with Christ and walk with Him, but please don't depart from Him.

DON'T LET ANGER

My brothers and sisters, don't let anger get the best of you. Many people have allowed anger to get the best of them. There is nothing wrong being angry, but don't let it cause you to sin (Ephesians 4:26–27). Many people have allowed anger to cause them to sin. If their boyfriend or girlfriend upsets them, they go out and cheat on them. Instead of them resolving the problem, they make things worse by going out and doing wrong. The beautiful relationship they had was ruined by anger. The couple has given place to the devil.

You see the devil is ready for you to get angry so he can try to manipulate the situation. Don't let him manipulate you into doing something wrong, because if you do, you are going to greatly regret it. You have to rebuke the devil in the name of Jesus, telling him that he has no place in your life.

The spirit of anger has broken families apart. People have allowed anger to control them. God wants you to be close to your family, not apart from them. A family is supposed to be tightly knitted together. The devil likes to ruin beautiful things because he is garbage. Don't let him pollute your relationship with your boyfriend or girlfriend, or your family. Continue to pray and read your Bible. I love you, my brothers and sisters, and remember, don't let anger get the best of you.

DON'T PULL AWAY

My brothers and sisters, don't pull away from God. Stay with Him. Pulling away from Him is not going to help you. Pulling away from Him is not going to get you spiritually blessed. Being spiritually blessed is more important than being physically and financially blessed. Being physically and financially blessed is not going to get you into heaven; just asked the rich young ruler (Matthew 19:16–24). And you can also ask the giant Goliath, for He was physically blessed (1 Samuel 17:4), but not spiritually blessed. If He was spiritually blessed, He would have never cursed the armies of the living God (1 Samuel 17:10).

Be patient, my brothers and sisters. Blessings are going to come your way. That is what separates us from the world: being patient. You see, the worldly ones want things fast and in a hurry. We as the people of God have to wait on God. You get the greatest blessings by being patient and waiting on God. You appreciate the blessing more when you wait on it, because you strived for it.

Don't pull away from God because you are losing hope. Don't pull away from God even if things don't seem right or are not going right for you. Keep your faith, hope, love, and trust in Him. I promise you, He won't disappoint you.

I'm telling you, my brothers and sisters, if you pull away from God, you have just missed out on your blessings that you were about to receive. I have seen it happen to many people. Just when God was about to bless them, they pulled away from Him. Don't let your emotions and flesh get the best of you. Don't pull away from Him. Stay. And I guarantee, you will not regret it.

FATHER GOD WANTS YOU

Just like Uncle Sam wants you, Father God wants you. God wants you to be a soldier in His army. No, you don't have to sign any paperwork; all you have to do is confess with your mouth the Lord Jesus and believe in your heart that God had raised Him from the dead and you shall be saved (Romans 10:9). From that point on, you shall not only be saved, but also be part of His army, where He is the commander in chief, and Jesus Christ is the general. The enemy is Satan and his demonic followers. They are who we fight up against.

Now, let me tell you, a bullet, bombs, or missiles can't destroy them; it takes the Word of God to destroy them, "For the weapons of our warfare are not carnal, but mighty through God to the pulling down of strong holds" (2 Corinthians 10:4). You can't destroy a spirit with a bullet. Satan will laugh at you. It takes the power of God and His son Jesus to destroy him and his followers. And I'm telling you, being part of God's army, you are in a fight of your life.

Jesus was in a fight of His life ever since He was a baby. A king wanted Him destroyed (Matthew 2), but God didn't allow it to happen. I'm not trying to frighten you, I'm just telling you the truth. There is nothing for you to be afraid of. God is not going to let Satan and his followers take you out. He will shield and protect you from them. He is not going to have you on the battlefield unarmored. He is going to equip you with all the power you need. Jesus Christ will love to have you to be among His host when He returns in battle fashion, sitting on His white horse, following Him for battle (Revelation 19:11–21), so come on and accept the Lord's invitation, an invitation you will not want to turn down.

FATHER'S BUSINESS

My brothers and sisters, be about your Father's business. You know that I'm talking about the Lord God Almighty. Be about His business. Don't let people get in your way from being about it. Do let them stop you. They are not going to reward you. He is. "He is a rewarder of them that diligently seek him" (Hebrews 11:6). And I'm telling you, His rewards are humongous. You be about His business, and you will see what I'm talking about.

You have to be willing to be about His business. You've got to have the desire for it. You've got to have love for Him. Jesus was about God's business. He told that to Joseph and Mary when He was twelve years old (Luke 2:42–49). He was a child being about His Father's business. I say this, if a child can be about God's business, we adults can be about His business too. There is no excuse. And what was Jesus' reward? His reward is being on the right-hand side of God, where He is today (Hebrews 8:1).

God is not a liar. You be about His business, He is going to bless and take care of you. He is not going to overlook you. He is not going to forget about you. He doesn't take you for granted. He loves you. Right now, He is getting ready to reward you, so be about His business so you can receive it.

GIVE IF YOU WANT

Listen to me clearly. If you want respect, you have to give respect. People are not going to give you respect unless you are giving it. It is not fair that you want others to give you respect, but you are not giving it to them. You have to treat others the way that you want to be treated. You can't be one-sided.

If you want love, you have to give love. People are not going to give you love if you are not giving it to them. Whatever you give will return back to you. If you give hate, it is going to return. If you give love, it is going to return. People are not going to give you love if you are abusing them. There is no love in abuse. Jesus says to love your neighbors not abuse them (Matthew 19:19).

Likewise, if you want support, you have to give support. Many people look for support, but they are not giving it. They expect others to give them support when they are not giving it. When you are not doing something and yet, expect others to do it, you are a selfish person. You think that everything is about you. But everything is not about you, so you need to get over yourself. The world does not revolve around you, it revolves around Jesus Christ, and I don't care what anyone has to say about that. If you want respect, love, and support or anything in general, you have to give it. Case closed, bottom line, and point-blank.

MY BROTHER, MY SISTER

My brother, God has a beautiful woman for you, but you have to be patient to receive her. While you are being patient, God is preparing her for you, and you for her. When you two meet, it is going to be beautiful. I wish I could be there to see it. I'm telling you, my brother, when God brings you two together, the angels are going to shout with joy. Just keep believing in God and continue to do His wonderful works. He is not going to let you wait for long. I'm telling you, my brother, this woman who God has for you is a knockout! She is going to sweep you off your feet! And once you receive her, you are going to give God all the glory.

My sister, God has a handsome man for you. Keep holding on to God, and He is going to send him to you. God knows you get tired and weary. You look at your peers and see they have a man, but that's okay because you are human. God is speaking through me to tell you that your husband is on the way. And I'm telling you, my sister, just like the queen you are, he is going to treat you that way. You deserve to be treated that way. You are not a peasant, but a queen. He is going to be everything you asked for in a man, like charming, respectable, trustworthy, faithful, and gentle. He is going to be a gentleman! Continue to wait on God and you shall have him. You are indeed going to give God the glory.

I love you, my brother. I love you, my sister. Stay uplifted! And continue to believe and wait on God.

NO DIFFERENT

Listen to me, my brothers. Listen to me, my sisters. We are no different from those in the Old Testament and New Testament days. We are no better than they. Just like they needed God, we need Him.

Many of us think that we are perfect. Many of us think that we can do without God. I'm telling you, that is a bold-faced lie because we can't do without Him. Self-righteousness is not going to put you through heaven's doors. I don't care how good, perfect, or righteous you are. If you are not righteous through Jesus Christ, you are not going to enter those doors. He is going to look at you and say, "Depart from me, I know you not" (Matthew 7:21–23).

The difference between us and the saints of old is that they knew how to call on God. We, on the other hand, don't know how. We try to be cute. We try to be grand. We don't know how to get down and dirty.

God doesn't love us any more than He loved them. We are going to be judged just as they were judged. Jesus said this generation shall not pass away till all be fulfilled (Luke 21:32). Meaning, just as it was in Noah's day, the earth was judged (Genesis 7:17–24), and Sodom and Gomorrah was judged (Genesis 19:24–29). This age too shall be judged.

What we need to do is give ourselves a self-evaluation. Inventory ourselves. Get on our knees and get to know God more and more. There is no limitation to seeking God's glory. God loves us, my brothers and sisters. Let's call on Him as they did in the Old and New Testament days, and He will surely answer. Be at peace, my brothers and sisters. I love you.

NO ONE IS PERFECT

Hear me out! Hear me out! One of the reasons why many of us don't have anyone in our lives is that we are looking for someone that's perfect. We have to understand that *no one is perfect*. We all have flaws, make mistakes, and do things that get on someone's nerve.

I'm telling you if you are looking for a perfect person, you are going to continue to be disappointed. No one is perfect but Jesus. You have to learn how to overlook a person's flaws. You are not perfect yourself. You have flaws. You make mistakes. What makes you think that someone wants to be with you? That person that God has for you could be staring you right in your face, but you would reject that person because he or she is not perfect.

I'm telling you, I would accept anything from God. If God tells me this female is my wife, I'm going to gladly accept her. Every creature God made is good. He would not give you a perfect person because no is perfect, but He will give you a person that is a perfect fit for you. "Trust in the Lord with all thine heart; and lean not unto thine own understanding" (Proverbs 3:5), and then you will come to the conclusion that no one is perfect, including you.

NOT GOING TO DISRESPECT AND GET AWAY WITH IT

Many people in the world are living in sin, even people in the church. The sad part is they think that they are going to get away with it. Let me be blunt, you are not going to disrespect God and get away with it.

I clearly understand that no one is perfect but Jesus Christ. I clearly understand "that all have sinned, and come short of the glory of God" (Romans 3:23). But you have people in the world, and in church, that are sinning purposely. They are sinning without a conscience. They are sinning without thinking about the consequences. They don't care about repenting. They don't care about asking God for forgiveness. All they care about is their flesh. All they care about is their greed, desires, and pleasures. They are selfish.

Take King Belshazzar, for example. What did he do? He disrespected God. How did he disrespect the Most High? He disrespected the Most High by drinking out of the silver and golden vessels that were taken out of God's Temple from Jerusalem. He, along with his princes, his wives, and his concubines, drank out of those vessels. To make God even angrier, they were praising the gods of gold, silver, brass, iron, wood, and stone while they were drinking out of the holy vessels. Even though his father, King Nebuchadnezzar, took the vessels out of God's Temple in the first place, that still didn't give Belshazzar the right to drink out of them along with his people. He gave God no glory. So what did God do? He left a message handwritten on the wall only Daniel could interpret. Daniel gave the king the interpretation, and that very night the king got slain (Daniel 5:1–31).

Furthermore, after the Lord God had delivered the children of Israel out of the hand of the Egyptians (Exodus 13:17–14:1–31), they had the nerve to have a golden calf made to worship. And you know the Lord God was not going to allow that. What does a golden calf have to do with Him? Absolutely nothing. So what did God do? He had those individuals that worshipped, sacrificed unto, and made the calf, slain (Exodus 32:1–35). They weren't supposed to worship a statue, they were supposed to worship God. A golden statue didn't deliver or save them from their enemies. He did.

This message is for the whole world. Don't disrespect God. He is nothing to play with. You don't disrespect Him or His Temple. What did Jesus do? In Jerusalem, "Jesus went into the temple, and began to cast out them that sold and bought in the temple, and overthrew the tables of the moneychangers, and the seats of them that sold doves; And would not suffer that any man should carry any vessel through the temple. And he taught, saying unto them, Is it not written, My house shall be called of all nations the house of prayer? but ye have made it a den of thieves" (Mark 11:15–17). And in 1 Timothy 1:20, Paul told Timothy how he had to kick Hymenaeus and Alexander out of the church. He handed them over to Satan because they were preaching false doctrine.

God is not going to let people continue to do wrong and get away with it. He is not going to let them disrespect Him and get away with it. You think you may be doing things in secret. You think no one sees what you do. God sees everything. There is no secret He doesn't know about. You can't keep things away from Him. He knows everything, and soon, very soon, we are going to be judged according to our actions.

PROFESS

Hey, my friend. I know what you need to do. You need to profess your love for God. Don't be too ashamed to do it. And don't be too shy to do it. You have been holding in your love for God too long. Now it's time for you to let it out.

Let the whole world know how much you feel about the Almighty one. You won't be trying to put on a show. You are not trying to be seen among men. You are just trying to express your love for God, and, my friend, there is nothing wrong with that. There is nothing wrong with you professing your love for Him, so come out of your cocoon and begin to bloom.

Every day, you hear people talking about crazy things, but there is nothing crazy about you professing your love for God. If people can profess craziness, you can profess God. Why should you profess God? You should profess God for He is the most awesome being in the universe. He is the most loving being in the universe. Every day, He professes how much He loves you, so you should profess how much you love Him. Come out, come out, and profess the living God.

SHED SOME LIGHT

My brothers and sisters, shed some light on others because others need your light. Many people are living in darkness; they need some light shed on them. It is our duty to shed light on them. We must bring happiness, joy, and gladness to their lives. Now, if they don't want to receive our light, that's a different story.

By us shedding our light on them, it will help bring them out of darkness. I'm talking about the darkness of hate, anger, depression, bitterness, oppression, and sorrow. There are people that desire our light, for they are willing and craving to get out of darkness.

Moreover, shed some love on others. Some people are not being loved. Some of them don't even love themselves. In their home it's chaos, and within themselves internally, it's chaos because they are lacking in love. It is a must that we give them love. Jesus told us to love our neighbor as we love ourselves (Matthew 19:19). So that is what we must do.

Furthermore, shed some peace on others. Many people have lived a violent life from childhood to adulthood. And many people have lived an abusive life from childhood to adulthood. They don't know what peace is. We have to be a living example of peace. We have to show and shed some peace on them.

My brothers and sisters, many people are dying due to not having light, love, and peace in their lives. They are dying mentally, physically, spiritually, and emotionally. They need us. We have to show them God, Jesus Christ, and the Holy Spirit, for they gave us the light, love, and peace to shed on others.

SILENT TREATMENT

Parents, don't give your children the silent treatment. Hear what they have to say because it may be critical. Many children are dying mentally, spiritually, and emotionally due to their parents giving them the silent treatment. Parents, they need your ears!

Moreover, you have to get involved in your children's lives. You just don't know how important it is to show up at their functions. It can be a school play or any sports activity. I'm telling you that would make a big impact in your children's life. Your children will remember that moment for the rest of their lives. They will remember you sitting in the audience giving them support. You are your children's confidence. You are who they look up to. Seeing you not there will hurt them.

Parents, let's be real. I know you have to work because you have bills to pay. Sometimes it's not easy, but that is still no excuse to neglect your children. You should never be too tired to sit down to talk to them. You should never be too busy to see how they are doing. And you should never be too busy to read them a bedtime story. Those things are not hard to do. You will be surprised at how doing the small things will bless you to have a beautiful relationship with your children. Don't give them the silent treatment. May peace be with you, and God bless you.

STAY IN THE RACE

My friend, don't give up, but stay in the race. You belong in the race. God selected you to be in the race. "Thou therefore endure hardness, as a good soldier of Jesus Christ" (2 Timothy 2:3). I'm telling you, my friend, you will not be enduring for nothing. You will be enduring for your crown in heaven. Now, there is nothing better than that.

You are not only enduring for yourself, but also for those who God has set out for you to help get their salvation. Paul endured all things for the elect's sake that they may also obtain the salvation which is in Christ Jesus with eternal glory (2 Timothy 2:10). Believe me, my friend, I know that it gets hard sometimes. I know that the devil is on your back, but you have to get him off your back in the name of Jesus.

"Wherefore seeing we also are compassed about with so great a cloud of witnesses, let us lay aside every weight, and the sin which doth so easily beset us, and let us run with patience the race that is set before us, Looking unto Jesus the author and finisher of our faith; who for the joy that was set before him endured the cross, despising the shame, and is set down at the right hand of the throne of God" (Hebrews 12:1–2).

Living in this world is not easy. The world has many tribulations, but you have to hold onto the Lord. The Lord is not going to let you go. You are not running the race alone for the Lord is with you. He started the race with you, and He is going to finish with you. There are going to be times that He is going to carry you, but that's okay because He is willing and loving enough to help you. He is your biggest supporter, pushing you along the race, and believe me, He is not going to give up on you. Stay in the race, my friend, because your reward is surely worth it.

STOP BEING SO DISRESPECTFUL

Stop being so disrespectful. How would you feel if someone disrespects you? You have to talk to people the way you want them to talk to you. It's not fair that you disrespect people, but don't want them to disrespect you. No, it doesn't work that way.

You can not be rude to people and expect them to be nice to you. You have to be nice. You get greater results by being nice. You get respect by being nice. People are not going to let you disrespect them and get away with it. They have the right to be that way for they are human, which means they have feelings. You get respect by giving it. You don't get it by abusing and disrespecting.

There have been plenty of times when people wanted to get violent with you, but they chose not to. There have been plenty of times when people wanted to curse you out, but they refused to stoop down to your ignorant level. Get your attitude in check and stop disrespecting people because, just like you want respect, they want it. Don't forget, God is watching everything that you do. Disrespecting people doesn't put a smile on His beautiful face.

TIME OF YOUR DAY

My brothers and sisters, don't give Satan the time of your day, but give it to God. All Satan wants you to do is fight, kill, argue, disrespect, and curse. He does not want you to be in peace with your brethren. He does not want you to be and speak positively. All he wants in your life is total chaos.

Satan gets a thrill out of seeing people fight. He does not want us to get along. He will try to destroy everything he gets his hands on, like people's excellent marriages and relationships. He does not want couples to get along. He hates good families. He will do all he can to confuse. He will do all he can to bring separation.

If someone close to you tries to start an argument, quickly diminish it by being peaceful. It takes two to fight. Don't be partakers of it. I'm telling you misery loves company. When evil rises up, begin to pray. When confusion rises up, begin to pray, for confusion is what Satan is all about. He does not want your mind to be stable, neither does he want your spirit or relationship to be stable. When your boyfriend or girlfriend, husband, or wife, or family member tries to lose control on you, remember, don't give Satan the time of your day, but give it to God, for He is all about love, peace, forgiveness, understanding, and unity. "Be not overcome of evil, but overcome evil with good" (Romans 12:21).

UPSET

My friend, stop being upset with yourself. You are only human. You are not perfect. We all did things that we are not proud of. We all did things that made us ashamed of ourselves. You are not the only person that's been in this position. You have to get over it and move on.

I know how you feel. You feel that you let yourself down. You feel that you let your family down, but most important, you feel that you let God down. The guilt, shame, and hurt are killing you. Believe me, my friend, I know. I've been there. You feel that you are just a big disappointment.

Well, I have some good news for you, my friend. You are not a big disappointment. You are a being made in the image of God. Whatever you did that made you feel the way that you feel, God has forgiven you. Your family has forgiven you. You have to forgive yourself. Believe me, I know that forgiving yourself is hard to do, but you have to do it because if you don't, the guilt, shame, disappointment, and hurt is going to slowly kill you. Guilt is a disease that slowly kills.

And God doesn't want you to go out that way. He doesn't want you to die. He wants you to be alive. He loves you. Your family loves you, and I love you. May peace be with you, and God bless you.

YOU ARE NOT A DOORMAT

My friend, you are not a doormat, so stop letting people walk all on you. Stop letting people disrespect and take advantage of you. Be like Jesus. Jesus was bold. Jesus was tough. He was not a coward. He was not weak. He did not let anyone or anything push Him around. He did not let anyone or anything take advantage of Him. He stood up for Himself, and that's what you have to do.

My kind friend, you have to love yourself. You have to tell yourself, I will no longer be pushed around. You have to tell yourself, I will no longer let anyone walk all over me and take advantage of me. I am somebody. You also have to let others know that you are not going to take their mess, and that you refuse to be abused.

Are you sick and tired of being pushed around? Are you sick and tired of being taken for granted? And are you sick and tired of being taken advantage of? Believe me, I know because I used to be in your shoes. I used to get pushed around, get taken for granted, and get taken advantage of. I know how it feels. And you know how it feels, so stop letting others walk all over you because you are not a doormat.

YOU MADE IT THROUGH

My friend, you made it through. You should be praising and thanking God that you made it through. You made it through that last relationship. That relationship hurt you because you tried your best to please that individual. You tried your best to satisfy that individual, but the individual was never satisfied. That individual was never happy or appreciative, so God had to take you out of that miserable relationship.

You gave that person the majority of your time, and it still didn't get you anywhere. It was a waste of your time, heart, and money. That individual was abusing you. Maybe not physically, but abusing you emotionally and mentally. Some days you could not sleep at night due to the peace you were losing over that individual. Never lose your peace over an individual.

You see, some of us have to understand that some people don't want a good person in their lives. Some people you just can not please. They are stubborn, ignorant, self-centered, and foolish. They don't know that they have someone good in their lives. Maybe they are not used to someone treating them good. All I know is that you deserve someone better because you are a wonderful person.

My friend, you have to understand that everyone does not want to be saved. I thank God for being in my life. Thank God you made it through, my friend, and don't worry because He has a wonderful person destined just for you. Stay uplifted, my friend. Stay uplifted.

BE LABORERS OF LOVE

My brothers and sisters, be laborers of love. God wants you to be laborers of love. He does not want you to be laborers of hate. He did not command you to be laborers of hate, but of love (Mark 12:31). Being laborers of hate does not get you anywhere. All it does is cause anger and bitterness to grow inside of you. And if you are not careful, hatred can kill you. It can kill your spirit. No matter what someone does to you, still labor love toward that person. In Romans 12:20, the Word of God says, "therefore if thine enemy hunger, feed him; if he thirst, give him drink: for in so doing thou shalt heap coals of fire on his head." This means that your love will make that individual feel ashamed for wronging you. You teach others love by showing it. When they see you labor in love, they will also do it. Labor in love, my brothers and sisters, because it is what Jesus taught us to do. And just like He taught us, we have to teach others as well.

BE MOVERS

My brothers and sisters, be movers. You are not going to get anything done by sitting down. You have to get off your tails and begin to do something. You have to work the gifts that Almighty God has given you. He gave you the gifts to work. Use that brilliant mouth you have. Use that brilliant heart and mind you have to bring people to

His kingdom. I looked to see if you were in your office, but you are not. You are at home, sitting on your bottom wasting valuable time. You have to use that time to reach out to people. You have to use that time to go after the businesses God has for you. He wants you to be successful. He wants you to be prosperous and rich. He wants you to reach out to people, but those things are not going to happen as long as you are sitting down. Wisdom is crying out, so hearken unto it. Be movers, my brothers and sisters, and the Father will move for you. He doesn't deal with laziness.

BE SINCERE

When it comes to God, my brothers and sisters, be sincere. Why? Because He is sincere when it comes to you. God always thinks about you. There is never a day that you don't cross His mind. Each day He thinks about how He is going to wonderfully bless you. Now, how many people do you know that do that? Some people don't even give you the time of day, but God loves you so much that He never skips a day thinking about you. And when it comes to blessing you, He not only comes through, but He comes through big. Of course, He comes through big because He loves you that much. He is not selfish when it comes to you. You mean everything to Him. So why would you not be sincere when it comes to Him, unless you are selfish? And if you are selfish, there is no reason for you to be. Be sincere when it comes to God, because like I said earlier, He is sincere when it comes to you.

BEAUTIFUL SPIRIT

God's Spirit is beautiful. And He wants your spirit to be beautiful as well. He doesn't want you to have an ugly spirit, but a beautiful one. He will grant you a beautiful spirit, but you have to allow Him to do it. God is not going to go to places where He is not wanted. If you don't invite Him inside of you, He is not going to force Himself inside of you. You are the one that needs a beautiful spirit. He already has one. He said He will not leave you comfortless (John 14:18), but He has no choice but to leave you comfortless if you don't invite Him in. You will be the one without peace due to your refusal of inviting

Him in. It won't be His fault, but yours. God's Spirit is beautiful, and forever it will be.

BEST INTEREST AT HEART

God has your best interest at heart. He loves it. He will not do anything to hurt or harm it. He will not do anything to jeopardize it. He cares about you. He cares about your future. No one, and I mean no one, cares about you the way He does. He will support you more than anyone. Many people say they have your back, but the majority of them are telling lies. They are only there with reaching hands to see what they can get out of you. They are supporting you with their own selfish motives and intentions. But God and a select few of people aren't that way. God wants you to be successful. He wants you to accomplish your goals. He is the one that is telling you to keep going on. He is the one that is telling you not to give up. He is real not fake. God will never break your heart, for He has your best interest at heart.

BROUGHT YOU OUT

God brought you out of your afflictions, so why are you being ungrateful toward Him? He didn't have to bring you out. He could have chosen to let you stay in them, but He was beautiful enough to bring you out. He was loving enough to bring you out. He is not a selfish God. He hears His children's cries when they cry out unto Him (Psalm 77:1). He is not going to let them suffer for long. It shouldn't be difficult for you to lift up your voice to give Him thanks for bringing you out. It's not difficult for you to give Him an offering. He doesn't ask for much. Give Him what's due Him. "God setteth the solitary in families: he bringeth out those which are bound with chains: but the rebellious dwell in a dry land" (Psalm 68:6).

CONTINUE TO ENDURE

My brothers and sisters, continue to endure. Don't lose hope. God is going to arrive for you. He is not going to lead you astray. You have to continue to press toward the mark for the prize of the high calling of God in Christ Jesus (Philippians 3:14). It is not a one-day thing, but an everyday thing. You don't just bless and serve God for only one day; you do it every day. In good times you have to push, and in bad times you have to push. You have to endure every day. Things are not going to always be peaches and cream. There is a devil in this world, and his name is Satan. Believe it or not, he does exist. And he has demons that work for him doing all the evil that they are bad enough to do, but I tell you what. They are not going to last for long because in the process of rescuing us, Jesus is going to destroy them. That is why I urge you to continue to endure and fight the good fight of faith (1 Timothy 6:12) because he that endureth to the end shall be saved (Matthew 10:22).

CRAZINESS

Hey, let me tell you something: God is not about craziness. There are a lot of people jumping off of buildings, bombing people and themselves, and doing witchcraft. They say that God is telling them to do those things, but I'm telling you, they are absolutely lying. Those people are crazy. They are out of their minds. God is not telling them to do those things. He is not insane. Why would God tell something He created to kill him or herself or to put spells on people? That is insane. God is not about voodoo. He is about love. He is not about suicide, but life. God doesn't promote evil things. He promotes love. We as the people of God have to pray for those individuals. A mind is a terrible thing to waste. God is not about craziness.

DESTINED TO WIN

My brothers and sisters, you are destined to win. Why? Because you serve the mighty Jesus Christ. In Jesus you have the victory. You should know that you are going to succeed for you can do all things through Christ which strengthened you (Philippians 4:13). You have no choice but to win, for you are made in the image of God. And we all know that God is a winner. Like His Son Jesus, we are destined to win. The apple doesn't fall far from the tree. And once we cross that finish line, we have reached our destiny like God told Jesus from the beginning: our children are destined to win.

DISCOURAGE

My brothers and sisters, don't let anyone discourage you. I don't care if it's your mother, father, sister, brother, preacher, or teacher. Don't let anyone discourage you. You are somebody. You are something special in the eyes of God. Stand up for yourself and believe in yourself. I don't care what people say about me. I'm going to continue to smile because the God I serve gave me the ability to smile. As long as He is in my life, I'm going to stay encouraged. You see, my brothers and sisters, you have to understand that there are a lot of bitter people in the world, and those bitter people are going to try their best to make you bitter. That's why you have to guard your heart with the breastplate of righteousness, so it can prevent them from getting to your heart. The first things the enemy tries to attack are your heart and mind. If you allow him to get to those things, he's got you, and that's when you become discouraged. But God has given you the power of joy. His joy is your strength, so don't let anyone discourage you. Stay encouraged. God loves you, and so do I.

DO SOMETHING FOR JESUS

Check yourself! When was the last time you did something for Jesus? My friend, you are busy wearing His ears out wanting Him to do something for you. Well, you have to do something for Him. It doesn't have to be something big. It can be something small. Bless Him, and unlike you, He will gladly appreciate it. Jesus Christ doesn't look at your pocket. He looks at your heart. He measures you by your heart. By you thinking about Him brings joy to His heart. Some people don't think about Him at all. They are busy focusing on themselves, but you don't have to be like them. Jesus was the one that clothed you. Jesus was the one that put food on your table. And here you go wanting Him to do something for you. He does something for you every single day. Now, my friend, it's time for you to do something for Him.

DON'T AVOID

My brothers and sisters, don't avoid the true and living God. Why would you want to avoid Him anyway? He is a beautiful God. He was the one that woke you up this morning. He was the one that gave you life. He holds the world in His hands. Let me also add, He is the one that protects you from all danger. All He asks is that you not be ashamed of Him. And all He asks is that you turn from your wicked ways and follow Him. Is that too much to ask for? I think not. How would you feel if He avoids you? If God avoids us, the world as we know it would be over. I pray and hope that will never happen. Follow God, and He will make you fishers of men (Matthew 4:19).

DON'T DEPART FROM JESUS II

Again, I say, don't depart from Jesus. Remain with Him. There is no need to depart from Him. There is no need to forsake Him. Don't take heed to the pleasures of the world. Don't take heed to the lusts of the world. The world has nothing good for you. The world has nothing to offer you but misery, hurt, and pain. Stick with Jesus because His yoke is easy and His burden is light (Matthew 11:30). He has your best interest at heart. He will not destroy your heart. He has no intentions of destroying your heart. He is the keeper of hearts. He will not let anyone or anything abuse it. Don't depart from Jesus. Stay with Him because He has all the love and tender care that you need, including eternal life.

DON'T HINDER

If you see someone serving God, don't hinder that individual. That person is doing his or her duty. Don't be a hater, be a participator. God wants you to serve Him as well. Join His party. You don't have to be left out. Some of us choose to be left out when we don't have to. God gives everyone an open invitation to serve Him. He gives everyone an open invitation to bless Him. When you see others doing it, don't hinder them and don't set a stumbling block before them because if you do, you have to answer to God. God doesn't want anyone stopping an individual from serving Him. Jesus checked a lot of people that hindered others from serving Him. He had to get them in order. Because when you hinder others from serving God, you are hindering them from receiving a blessing. And God is going to punish you for doing so because you are being selfish. God has space for you. He has more than enough space. Instead of hindering others, get in on the action, for you should be eager to serve the most beautiful King in the universe.

EVERYTHING REVOLVES AROUND JESUS

Everything revolves around Jesus. If you didn't know that, I don't know what's wrong with you. Through Jesus everything was made, and because of Him, everything was made (Hebrews 1:2). God saw fit to make everything through Jesus. God saw fit to make Him King of kings and Lord of lords. God saw fit to make Him ruler of all mankind. Jesus was the one that saved the Hebrew boys in the fiery furnace (Daniel 3:23–27). Jesus was the one that overcame Satan's temptation (Matthew 4:1–11). Jesus was one who died for all of mankind's sins on the cross, defeating sin and death through His resurrection (Mark 15–16). I do not blame God for letting everything revolve around Jesus. I do not blame God for letting Jesus sit on the right-hand side of Him (Hebrews 8:1). Many people say that God did that because Jesus is His Son. I say to those people, no, and stop hating because Jesus earned that right to be honored. He went through more suffering than any of us can ever imagine. Everything does revolve around Him, and I can gladly say it's all good.

FEEL GOOD ABOUT YOURSELF

Why not feel good about yourself? You are a beautiful being made in the image of God (Genesis 1:27). And knowing that, you should be feeling good about yourself. God wants you to feel good about yourself. He created you to feel good about yourself. Feeling good about yourself shows that you have confidence. It shows that you love yourself. It shows that you adore yourself. And it also shows you are proud, and not ashamed of yourself. And someone as great as you should never be ashamed. Everywhere you go, speak kindly to people. Everywhere you go, greet people in a respectable manner. You just don't know how many people admire you. You just don't know how many people adore you. Now it is time for you to do it for yourself, so stop being so hard on yourself and begin to feel good about yourself.

FEEL GOOD ABOUT YOURSELF II

God doesn't want you to feel bad about yourself, but good about yourself. You are a wonderful being so you shouldn't be feeling bad about yourself. You are made after the similitude of God (James 3:9), so there shouldn't be any reason to feel bad about yourself knowing that. You have to look deep within yourself and say, "I am somebody, and I am something special. I am not going to pull myself down." You have to say that because sometimes you can be your own worst enemy. I know because I've been there. I haven't always been good about myself. I used to have low self-esteem, but I got sick and tired of having it. I built my confidence with the help of God. You too can do that, my friend. God is right with you, and He is willing to help with open arms. Receive His help. When you feel good about yourself, others will notice. They will notice by your walk, talk, conversation, and smile. And I'm telling you, my friend, there is nothing wrong with that, so feel good about yourself, not bad, because you are amazing.

FOCUS ON JESUS

Focus on Jesus. Why? Because everything about Him is good, and everything about Him is right. There is no wrong in Him (Hebrews 4:15). From a child to a man, Jesus was awesome. Jesus was powerful. And sitting on the right-hand side of God He is still awesome. Why should I tell you to focus on anyone or anything else? There is no one or nothing greater than He. There is no one or nothing more awesome than He. How many people that you know walked on water? How many people that you know quiet the storms and the seas? No one did those things but Jesus. Focusing on Jesus gives you hope. Focusing on Jesus is positive. With your mind on Him, you feel that you can do anything. You feel that you can overcome any obstacle. Focusing on Jesus gives you confidence. It gives you strength, so stay focused on Him because in Jesus you will gain all that is wonderful.

GET WITH JESUS

Get with Jesus. Why? Because Jesus is loyal, beautiful, and has everything you need. He has everything that your heart desires. The things that Jesus has never go out of style. The things that Jesus has never wash away. His love, peace, and joy never fade away, and that is what we all need. Jesus has it all for us. All we have to do is seek after Him to get Him. We have to get with Him. The best thing about getting with Him is that He would not push you away. He will not reject you. You have to continue your pursuit just like the Canaanite woman told Him, "Yet the dogs eat of the crumbs that fall from their masters' table" (Matthew 15:27). Jesus wants you to get with Him. He wants you to hang with Him. Your blessings come by getting with Him. Your deliverance comes by getting with Him, and so does your healing and salvation. Jesus has enough love for the whole world. His love covers the world. Respect Jesus and get with Him and you will experience what I'm talking about.

GOOD CHARACTER

My friend, keep your good character; don't change. God made you to be a good person, so stay that way. He and His Son are the only beings you have to answer to, not anyone else. If others choose to be evil, so what? Let them be evil. You just continue to be the wonderful person you are. There is nothing wrong with being good. There is nothing wrong with treating people with kindness. There is no shame in doing that, so keep it up. God is proud of you. He loves the way you carry yourself. He is impressed but not surprised because He knows you are magnificent. He was the one that created you. He knows everything about you. He knows how hard you work to show love toward your neighbors, and He commends you for that. And, of course, He is not going to forget about you, so stay strong. Keep your good character, my friend, because that is what makes you so beautiful.

GOT YOU

First of all, you need to stop worrying. Why? Because God has got you. Of course, He got you, for you are His sheep. You belong to Him. He created you for Himself for His glory. He is not going to let anything happen to you. He's got you covered. When the wolf (Satan) approaches, he is going to flee because he is going to see that you are covered by God. He doesn't want anything to do with God because God will destroy him. The wolf is no fool. On your job, God has got you. When it comes to your bills, He's got you. In trials and tribulations, He's got you. He's got you in all areas of your life. You are surrounded by His goodness, love, peace, joy, and protection. When He says that He is never going to leave or forsake you, He is not lying. God has got you, my friend, so please stop worrying.

HOME

The reason why so many of our homes are in total chaos is because the Lord is not present. Once you invite the Lord into your home, it is not going to be in chaos for He is going to bring peace into it. You wonder why you fight so much in your home. That is because the Lord is absent. He will not be absent if you invite Him in. Ask the Lord to come into your home. Pray, read the Bible, and play Gospel music in your home. I guarantee, His presence will arrive. Hang words of inspiration on your walls. And once you invite the Lord into your home, all of those demonic spirits are going to leave your home. They will flee once the Lord is present. They know that they don't stand a chance against Him. God wants to be in your home. He wants to dwell there. He wants to protect your home from demonic spirits. And when He arrives, you will know He's there because love, peace, joy, and unity are what you and your family are going to be all about.

JESUS IS VERY IMPORTANT

Jesus is very important, so get to know Him. He is your way to the Heavenly Father (John 14). He is the special key to opening the gates of heaven. Without Him there is no way that you are going to get through those gates. You can not sneak, break, or bribe your way in. There is no amount of money that can get you through those pearly gates. Money is nothing compared to the salvation that is given through Jesus Christ. Money is beneath Him. His name is greater than riches and fine gold. His name is greater than fine silver. His name is greater than you and me. Get to know Jesus because He is very important for your earthly and eternal estate.

JESUS IS WONDERFUL

Jesus is wonderful, my brother. And Jesus is wonderful, my sister. He died for your sins and made you righteous. He made you a new creature. The old, polluted, and sinful you is dead. You no longer have to walk in sin. Jesus delivered you from the old you. He took away all of your sins. He delivered and saved you from going to hell. Now *that* is something to shout about. I told you Jesus is wonderful. He did many amazing things for you. He protected you from those who were out to destroy you. He protected you from those who were out to ruin your reputation. You should be filled with joy because He is still protecting you. Bow down to Him and tell Him that He is wonderful. Praise Him for being wonderful because wonderful is what He surely is.

LOVE JESUS CHRIST

My brothers and sisters, love Jesus Christ. Why not love Him? He loves you. He did all that was good for you. He did all that was good for your benefit. For your sake He died on the cross. He did not want you to be eternally separated from His Father (God). He wants you to see the goodness of His Father. He wants you to share the kingdom of heaven with Him. Jesus needs someone to party with Him. And He wants that someone to be you, so thank Him for sacrificing Himself. Thank Him for loving you. Love, serve, and honor Him for all that He has done for you.

LOVES YOU

Of course Jesus loves you. There shouldn't be any doubts in your mind about it for He loves you. Jesus is crazy about you. He loves you with everything within Himself. He loves you so much that He died for you (Luke 23:26–56). And then He resurrected for you (Luke 24). Jesus has a place set up for you in heaven, and here you are down on earth thinking that He doesn't love you. You should be ashamed of yourself! But I'm not going to be too hard on you. I just want you to know and understand that Jesus never hated you. He loved you before you loved yourself. He loved you before you even existed. And He always will. Keep in your mind, heart, soul, body, and spirit that Jesus loves you. Rejoice and be glad, my friend. Rejoice and be glad.

MERCIFUL GOD

God is a merciful God. He is a good, kind, compassionate, and loving God. When you sin, He doesn't rip you to pieces. He forgives you. He doesn't come down on you like Satan comes down on his demons. God loves you, and He is merciful toward you. He knows that you are not perfect. He knows you are human. And He knows that you live in a world full of sin. God is full of mercy. He is not a monster. It is we who have got to have mercy on ourselves. It is we who have to forgive ourselves and stop being so hard on ourselves. We have to love ourselves enough to forgive ourselves. God forgave us a long time ago. Now it is time for us to forgive ourselves. "O give thanks unto the Lord, for he is good: for his mercy endureth for ever" (Psalm 107:1).

MISSION

My brothers and sisters, don't you have a mission to accomplish? You most certainly do. You have a mission to accomplish for the Lord God Almighty. He commissioned you to reach souls, so go out and do it! I'm telling you, my brothers and sisters, time is running out. Jesus is on His way back. You can tell by the destruction of the world: crime is increasing, and hate is constantly growing. The world is about to end! You have to get out there and save as many people as you can. Don't just think about your soul's salvation, but think about others as well. Of course, you have your ticket to heaven, but help others get theirs as well. It is not going to be a pretty sight after the Rapture. God Almighty is going to pour out His wrath upon the earth. That is why I am encouraging you to fulfill your mission. People think that it is hell on earth at this exact moment, but this moment can't compare to the time when God is going to pour out His wrath (Matthew 24:21). My brothers and sisters, the world is in a state of emergency. It needs our help, so let us do what God has commissioned us to do. Remember, we are the light of the world (Matthew 5:14).

NO ONE IS BETTER THAN YOU ... BUT JESUS

My friend, dry your eyes because no one is better than you ... but Jesus. People are not better than you, only Jesus is better than you. I don't care how beautiful women may be, and I don't care how handsome men may be; they are still not better than you. You have to speak up for yourself and stop letting people talk to you as if you are a nobody. Have confidence in yourself and believe in yourself. That female who rolled her eyes at you is not better than you. That male who turned his nose up at you is not better than you. The one who died and resurrected for you is better than you, and He is Jesus Christ. You are great, my friend, but you have to believe that for yourself. I can tell you that day and night, but it's all up to you to believe it. Those people who are trying to intimidate you are not better than you. Just like you, they have issues; they're not perfect, they have sinned, but who has no sin? Only Jesus Christ (Hebrews 4:15), the author and finisher of your faith. My friend, always remember, no matter how rich, middle class, or poor someone may be, no one is better than you ... but Jesus.

NOT A PEASANT

My friend, you are not a peasant, so stop acting like one. I don't care what someone has said about you; you are somebody. Stop letting people treat you like trash. Stop letting people talk to you like you are a nobody. You are a child of the Most High God. You are a joint heir of Christ, and there is nothing peasant or low about that. You are royalty (1 Peter 2:9), so walk like it, talk like it, and be confident about it. If others are jealous of you, so what? Let them be jealous. Don't stop being who you are just because of their jealousy. They are the ones that chose to be that way. They can have Jesus as well, but they refuse. They are peasants. You have Jesus, so be in good spirits.

Walk with your head up, not arrogantly, but confidently. And always remember, you are not a peasant (smile).

NOTHING TO FEEL BAD ABOUT

My friend, there is nothing to feel bad about. You serve the Almighty God, so you shouldn't be feeling bad about a thing. You are blessed. Every day, God shines His light upon you. And every day, He blesses you, so what are you so down about? You have good health, strength, money, clothes, shelter, and transportation. I don't even know why I am talking to you. You have everything you need. Some people don't even have what you got, but you don't see them complaining. Instead of you feeling bad, you should be praising Almighty God. You've got it good, my friend. What more do you want? Ask God for more of His spirit, instead of asking Him for more of meaningless things. There is nothing to feel bad about, my friend, so get up and do your duty for the Lord God.

PUT PRAYER BACK IN SCHOOL

To restore order in school, prayer must be put back. Only God can make things right. Only He can restore. His order is the right order. There is no authority higher than His authority. He rules with an iron fist. Things started to get out of hand when prayer was taken out of the school system. For the students to be in a safe and positive environment, God must be present. I'm not saying to have church in school, but at least have something to do with God, which is prayer. God keeps everything calm and cool. He doesn't bring chaos. He brings peace. Only God can make a storm disappear (Matthew 8:26). All the negative things you hear going on in school are called storms. If you put prayer back in school, I assure you God will diminish the storms. God doesn't want His children to be in a hazardous environment. He wants them to be in a safe and peaceful environment. If you put prayer back in school, you get rid of the wolf, which is Satan. He is having a field day in school because He knows God is not present. Satan is going to continue to rule the school system until the people make a stand and put prayer in school. It is all up to us. Are you sick and tired of seeing violence in school? Put prayer back in school. What do you have to lose? The decision is up to the people. Welcome God's presence, and He will protect.

REAL MEN AND WOMEN

Well, let me tell you about real men and women. Real men and women love Jesus. They know that He is the mightiest Savior in the universe and that He is the most beautiful Savior in the universe. Real men and women know that they can always depend on Him to supply their needs. Their faith in Him is unshakeable. They are the people who are not disobedient. They are the people who serve Him with everything within them. They put Jesus before everything. He is their life. Real men and women sacrifice themselves daily for Jesus; that is how much they love Him. When it comes to Him, they are never selfish. They appreciate Him for dying for their sins. They appreciate Him for preparing a place for them. Their love for Jesus is everlasting. He is who they live for. He is their everything. He is who they desire. Real men and women love Jesus with all of their heart because they know that He loves them with all of His heart.

RIDING ON HIGH

I'm telling you, my brothers and sisters, when you are riding with Jesus, you are riding on high. There is nothing low about Jesus. Don't get it twisted, when He says He is lowly in heart (Matthew 11:29), that means He is humble. That doesn't mean He is depressed and sorrowful. Jesus is full of joy, and riding with Him, you too will be full of joy. Jesus doesn't give people a spiritual low. He gives them a spiritual high. His high doesn't kill, but builds. His high is the type of high that you need. A high that will get you through storms. A high that will be with you through good times and bad times. Jesus' high is consistent, but you have to be consistent with Him. You have to follow Him daily, meaning that you have to read the Bible, pray, and consult Him on a daily basis. You have to study to show thyself approved unto Him (2 Timothy 2:15). Riding with Jesus you are riding on high, a high that lasts forever.

ROCK WITH JESUS

My brothers and sisters, rock with Jesus. Jam with Jesus. It is fun rocking with Him. It is fun jamming with Him. When you rock with Jesus, the fun, music, worship, and praise never stops. It never ends. Jesus is the Savior that has fun. He is the Savior that enjoys Himself. He does not believe in being bored. He refuses to be bored. He has too much fun to be bored, and rocking with Him, you too will not get bored because Jesus is the King that rocks. He parties 24/7. Don't worry about party poopers because Jesus will get rid of them. He does not associate Himself with party poopers because He knows party poopers will spoil the fun. Come on, my brothers and sisters, don't be shy and don't sit this one out. Rock with Jesus. He wants you to join the party.

SMILE FOR A CHANGE

You know what you need to do? You need to smile for a change. You need to try it sometimes. What do you have to lose? You see, being angry and depressed is not getting you anywhere. Why don't you try something new, and that is smile. You will be amazed at the positive results you will get by smiling. When you smile, the sun shines brighter. When you smile, it brings warmth and comfort to your heart. When you smile, it encourages others to smile, and that is what you call the power of smiling. You never know what a person may be going through, but when he or she sees your smile, it will bring excitement to his or her spirit. I'm telling you, my friend, there is nothing negative about smiling. Smiling encourages you to live. Smiling encourages you to motivate and inspire others. Smiling makes your day and others' day around you a whole lot easier. I love to smile, and I encourage you to love it too, so smile, my friend, and you will see the blessings it brings.

STAY PRAYED UP

My brothers and sisters, for you to make it in life, you have to stay prayed up. Without prayer, there is no surviving, success, or power. You need prayer for those three things. You need prayer for power to conquer over your enemies and to press through life. You need prayer for success to live a beautiful and happy life. You need prayer for surviving because when hard times come your way, prayer, through Jesus to the Father, will provide you with the sources to survive. "For whosoever shall call upon the name of the Lord shall be saved" (Romans 10:13). All you have to do is pray, and the Father will hear you. He will gladly hear you because you humbled yourself unto Him. He is not going to ignore you. He is not going to turn His head away. Praying is what He wants you to do! And I'm telling you, my brothers and sisters, with prayer, there is love and victory, so stay prayed up because without it, there is simply no hope.

STAY WITH GOD

I know that things get rough for you at times. And I know that things seem like they are not going to get better. But stay with God and you will see that things are going to get fine for you. Be a soldier and stay in the race for your King. Don't give up on Him so easy. He is going to show you that He is God, and that there is nothing impossible for Him. God can do anything, and He can get you through anything. His name is not God for nothing. He holds all the power. He controls everything. He is the one that you should trust. His hands are the hands that you put your life into. There is no problem or situation too big that He can not handle. And when everything is all said and done, your blessings are going to be as beautiful as you are. Stay with God.

STOP CRIPPLING YOURSELF

My friend, stop crippling yourself and begin motivating yourself. You gain nothing good by crippling yourself. You ask me, when are you crippling yourself? You are crippling yourself when you speak negatively. You are crippling yourself when you are not believing in yourself. And you are crippling yourself when you are sitting on your goals, hopes, talents, skills, gifts, and dreams. You have to get off your tail and work them. Don't let them fade away. What are you afraid of? With God on your side, along with Jesus and the Holy Spirit, all things are possible. You are more than a conqueror, but right now, you are your own worst enemy. It's not Satan. It's you. You have to speak and be positive, have faith in yourself, and do what you've got to do. And remember, if God be for you, who can be against you? (Romans 8:31) So stop crippling yourself.

STOP LOOKING FOR BAD TO HAPPEN

The problem with most people today is that they look for bad to happen. They never look for good to happen. It is always bad. If only they would stop looking for bad and begin looking for good, life would be so much more beautiful for them. Life is beautiful when you look for good. Life is beautiful when you are being positive because you know that everything is not going to have a negative outcome. I don't care how evil the world may be, still look for good to happen. Good outweighs evil, and God outweighs Satan. Evil doesn't stand a chance against good, and Satan doesn't stand a chance against God. He and his followers were the ones that were cast out of heaven—which was a good outcome not bad. In the world of faith, good always prevails, but if you continue to think negatively, that is the outcome you are going to get. Stop looking for bad to happen and begin looking for good.

THE BEST IN THE BUSINESS

God is the best in the business. No one can save or deliver the way He does. God delivered people out of situations that you believed could not be possibly accomplished. For example, He parted the Red Sea for the Israelites so they would not be destroyed by Pharaoh and his army. He delivered them out of the mighty hand of Pharaoh! God also delivered Daniel out of the lions' den. Everybody knows that the lion is the king of the jungle. God delivered Daniel from such a ferocious creature. He also delivered Paul and Silas out of prison. This God whom I'm talking about is an awesome God. This God whom I'm preaching about is a mighty God. His mercy is new every day. It just gets sweeter when it comes to Him. Shout unto the Lord, my brothers and sisters. Let Him know that you appreciate Him for delivering you from situations and circumstances that you thought you would not be able to escape. He is the Great Deliverer! He is the one that leads the captives free. Father God, I thank you for saving me from all my troubles. I thank you for delivering me from troubling situations. You are so mighty in all your ways. Your mercy is everlasting! Your peace is everlasting! Your love is everlasting! Without you, I'm nothing. Without your help, I would have been destroyed by my enemies. I thank you, God, for your saving and delivering grace. You are the best in the business.

THE GREATEST OF ALL TIME

Who is the greatest of all time? Jesus Christ is the greatest of all time. There is no other being greater than He. There is no one that can be compared to Him. Who else do you know walked on water? Who else do you know brought a man back from death? Who else do you know fed over 5,000 people with a couple loaves of bread and a few fish? It was Jesus Christ that did those things. Jesus is amazing! He is the one that calmed the winds and the waves. He is the one that God appointed heir of all things. He is the one that sits on the right-hand side of God. My friend, you may be great, but I guarantee you that you are not greater than He. Don't be offended. I'm just telling you the truth. Jesus Christ will run circles around you. He is the greatest of all time and forever will be.

THE KING THAT SHINES

Jesus Christ is the King that shines. His light shines so bright that you will get blinded. All His ways are absolutely kind. Jesus is truly divine. Everywhere He goes, He draws attention for His ways are cool not cruel. When you walk with Jesus, He gives you hope not dope. Jesus is the holy King. He is a righteous King, and walking with Him you will truly bling with His magnificent light. Jesus is a master and a pastor that is filled with joy and laughter. He is a King that has great self-esteem. He walks upright not uptight. He is prestigious not religious. Jesus is the King that shines whose glory is exemplifying.

YOU ARE ALIVE

My brother, you are alive! My sister, you are alive! Thank the Father you are alive. Be glad that you are alive because you're supposed to have been dead a long time ago. It was God that saved you from death. It was God that kept you alive, so rejoice in His holy name. God loves you that much to continue to let His breath be in your body, so you can see and be in awe of His beautiful days. Breathe the fresh air of His beautiful planet. Proclaim the name of the Lord for He is your God. He is the God of life. Thank Him for keeping you alive spiritually. Now that's a wonderful blessing being alive spiritually. There is nothing greater than that. Being alive spiritually lets you know that there is a God, and He lives in you. You are alive, my brother! You are alive, my sister! And I'm glad, and thank God that you are.

YOU ARE NOT A THREAT TO JESUS

Many people think that they are a threat to Jesus. They think that they intimidate Him, but they are only fooling themselves. No one is a threat to Jesus. No one intimidates Him. What does Jesus look like being afraid of someone? What does He look like being intimidated? I'm talking about a man that stared death in the eyes and defeated it. A grave can't hold Jesus. I'm talking about a man who had demons trembling at the sight of Him. Saying that Jesus is afraid of someone is a joke. It's hilarious. Jesus will never be afraid of someone. He will never be threatened. He is clothed with power. He rules with an iron fist. He is clothed with majesty (Psalm 93). If you don't know that, you better ask somebody. What does He look like being afraid of or threatened by something He helped created? Come on, use a little common sense. You are not a threat to Jesus, and you will never be a threat to Him, so please stop fooling yourself.

CHAPTER 5

THINK ON THESE THINGS

ADORES YOU

My friend, don't be down. Why? Because God adores you. Ever since He thought about you, made you, and set His eyes upon you, He adored you. Up till now, He still adores you.

People may not adore you, but He does. He adores everything about you. He adores your spirit, the way you treat and talk to people, and the way you help out in His kingdom. He appreciates your contributions and sees the excellent job that you are doing. Others may not acknowledge or recognize you, but He does. As long as He acknowledges and recognizes you, that is all that should matter.

I'm telling you, my friend, as long as God sees what I'm doing, that is all that matters because people can talk good in front of my face, but behind my back they may not speak well of me. Some people are flip-floppers, but God is not a flip-flopper. He always remains the same. He speaks well of you in front of your face and behind your back. God never speaks negatively about you. There is no darkness in Him.

My friend, keep your eyes set on God. Keep doing what you are doing. You are not living in vain. You are not wasting your time. And remember, whenever depression tries to rise up again, know that you have someone who adores you, which is your Heavenly Father, God Almighty.

BE A BLESSING

My spiritual friends, be a blessing. Why? Because it feels good being a blessing. I'm not going to lie to you. One of the main reasons I love being a blessing is because of the compliments I receive. After I bless someone, I love to hear him or her say, thank you. And that I'm a great person. When someone tells me thank you, it makes me feel good because it lets me know that the person appreciates me.

Many people don't appreciate a thing, but it's okay as long as you've done what God told you do, and that's being a blessing. You have to understand that many people are bitter, and they don't know how to receive things. They are too stubborn, but don't let that get you down. Continue to be a blessing because God is going to reward you for your selflessness, kindness, and obedience.

Furthermore, be a blessing by your words. Speak kindly and positively to others. Tell them that they are an achiever. And that there is nothing that they can not accomplish. Give them confidence by your words. I'm telling you, my brothers and sisters, that is a huge way of being a blessing. You see, you have to understand that words are powerful. You can either make or break a person by your words. I choose to make, not break. I don't want any human being to be destroyed by my words, only Satan and his demonic followers.

We as people have to encourage each other. We as people have to look after and be there for each other. I'm getting sick and tired of people being a curse to each other and not a blessing. They are cussing each other out, not blessing each other out. They are fighting each other, not loving each other. God gave us the gift of love, and now it's time to use it. Evil is evil, and love has no hate or evil. So be a blessing, and I guarantee God will shower you with more of His love, grace, and blessings.

BE A MATURE ADULT

Be a mature adult. There was a need for me to write this one. Oh yes, it was because many adults act like children. They are in adult bodies, but have the mentality of a child. They need to grow up. Act their age. You have children that act more mature than adults when it is supposed to be the other way around. That is so sad when you see grown people acting like children. We're supposed to teach the children, not the children teach us. We're supposed to be their role models.

It is so sad when you see adults constantly argue and can never come to an agreement. Someone has to be the mature one. I recommend that both be mature, but you are going to always find someone who is going to be too stubborn to humble himself, which is also immaturity. You have to come to an understanding. You have to compromise. There is nothing wrong with humbling yourself. Humbling yourself is a blessing. And you will be surprised how humbling yourself will bless you and your relationships. Many companies and businesses have flopped due to individuals fighting with each other. I'm talking about big-name companies and businesses. If only they would have come to an agreement, they would still be up and running today.

We as a people need to grow up. We need to stop bickering and arguing over petty things. It is not that serious. Just think about this, there's someone out there in the world that's in a worse situation than you, and here you are being immature about your situation. Be thankful. Some of us let small things drive us crazy. You have in-laws fighting against each other; that is crazy. The bottom line, my brothers and sisters, be mature. And if someone tries to start a fight with you, tell the individual you don't have time for the nonsense. Grow up!

BE HAPPY IN THE LORD

My brothers and sisters, don't be sad in the Lord, be happy in Him. There is no reason for you to be sad because you serve the greatest God in the universe. Just thinking about Him should make you happy. Just saying His name should bring joy to your heart.

God does not give you the spirit of depression, but of love and joy. Ask Him to release it on you, and He will gladly do it. God has enough love and joy for everyone. He is not stingy when it comes to giving it away. You have to be willing to want it.

He is not angry with you. He is not disappointed. So why are some of you so sad? God wants you to be happy. His goal is for you to be happy. What makes you think that He wants you to be sad? Even in the midst of chaos, He wants you to be happy. His joy is going to be the source that brings you through the chaos.

Be happy at all times. I know that there are going to be times that it's going to be hard to be happy because I know living in this world you experience difficulties which make it difficult to be happy. But I tell you this, if you are happy in the Lord, it will give you the strength to be happy during the difficult times.

Don't let material possessions, things, and money be the reason for your happiness, and don't center on them. Let it be God, for He is greater than those things. Only He can bring you true happiness. None of those things can stand up to His stature. He is the one that created those things. Be happy in the Lord, and stay happy.

COME OVER

This is for those of you who are unsaved, and yes, I'm talking to *you*. Why don't you come over onto the other side? On the other side there is love, peace, joy, power, happiness, and freedom. Let me also add, life. God is waiting for you on the other side. His arms are open. Jesus has eternal life waiting for you. All you have to do is accept His offer of salvation. "That if thou shalt confess with thy mouth the Lord Jesus, and shalt believe in thine heart that God hath raised him from the dead, thou shalt be saved. For with the heart man believeth unto righteousness; and with the mouth confession is made unto salvation" (Romans 10:9–10). You shall be saved from eternal damnation; that is eternal separation from God.

Once you come over onto the other side, God will give you anything that your heart desires. You don't have to worry about condemnation. You don't have to worry about His wrath. Believe me, it is going to be an ugly day when God pours out His wrath. I'm not trying to frighten you, I'm just trying to get you to understand that God loves you so much that He doesn't want you to experience His wrath, but He has no choice but to pour it out because of the sins of men. God is not going to let any unsaved people enter into His kingdom. Sin is not allowed in heaven.

"The Lord is not slack concerning his promise, as some men count slackness; but is longsuffering to us-ward not willing that any should perish, but that all should come to repentance" (2 Peter 3:9). You see, the Lord is not a cruel God. He gives men time to repent. He doesn't want anyone to perish, but you have to understand that Jesus is on His way back, and if you are not saved you are not going to give God any choice but to bring His judgment upon you, so come on over onto the other side so you can enjoy life everlasting.

DO FOR GOD

Many people want God to do for them, but they don't want to do for Him. How are you going to expect God to do for you when you never do for Him? You have to do for God, and that is by reading your Bible, praying, helping the sick and the needy. You most definitely have to be obedient to Him.

Being obedient to God is a huge plus. That is when you can most definitely expect blessings (Deuteronomy 28:1–14), but some of you don't want to do that because you are selfish. You think everything is supposed to be about you. If you think everything is about you, you are sadly mistaken. Everything is about God. You should be happy to do for Him because He is the one that wakes you up every day. He is the one that shines the sun for you. God sent His only begotten Son on earth to die for your sins (John 3:16).

When you are in church, you are too cute to clap your hands, but you expect God to bless you. When you are in church, you are too fresh and clean to get on your knees because you think you may dirty your clothes, but you expect God to bless you. I'm telling you, that is pathetic! How would you feel if God was too cute and too fresh and too clean not to provide for you? Well, He is God, meaning that He could do anything that He wants to do. What can you do if He does decide to do that? Nothing, because He is God, and you're not. No one can stop Him. He doesn't take orders from anyone. Do for God, my brothers and sisters, and He will gladly do for you. And when you do for Him, be joyful about it.

DON'T BE FAZED

Check it, check it, check it, check it. My brothers and sisters, don't be fazed by the enemy. There is nothing that you should be fazed about. Satan doesn't have any power over you because Jesus gave you the power to tread on him (Luke 10:19). As a matter of fact, Jesus *is* that power.

"Greater is he that is in you, than he that is in the world" (1 John 4:4). Jesus is more powerful than Satan. He is greater than he. That is why I'm telling you, don't be fazed by Satan. He can not harm you. Once you call upon the name of Jesus, he is going to flee. He is afraid of that name. Use the power that Jesus has given unto you. He didn't give you the power to sit on it. He gave you the power to use it. If you don't use it, the enemy is going to continue to get the best of you.

Why do you think people constantly get defeated? They constantly get defeated because they think that they can beat Satan on their own. It is impossible to defeat him alone. How did Jesus defeat Satan? He defeated Satan by using God's Word (Matthew 4:1–11). Don't you get what I'm saying? I hope you do. Don't be fazed by Satan. Just use the power that Jesus has given unto you, and he will flee. And you will see that there is nothing that you should be fazed about.

DON'T BE SORROWFUL

My brothers and sisters, don't be sorrowful but be joyful. Being joyful is what you should be not sorrowful. Being joyful can get you through anything. It will get you through good, bad, hard, and trying times. It will get you over obstacles. Being sorrowful won't get you through anything because you will be stuck in depression, which is one place.

We all go through bad, hard, and trying times, but it doesn't mean that we should be sorrowful about it. Bad, hard, and trying times are necessary for they are the times that you gain strength if you don't faint and get weary. Use the bad, hard, and trying times to your advantage. Know that there is a God that will bring you through those times, and once He brings you through, you are going to be stronger than ever.

Furthermore, you are going to be glad that you went through those times because going through those times is going to make you a mighty and powerful vessel. I see you right now giving God the glory. There is nothing that you should be sorrowful about, for you were created by a beautiful God who made you beautiful. God's earth is beautiful, so make it even more beautiful by being joyful, not sorrowful.

DON'T CHASE AFTER

My brother, don't chase after any woman. My sister, don't chase after any man. If a person is not interested in you, don't pursue that person. Don't chase after that person. You don't need to waste your time.

My brother, there are plenty of women out there in the world. My sister, there are plenty of men out there in the world, so why do you want to waste your time chasing after that one who doesn't want to give you any play? You are wonderful, so you don't need to chase after anyone. If you are going to chase after someone, let it be God. He is the only one that's worth chasing after of. Pursue Him and His kingdom, and I guarantee that you won't have to chase after anyone for He will send you someone. No ifs, ands, or buts about it.

God wants you to have someone. He doesn't want you to live a lonely life. No human being is that great that you have to chase after. Either they like you or they don't. And if they don't, move on. Don't beg anyone to go out with you. Don't beg anyone to be in a relationship with you. I would rather be alone than have to keep asking someone to give me a chance. Do you get what I'm saying? My brother, you are amazing. My sister, you are beautiful, so love yourself enough not to chase after anyone but God.

DON'T FORGET ABOUT ISRAEL

"Brethren, my heart's desire and prayer to God for Israel is, that they might be saved" (Romans 10:1). My brothers and sisters of America, let us not forget about the land of Israel. Israel is the nation of God, so we must not forget about it. If we bless it, God will bless us. If we help it, He will help us.

We will gain a lot of blessings from God by helping the land of Israel. Our nation will truly flourish. God will not take His hand from upon us. He will shield and protect us from our enemies. He will heal our land. You talk about being a rich nation, well, we would truly be a rich nation by helping out the nation of Israel. I'm not just talking about with warfare, but financially, sending it goods and supplying it with anything that it may need.

The people of Israel need us. We have to stop thinking about ourselves. We have to preach the Gospel more and more in Israel. We have to show more love to the people of Israel. Life is more than living in luxury. It is also helping out those in need. And I say we should help Israel not only for what we can gain from God, but also to show other nations that we have a heart and that we are concerned about them. It is so sad to be living in a world corrupted by greed and selfishness. Let us not be overtaken by the corruption of the world. Let's help Israel to show God we are concerned about the well-being of His nation, and that we will never forget about it.

P.S. Let us preach and teach the Gospel more and more to all nations of the earth. In Jesus' holy name.

DON'T GO TO HELL FOR ANYONE

I'm telling you, my brothers and sisters, don't go to hell for anyone. I don't care how fine, sexy, bad, rich, or wonderful a person is—don't go to hell for that individual. You do what's right, and that is live by the ways of God. If that individual is not doing what's right, so what? That's that individual's prerogative. Let him or her go to hell. You don't have to join that person because when Jesus judges you, He is going to say that it is your fault that you are going to hell, for you chose to partake with that individual.

My brothers and sisters, you have the right and the might to tell someone no if they are not doing what's right. You don't have to get involved. Don't compromise your position. Know better. You have a mighty God to answer to, and you know He's mighty. Who should you fear most? That individual or God? Your answer should be God.

No one is more powerful than God. No one is mightier than He.

He rules and owns everything. He created heaven and hell. He created the whole universe. There is no life without Him. There is nothing without Him.

When someone tells you to do something ungodly, you shouldn't hesitate to say no. Don't get me wrong; God is a forgiving God, but you know when you are trying to take advantage of Him. It is not fair to take advantage of someone. How would you feel if someone takes advantage of you? Think about that for a moment. Don't go to hell for anyone, not even yourself.

DON'T REBEL

Listen to me, my friend, I know that you are hurting. And I know that you are angry, but please don't rebel against God. God is not the cause of your hurt. He is not the cause of your anger. He loves you and would never do anything to hurt you. Rebelling against Him is not going to help your situation.

God is the one you want to run to, not run away from. God will comfort you through your hurt. He will comfort you through your anger. He is someone you can talk to anytime. He always has room for you because He loves you. His love is greater than your father's. His love is greater than your mother's. As a matter of fact, He loves you more than you love yourself. Now does that sounds like someone you want to rebel against?

My friend, we all struggle in life. We all have problems, but it doesn't mean that we should give up. It doesn't mean we should turn away from God. Jesus Christ said, "In the world ye shall have tribulation: but be of good cheer: I have overcome the world" (John 16:33). Now what does that tell you? It tells you that you don't have anything to worry about because your Lord and Savior is a Conqueror. He defeated the world. And you too have the power to overcome the world because Jesus lives in you.

By me talking to you, I hope you feel much better. My friend, God is on your side. Never think that He's against you. You may do things that He doesn't approve of, but that doesn't mean He hates you. None of us are perfect but He and His Son Jesus Christ. God knows that you are going to make mistakes. He knows that you are going to fall, but it doesn't mean He is going to cast you away. God is well aware that we live in a world of sin, and that is why we have to come to Him for strength, but if we rebel, where does that leave us? Don't rebel, my friend, stay with God.

GET HIP TO JESUS

People, get hip to Jesus. Jesus is cool and fun to be around. He is not a party pooper. He will not bore you. The beautiful thing about being hip to Him is that you don't have to drink alcoholic beverages, smoke, use drugs, or curse. Many people think that doing those things makes them cool. They think that doing those things makes them popular. Doing those things doesn't do anything but kill your health. Being hip to Jesus will not kill your health, but increase it. Jesus is the Savior and Provider of health care. He will keep your body in great condition.

I am hip to Jesus. I love Him. He tells me that I don't have to smoke, use drugs, or drink alcoholic beverages to have fun. Many people think that they have to do those things to have fun. They fall because of peer pressure. They allow others to influence them to do those things. If I have to do those things to have fun or fit in with others, I'd rather be alone. I'd rather not have friends. I refuse to drink, smoke, or use drugs.

Being hip to Jesus is not a bad thing but a good thing. It is a good thing because being hip to Him makes you rich in spirit and health. Being hip to Him gives you happiness and joy. It gives you security. Jesus makes you feel good about yourself. If you are depressed and you turn to drugs or alcohol, it will make matters worse, but if you turn to Jesus, He will uplift you from your depression. Get hip to Jesus and stay hip to Him because His fun is good for the soul.

HAVE A SENSE OF HUMOR

A great thing to have is a sense of humor. I, personally, do not like to be around a person who doesn't have one. I don't like to be associated with a person who doesn't have one. There's nothing wrong being serious, but don't be serious all day. Being serious all the time will run people away from you. I remember when I was having a conversation with a female on the telephone. I started to play and have fun with her, but she took it seriously. I told her I was only testing her to see if she had a sense of humor, and by her response, I could tell she did not. She got upset with me and hung up the phone in my face.

A person who doesn't have a sense of humor is a boring person. They have nothing to make you laugh about. They have nothing to make you smile about. I don't like being serious all the time. I want to laugh and play sometimes. If you are serious all the time, life and good people will pass you by.

Jesus Christ was not serious all the time. He went to parties. He went to festivals. Jesus had fun. Jesus enjoyed life. He laughed and was full of joy. He did not associate Himself with party poopers. The Pharisees and Sadducees were party poopers. They tried their best to take His joy, but He didn't allow it to happen.

My brothers and sisters, it is not a sin having a sense of humor. Have some fun. Spread some happiness on others. Make others laugh at your wonderful jokes. Put smiles on their faces. Let others know that you do have a funny bone, and you are a whole lot of fun to be around. Have a sense of humor because no one likes a dull person, and no one likes to hang around a person who is serious 24/7.

IT'S NOT COOL

May I please have your undivided attention? Listen to what I have to say because it is very important. It involves our tongues and how dangerous they can be. In James 3, James tells us how dangerous our tongues are. My brothers and sisters, it is not cool making people feel bad. Many people are trying to destroy other people's reputations. Many people are trying to ruin other people's images and names. It's not cool to do that, and it's certainly not right.

There are people that are just speaking against others, trying to embarrass and put them to shame. They are trying to make others feel like dirt. They are trying to hurt their feelings and trying to bring them down. Jesus Christ says to love your neighbor like you love yourself (Matthew 19:19). He did not say speak against your neighbor, but to love your neighbor. He did not say to make your neighbor feel like dirt, but to love your neighbor.

I, personally, love everyone. I would never try to make anyone feel like dirt. There are people that are doing that. They are doing that just to make themselves feel good. They get a kick out of it. They get happy by doing it. I'm here to tell them that it's not right. God is looking at everything that each of us is doing. How would you feel if God embarrassed you? How would you feel if God made you feel bad? What you need to do is close your mouth unless you have something positive to say because it is not cool making others feel bad.

KEEP LIVING

My brothers and sisters, don't let what people say or do to you stop you from living. Keep on living. Don't give anyone the power to stop you from living. God created you to live, so that's what you need to do. He is the only one that has power over you, so if He's okay with you living, live.

Don't let the haters stop you. Don't let your enemies stop you. They are just jealous because you are living a wonderful, beautiful, peaceful, joyful, blessed, and good life in Jesus. They can live that life as well, but they refuse because they think that living a spiritual life is a waste of time. They enjoy the pleasures of the flesh, but soon they are going to find out that living in the flesh is a waste of time, especially when they are on the highway to hell.

Those who are living a fleshy life are on the highway to hell. It's not beautiful being on that highway. It's horrible, but they don't see it that way because they are living in the flesh, and when you are living in the flesh, you don't see things in the spirit. Things of the flesh in the world look good in their eyes. They can not look past the pleasures of it. Living in the spirit, you will clearly see that living in the flesh is not good for you.

My brothers and sisters, don't regret the life you are living. Keep living it. Enjoy it. Have fun living your spiritual life, and have fun living the life that God provides for you, like going on cruises, going to the movies, to the beach, taking vacations. Those things are okay. And if people have a problem with you doing those things, so what? You don't answer to them, you answer to God. Keep living. God wants you to enjoy yourself and not be stuck up in a box.

MOVE UP

My brothers and sisters, it is time for us to move up. Are you ready to move up? Are you sick and tired of seeing those living in the world move up? They are no better than we. We know God. We serve Him! Our Father created this planet. Of course we have the right to move up in this world. We don't have to do things the way they do them. We don't have to compromise ourselves. All we have to do is do things God's way and keep holding on to Him.

My brothers and sisters, we can't give up. We can't give in to the way of the world. Don't lose hope. Keep pushing and striving. God is going to move His people up. We must not get weary in well doing (2 Thessalonians 3:13). Good things happen to those who wait. Waiting doesn't mean sitting down on our tails. It means keep doing what we are doing, and in God's season, He is going to bless us (Deuteronomy 28:12). Keep believing and it shall be done.

Believe me, God knows everything that is going on. He sees how His people are being treated unfairly. He sees how others are doing crooked, wicked, and mischievous things to move up in the world. God is going to put a stop to it. He also sees how crooked the school systems are. How they are piling all these tests on the kids to keep them from making it. Oh yeah, God sees it all, and it's not fair how corrupt the school systems have turned out to be. God is upset.

My brothers and sisters, I want you to know that you are not doing anything bad. God is not upset with you. He is upset with the world. He sees the good that we are doing, and you can rest assure He is going to reward us. He is going to come through for us. He doesn't want us to take shortcuts. Taking shortcuts is the way of the world. He wants us to do things the right way. He wants us to earn everything we get. We are better than the world. We can not live like it. We are holy and righteous. Be still and know that the Lord is God. He is going to fight for us (Nehemiah 4:20), and indeed, move us up.

NEVER TURN AGAINST YOUR FAMILY

My brothers and sisters, there was a need for me to write this one; never turn against your family. Your family is your loved ones. They are your blood. They will be there for you when nobody else will. Your family will never turn you down.

Many people are turning against their families. They are turning against their families over things that are meaningless, such as money and material possessions. Don't get me wrong, you do need money and material possessions, but I want you to know that they are not more important than your family. Money and material possessions will vanish away, but your family won't. Money and material possessions don't have a heart, but your family does.

Nevertheless, many of us are turning against our families over meaningless relationships. We tell our naive relative that the person he or she is in a relationship with doesn't give a crap about him or her, but what does he or she do? That person turns against the family and chooses to be with that individual. And as time goes on, our relative is getting abused until he or she finally realizes that the family was right, and then wants out of the relationship.

God uses your family. He gives your family discernment. That is why you see individuals introducing their boyfriend or girlfriend to their parents because the parents will discern if the person is the right one for their child. God knows best. And He places what He knows into your family. Now if your family is crazy, pray for your family. We all have crazy family members. That's another story. I hope you all know and understand what I'm talking about. Never turn against your family, for it is great having one.

PRAY FOR OTHERS AS WELL

My brother and sister, don't just pray for yourself, but pray for others as well. The reason why I say pray for others is because others need prayer. You never know what an individual may be going through. Your prayer can help that individual make it through the trial that he or she is facing.

We all have hard times. We all have trials, but if we pray for each other, it can help us make it through the trial. Prayer makes you strong not weak. Prayer helps. It doesn't hinder. If you see a person being rude, pray for him. If a person disrespects you, pray for her. Don't curse her out, but pray for her.

I, personally, had to work hard to get to this level where I'm at. In the past, when someone disrespected me, I cursed him out. I went off on her because I thought I was big and bad, but cursing someone and going off doesn't make a situation better; it makes it worse. But I learned from my mistakes and asked God for forgiveness. And like the great God He is, He forgave me.

My brother and sister, you have to learn that you are not the problem. When you pray for someone, God will reveal what's bothering the individual that you saw cutting a fool. Maybe the individual was having problems at home. Maybe the individual was having financial problems. Maybe the individual was having problems with knowing himself, but whatever it is, pray for the individual. Don't forget, someone prayed for you, so don't just pray for yourself, pray for others as well.

SERVING GOD IS A BLESSING

I'm telling you, my brothers and sisters, serving God is a blessing. Many people think it's a curse serving Him, so they refuse to do it. They are afraid. They just don't know that when you serve Him, beautiful things happen. Now, the one they should not serve is Satan. They just don't know that when you live for the world you are actually living for him. And what does living for the world lead to? Living for the world leads to eternal damnation, whereas living for God leads to eternal life which is in Jesus Christ.

You can not serve both God and the world. You must serve one or the other. I'm telling you, God will spew you out if you think you are going to serve both Him and Satan. He doesn't want you being lukewarm. You either must be hot or cold; you can not be both

(Revelation 3:15–16). There is nothing to be afraid of for God has all the things you need. He will not leave you comfortless. When things go wrong, God will be there to help you. If you serve Satan, and when things go wrong, he is going to leave you there to sort things out by yourself. He doesn't care about you, but God does.

God loves you with all of His heart—not part, but all. He expressed His love for us all when He sent His only begotten Son Jesus Christ to earth to die for our sins. And by Jesus Christ doing that, it opened up many benefits to those that would receive Him and serve the Lord God. With God there is life, not death. I'm talking about spiritual life. Some day we all must die physically. But while you are living physically, God will take care of you both spiritually and physically, and let me also add, financially. And when you die, Father God has eternal life for you because serving Him is a blessing.

SPIRITUAL EQUIPPING

Listen up! My friend, I know what you need. You need spiritual equipping, and there is nothing wrong with that. We all need God to sharpen our spirits. We all need Him to work on our mind, heart, body, and soul; the only thing it is going to do is strengthen us. If someone says otherwise, he or she is telling a lie.

Every day I want a change. Every day I want to be new, and that is what spiritual equipping does. It brings you to another level. It empowers you. It pushes and helps you move on through life, especially through the hard times. Don't resist God, but accept Him. Don't deny His power. A person that denies His power has a form of godliness (2 Timothy 3:5). Spiritual equipping doesn't hinder you, it liberates you.

Living in this world, you are going to need spiritual equipping here and there. You are going to need spiritual equipping after dealing with a depressed person. You are going to need one after dealing with negative, bitter, angry, jealous, and evil people. And you are going to most definitely need spiritual equipping after dealing with Satan and his evil forces.

Jesus had spiritual equipping after He was tempted by Satan (Matthew 4:11). Now, what does that tell you? It tells you if Jesus needed spiritual equipping, His servants need some as well. "The disciple is not above his master, nor the servant above his lord" (Matthew 10:24), and we all know no one is greater than Jesus except the Father. Proceed to get your spiritual equipping, my friend, so your life can continue to be powerful.

TALK IT, AND WALK IT

Many people talk the talk, but they don't walk the walk. They look at others and judge them. They look at others and point the finger. Jesus said, how can you judge someone when you have a mote in your eye? He said first get the mote out of your eye, and then proceed to help get it out of your brethren's (Matthew 7:3–5). That's what gets me upset about people; they judge others, but they are not living righteously. They do wicked things behind close doors, and they are phony bologna.

James said don't be hearers of the word and not doers. He said you have to be both hearers and doers of the Word (James 1:22–25). What he is basically saying is to talk it, and walk it. You can't talk it if you are not walking it. If you are doing that, you are living in vain. How can you lead others if you are not living what you preach? The answer is, you can't. You have to lead by example.

"Take heed that no man deceive you. For many shall come in my name, saying, I am Christ; and shall deceive many" (Matthew 24:4–5). "Beware of false prophets, which come to you in sheep's clothing, but inwardly they are ravening wolves" (Matthew 7:15). Many people today are being led by false prophets. If only they would just get on their knees and ask God for the spirit of discernment so they would not get deceived. That is why you have to read the Bible for yourself. "Study to shew thyself approved unto God, a workman that needeth not to be ashamed, rightly dividing the word of truth" (2 Timothy 2:15). I'm not getting off the subject of talk it and walk it. I'm just trying to get you to be aware because the world has many false prophets (1 John 4:1). "See then that ye walk circumspectly, not as fools, but as wise, Redeeming the time, because the days are evil" (Ephesians 5:15–16). And once you read the Bible, my friend, get that knowledge of God, talk it, and make sure you walk it as well. I love you. Be blessed.

TEAM

We as the people of God are supposed to be a team. We are supposed to be united, so why are we contending with ourselves? Why are we competing with each other? We are supposed to be on the same side. We are supposed to be for each other, not against each other. Many of us are trying to be better than the next person. Many of us are trying to outshine the next person. God does not want us to be that way. He wants us to be as one. We are one family in Christ, meaning that we should be on the same page.

Just because we go to different churches doesn't mean we should not be together. It does not mean that we are on different teams. We have the same spirit, which is the Holy Spirit, the Spirit of God. We should not let going to different churches separate us. We serve the same God. We are here for the same purpose. We are on the same team.

God did not give us His power to feud against ourselves. He gave us His power to conquer the enemy, which is Satan. God gave us His power to praise, acknowledge, and worship Him. He gave us His power to draw those that are lost to Him. Many of us are misusing that power. Many of us are abusing that power. And many of us are using that power for our own selfish gain.

My brothers and sisters, we are a team, so let's be a team. Let's pull together and use the power that God given to us to conquer the world. Let us take control of this world. Jesus did His part. Now it's time for us to do our part. He does not want to come back and see us fighting among ourselves. He wants to come back and see us loving ourselves. People of God, we are a team, now it's time for us to act like it.

P.S. We should not be our own enemy. Let's stand together and fight together because that's what a team does.

THINK BEFORE YOU SPEAK

My friend, let me give you some advice: think before you speak. I say think before you speak because if you don't, you may say something that could hurt someone. My friend, you have to be sensitive toward people. It's not cool killing someone's spirit. It's not cool hurting someone's feelings. It's not cool saying something to hurt someone, even if he or she said something to hurt you, because two wrongs don't make a right. "Recompense to no man evil for evil" (Romans 12:17). You have to be the better person.

God does not reward people for being ignorant or abusive. He rewards them for showing love, consideration, and peace. If you feel angry toward someone, you are bound to say something hurtful in that situation. It would be best for you to leave that individual. My friend, just because someone else is crazy, that doesn't mean you must be crazy. Have some class about yourself.

"Be ye angry, and sin not: let not the sun go down upon your wrath: Neither give place to the devil" (Ephesians 4:26–27). Let's be real, nine times out of ten when you are angry, you are not going to say something nice. You are going to say something harsh, and that why it is best to leave an individual when you are angry because if you don't, I see you giving place to the devil. What you have to do is collect yourself and pray about it. Ask God to release His peace upon you because if you try to do things your way, you are going to curse someone out, and that is a sin. God knows you are a good person, but even good people have angry days. For those days to be decreased, think before you speak, and if someone angers you or if you are angry for no apparent reason, ask God to pour His peace upon you. "If it be possible, as much as lieth in you, live peaceably with all men" (Romans 12:18).

WONDERFUL

Hey! How are you doing? I'm doing just fine. My brothers and sisters, I love you. I'm glad that God created us because we are beautiful people. Of course, we can't help but to be beautiful when we are made in His image (Genesis 1:27). He loves us so much that it was His good pleasure to make us in His image. And what a wonderful job He did! He is mighty.

My brothers and sisters, don't let anything worry you, and don't let anything get you down. You are wonderful beings, so don't let anyone tell you otherwise. All you have to do is continue to reflect upon God, and His peace will come upon you. His peace is more powerful than your enemies. His peace is more powerful than depression and stress. His peace will keep you from worrying about the cares of this world. He knows all of your needs, and believe me, He is going to provide them to you.

God is not a God of emptiness, but a God of fullness. He is full of all the things you need, such as love, peace, joy, power, and strength. He has those things available to you. All you have to do is just ask Him for them, but some of us are just too busy searching after the things that the world offers. Compared to God the world is meaningless, for He is bigger than it.

Who would you rather have, the world or the one that is bigger than it? The world is going to pass away, but He is not. He is forever. God never falls apart. He is stable every single day. "Love not the world, neither the things that are in the world. If any man love the world, the love of the Father is not in him. For all that is in the world, the lust of the flesh, and the lust of the eyes, and the pride of life, is not of the Father, but is of the world. And the world passeth away, and the lust thereof: but he that doeth the will of God abideth for ever" (1 John 2:15–17).

A BEAUTIFUL CREATION

My friend, you are a beautiful creation. There is nothing wrong with you, so why are you hard on yourself? After God created you, He saw that you were good (Genesis 1:31). It is you that have to believe it. Many people can tell you that you're beautiful, but if you don't believe it for yourself, it is all vanity. Stop being your own enemy talking against yourself. Begin to love yourself because you are beautiful, and no devil in hell can take your beauty away from you. Why? Because God gave it to you. You are made in His image, and what a glorious image it is! (Genesis 1:27) Start encouraging and uplifting yourself. Tell yourself you're beautiful, and believe it, for you have a Father in Heaven that absolutely does.

BE HONEST WITH YOURSELF

How could you be honest with others when you're not being honest with yourself? You have to be honest with yourself so you can be honest with others. You can't be honest with others if you are not honest with yourself. If you lie to yourself, you will lie to others. You have to ask God for the spirit of honesty. Ask Him to deliver you from the spirit of lying. That's right, you have to call it what it is: a spirit of lying. Having a spirit of lying makes you a liar. You must be delivered from it. It is an evil spirit. It is very cruel and manipulative. And it is not of God. God hates liars (Proverbs 6:16–19). No one likes a liar. No one likes to be lied to. It all begins with you. Once God delivers you from it, begin being honest with yourself, and proceed to being honest with others. I'm telling you it feels so good being honest, knowing that you can be trusted by others. Keep this in mind, "A false witness shall not be unpunished, and he that speaketh lies shall perish" (Proverbs 19:9).

BIGGER, BETTER, AND GREATER

You want to know why doors have been shutting in your face? Doors have been shutting in your face because God has bigger, better, and has greater things in store for you. God doesn't want you to be in mediocrity. He doesn't want you to step into a door that is not worthy of you. He wants you to be in greatness. He wants you to have the best. Remember, He is the one that knows best. God knows you have bills to pay. He knows that you are in debt, and He knows that you want money in your pocket. He is not ignorant of that. Don't be anxious, but be patient. Soon, very soon, He is going to open the right door for you. I'm telling you when He opens that door, you are going to be praising Him all over the place. God has bigger, better, and greater things for you, so just keep persevering and you will step into what I'm talking about.

BREAK YOUR SPIRIT

My brothers and sisters, don't let anyone break your spirit. Be tough. You are mighty in the Lord. You are more than conquerors (Romans 8:37). Don't let anyone take what belongs to you. Defend what's yours. Protect what's yours. You are in charge of it. Don't be like Adam and Eve. Be better. Don't let the devil take what belongs to you. He would if you allow him to. You have to put your feet on his throat and take him out. You can not be cute with him; you have to be bold. Being cute will get you defeated. The devil wants you defeated. The devil wants you to have low self-esteem. You have to refuse to be the way that he wants you to be. Continue to be positive. Continue to show love toward your neighbor (Matthew 19:19). Don't be evil toward them, but good toward them. Being good and showing love is the way of God. And what a beautiful way it is! Don't let anyone break your spirit, my brothers and sisters. You are wonderful, beautiful, righteous, caring, and loving people.

BRIDEGROOM

My brothers and sisters, our groom is on His way back. You know who I'm talking about. I'm talking about Jesus Christ. He is ready to come back for His bride. He is getting prepared to come back for us. "Watch therefore: for ye know not what hour your Lord doth come" (Matthew 24:42). Jesus is ready to bring us to the place that He and His Father prepared for us—heaven, a place that is filled with riches, love, and glory. Each day brings a smile to His face because He is ready to sweep us off our feet. He loves the work that we are doing on earth. He is proud of us. Day and night we are teaching, preaching, and sharing the Gospel with others. We are helping the unsaved get saved. We are bringing Him lost souls. We are praying for others. Jesus is in heaven dancing, and the angels are joining in on the party. In heaven you can't help but to join in on the party because there is life. There is no death, corruption, sin, and depression. In heaven you are debt-free. It is the place where Jesus is going to have us for all eternity, therefore, rejoice and be exceedingly glad because the marriage that we have been waiting for is about to take place.

CAN BE TRUSTED

My friend, who has been lying to you? God can be trusted. He never lies. He always keeps His Word. People never keep their word, but He does. People lie, but He doesn't. You can count on Him on anything. You can trust Him on anything. He will never deceive you. He will never mislead you. His way is the way of truth, love, and righteousness. If it wasn't for Him, I would not be where I am today. With God's help, I never drink, never smoke, never done drugs, and never been in jail. With God's help, you too can be that way. If you are already that way, good, but you need Him in your life to stay that way. Many people were just like you, but when something tragic happened to them, they turned to drugs, alcohol, and cigarettes. By having God in your life when something tragic happens, you don't have to turn to those things. Instead, you turn to Him, and you can rest assure He will make everything all right. God can be trusted; just try Him, and you will see that He is the Truth.

CARRY YOUR LOAD

You know what you need to do; you need to let Jesus carry your load. Once you let Jesus carry your load watch how light your spirit will become. Right now, your spirit is heavy because you are carrying too much weight. What I mean about that is you have too many burdens on you. As long as you keep those burdens on you, you are not going to make it far. It is just like packing your book bag with a lot of weight plates. All it's going to do is slow you down. Why should you carry burdens when you don't have to? My friend, introduce yourself to Jesus, and He will take it from there. He will take your worries away. He will help you budget and manage your bills. Jesus is your answer for everything. He knows everything, and He is willing to help you in every area of your life. You have to give Him a chance. All you have to do is try Him. Give Him a shot. You gave everything else a shot, and what happened? Everything else failed you. Give your load to Jesus and watch how free you will be.

CARRY YOURSELVES IN LOVE

My brothers and sisters, carry yourselves in love, not hate. God carries Himself in love, so He expects you to carry yourselves in love. He commands you to carry yourselves in love. You are a reflection of Him, so act like it. He does not reflect evil, but love. Though others may hate you, love them. Though others may be jealous of you, love them. God does not want you to be cruel and ignorant like they are. He wants you to have class and respect about yourself. Being like them is ignorant. Stooping to their level doesn't solve a thing. Two wrongs don't make a right. Put on a loving attitude. Show others that love is not going to play out. It is everlasting. I don't care how much evil and hate is in the world. Neither of them have more power than love. Jesus defeated evil and hate with love. Though the world was against Him, He overcame it. He was not moved by the evil in it. "And walk in love, as Christ also hath loved us, and hath given himself for us an offering, and a sacrifice to God for a sweetsmelling savour" (Ephesians 5:2).

CLEAN SLATE

God has given you a clean slate, so rejoice about it. There is no need for you to dwell on your sin. God has forgiven you, so accept His forgiveness. He doesn't want you carrying your sin. He doesn't want you beating yourself up about it. He wants you to release it. There is only one Jesus Christ, and it is not you. He is the only one without sin. But thanks be to God, He died for all of our sins so we too can have eternal life. My friend, no one is perfect but Jesus Christ. By Jesus dying for your sins, God has given you a clean slate of living a holy life. He knows that you are going to fall sometimes. He knows that you are going to make mistakes, so don't be too hard on yourself. You are only human. God loves you, my friend, always remember that. There is nothing that won't keep Him from loving and forgiving you. Be in peace, my friend. I love you. God has given you a clean slate, so enjoy your life in holiness, righteousness, love, freedom, and fun. Live, my friend, live, because you have abundant life in Jesus.

CONTINUE TO BE WHO YOU ARE

My friend, continue to be who you are because there is nothing wrong with you. If someone doesn't like you for who you are, so what? That is his or her problem. The only being you need to please is

God. Pleasing Him is a big plus. Pleasing Him is a big deal. God loving you for who you are is all that should matter. If there are changes you need to make concerning yourself, God will tell you. Other than that, you need to stop stressing yourself trying to satisfy people who will never be satisfied. People like that have issues. If they are not satisfied with themselves, how are they going to be satisfied with you? That is why I am telling you to continue to be who you are because the majority of the people in this world don't know who they are, and due to them not knowing who they are, they will try to abuse you with their low self-esteem. You are a beautiful human being, so continue to be that way. You are made in the image of God (Genesis 1:27). Now what is wrong with that? Nothing. So continue to be who you are and live joyfully.

DON'T BE SELLOUTS

My brothers and sisters, don't be sellouts. Continue to serve the Lord God. Don't sell the Lord God out for anyone or anything. That person or thing you are selling Him out for is not more valuable than He, or more worthy than He. God is the greatest jewel in the universe. There is nothing more precious than He. "For what shall it profit a man, if he shall gain the whole world, and lose his own soul?" (Mark 8:36) Gaining the world is meaningless compared to keeping your soul. The world is going to pass away. All materials and possessions are going to pass away. It is all vanity. It is temporal. But serving the Lord and gaining your reward is not. Eternal life is not vanity. Eternal life is not an illusion or fantasy. It's the real thing. It is what Jesus Christ has prepared for you. There is no depression, slumber, dying, or sickness. There is no murder, raping, cursing, or abusing. There is love. And I'm telling you if you stick with God, you shall have it. Keep trusting in the Lord. Keep following Him. Don't get weary, and you can rest assure you will get everything that your heart desires. Don't be sellouts!

DON'T COMPLAIN

When you do things for God, don't complain about it. Why? Because when He does things for you, He doesn't complain about it. He doesn't mind doing things for you because He loves and cares about you, and you should feel the same way about Him as well. You are made in His image, so love and be right about Him. It is a crying shame how some of us are selfish. God is not selfish, so neither should we be. It doesn't make any sense. Did God complain when He created you? Nope! Did God complain when He delivered you from your enemies? Nope! Did God complain when He woke you up this morning? Nope! Did God complain when He sent His beloved Son down here on earth to die for your sins? Nope! Neither should you complain when He tells you to pay your tithes and offerings. Neither should you complain when He tells you to donate something to the building fund. And neither should you complain when He tells you to help out the children and the poor. You should be eager to do those things for God because your Heavenly Father is eager to do things for you. Stop crying and mourning 24/7. Stop being selfish and self-centered. Stop complaining and begin to love; be eager and be positive to do things for God.

DON'T CONDONE EVIL

My friend, don't condone evil. Many people are doing it, but it doesn't mean that you have to do it. Be your own person. Don't follow after those that do evil. And don't let them pressure you into doing it. Don't tell your neighbor to slap someone. Don't tell your neighbor to shoot someone. Don't tell your neighbor to curse someone. Because if you do, you are condoning evil. You are motivating someone to do evil, and that's not right. Instead of following after unrighteousness, follow after righteousness. If your peers call you a coward, so what? Don't worry about what they say about you. Believe it or not, your peers want to follow after righteousness as well as you do, but the problem is they are afraid what others will say about them. They don't have their own mind. They let what others say control them. They let what others say dictate their behavior. Walk in peace and walk with an upright heart so you can condone good and not evil.

FIGHT BACK

Stop being a wimp and fight back. Stop letting your enemies defeat you. Stand up to them. You are a soldier in the army of the Lord, so stop letting your enemies bully you around. Pull out your sword and begin to slay. Your sword is the Word of God. You have to speak it, and your enemies will scatter. They can not stand up to the power of God. They are afraid of it. You have all the power within you, so use it. God gave you the power to use it. He didn't give you the power to be cute. There is spiritual warfare going on. You will get destroyed trying to be cute with those demonic spirits. They don't care how cute you are. Their mission is to destroy you. Many people have been destroyed by demons because they didn't use the power that God has granted them. They thought the power they had was for show, but they found out the hard way that it's not. God doesn't want you to be destroyed by Satan and his demonic followers. He wants you to defeat them, so stop being a wimp and fight back.

FRET NOT

Fret not, my friend, for God knows what He is doing. He has you covered. He will not do anything to jeopardize you or your life. Jeopardizing your life is not what He's about. He is about giving life, not harming it. He is life. He is the light of life. There is nothing to fret about having Him in your life. God is a tremendous God, and having Him makes you and your life tremendous. Having Him in your life is a plus, not a minus. Having God in your life makes you cool, for He is cool. God is not a party pooper, but a party starter. His party is for all eternity. I'm telling you what I know. This is not something that I'm making up. Fret not about car payments. Fret not about house payments. Fret not about anything. Period. God is going to work everything out for you. Believe and have faith. Trust in Him. God will never leave you alone, so fret not, my friend, fret not.

GO

Why are you still sitting down on your bottom? Jesus Christ told you to go to the highways, the byways, and the streets to preach and teach the Gospel. People are in need of the Gospel. They are in need of hearing it. They are in need of establishing a relationship with God, Jesus Christ, and the Holy Spirit. Their souls need to be saved. I'm not joking; I'm serious. God doesn't want anyone to go to hell, so if you can help someone from going there, then do it. Get off of your bottom and do your job. God is holding you accountable. You have His knowledge within you, and He wants you to apply it. Stop being lazy. You are too important to be lazy. "Go ye into all the world, and preach the gospel to every creature" (Mark 16:15).

GOD IS AROUND

I don't know what some people are talking about, but God is around. If He wasn't, how does the sun continue to rise? If He wasn't, how do we continue to wake up? God causes the sun to rise, and He causes life to continue to exist. He is around and is going to remain around. He created this planet and everything in it, of course. He's around. You ask, "If God is around, why is the world the way that it is?" The world is the way that it is because of the lawlessness of mankind. Man refuses to follow God's principles. That's why the world is full of chaos, not because of God, but because of the wickedness of man. God gave man the authority to rule the earth, not to corrupt it. Man is responsible for the affairs of the world. The only thing that God wants us to do is to serve and fear Him. He also wants us to keep His commandments. And part of His commandments include not serving false gods or any graven image (Exodus 20:3–4). Though man is ruler over earth, God is ruler over both man and earth. "The earth is the Lord's, and the fulness thereof; the world, and they that dwell therein. For he hath founded it upon the seas, and established it upon the floods" (Psalm 24:1–2). "Let all the earth fear the Lord: let all the inhabitants of the world stand in awe of him" (Psalm 33:8) for He is around.

GOD IS LOVE

God is love. What makes you think that He's not about it? He is not the reason for the chaos in the world. He is not the reason for the corruption and violence in it. He does not promote those things. Neither does He campaign for those things. He promotes and campaigns love. He created this world in love. He created you in love. You've got to be out of your mind thinking that He's not about love. Everything He does is as all about love. Just like He sent His only begotten Son to the world to save us from sin (John 3:16–17). Now that is what you call love. In good times and bad times He is love. In stormy days and stormy nights He is love. He is always love. That is one thing I know I can always count on, that God is love. That is how I make it through life, knowing that He loves me. And He also loves you too, so never forget that God is love (1 John 4:7–21).

GOD MOVES

I don't know what some of you are talking about, but God does move. He moves for us every day. He even moves in His silence. He is the one that keeps the earth revolving around the sun. He is the one that keeps the stars shining. He is the one that protects the earth from being destroyed by comets. I dare you to say that He doesn't do anything. God's favor is upon all of us. If it wasn't, He wouldn't have created us, and if it wasn't, He wouldn't have sent His Son to this world to die for our sins. God's sun shines on the just and the unjust, and His rain pours on the just and the unjust (Matthew 5:45). He is not a biased God. He loves us all. He gives everyone equal opportunity to receive His salvation through His Son Jesus Christ. It is up to us to receive it or not. God is a good God. He is a loving God. There is no hate in Him. He keeps the oceans, seas, lakes, and rivers separated from dry land. What more do I need to say? Stop being in denial and submit yourself unto Him because you know that deep down in your heart, God moves for you.

GREAT GOD

My brothers and sisters, God is a great God. He's an excellent God. Without Him, we would not be alive. He always goes out of His way to bless us. He is an unselfish God, and whoever denies that is a liar. God enriches us with His love. God enriches us with His peace.

God enriches us with His strength. We never beg for bread for God is our Provider and a great Provider He is. When God blesses us, He never complains. He is so sincere! That is why I love Him so much because there are a million other things that He can be doing, but He always finds the time to provide for us. God is cooler than cool. He is hotter than hot. He is greater than great. Those are other reasons why I choose to serve Him. Come on, who doesn't want to serve an awesome God such as Him? I know I do, and that is why I am going to keep on doing it. God is a great God, and great He will always be.

HAVE FAITH AND DOUBT NOT

Have faith and doubt not. Great things happen when you have faith, but when you doubt, things don't happen because you don't believe. You have to believe to be successful. You have to believe to get pure things in life. As long as you keep doubting you are going to be stuck. That's all doubting does is keep you still. When you have faith, mountains move. When you have faith, obstacles get overpowered. Having faith makes you powerful and unstoppable. God wants you to have faith. He wants you to be powerful and unstoppable. That is why He made you in His image, but you have to operate in faith. Don't be afraid to have faith; take full advantage of it. Apply it in your life for it is free. With faith many positive benefits come. Take it up on its offer. There is nothing stopping you from having it. It is all in your will. You have to make the choice of having faith or not having it. "Verily I say unto you, If ye have faith, and doubt not, ye shall not only do this which is done to the fig tree, but also if ye shall say unto this mountain, Be thou removed, and be thou cast into the sea; it shall be done" (Matthew 21:21).

HAVE FAITH AND WORK IT

What you need to do, my friend, is put your faith in Jesus. Jesus is King of kings, and Lord of lords. He will not fail you, my friend. All you have to do is trust Him, and He will provide you with everything you need. He knows what your heart desires. He knows the necessities of life. Don't forget He was here before you, that He was human before you. He knows what we need. He knows what we hunger for, and He knows what we thirst for. He knows we need money to live. Jesus is not ignorant, but you have to understand that you are not going to get things on a silver platter. You have to get off your tail and work for it. You have to work your faith because Jesus is not going to move for you unless you work it. Have faith in Jesus, and work it and you can rest assure He will come through.

P.S. Always keep this in your spirit: faith without works is dead (James 2:17).

KEPT YOU ALIVE

"O Lord, thou hast brought up my soul from the grave: thou hast kept me alive, that I should not go down to the pit" (Psalm 30:3).

My friend, you are alive because of God. He is the one that kept you alive. He is the reason for your survival. You may be a strong individual, but God is the reason why you made it this far, so what you need to do is give Him the glory. By you giving Him the glory, He would add more years to your life. By you giving Him the glory, He will continue to strengthen you. Why? Because you acknowledge Him. I'm telling you, my friend, God is not hard to please. He just wants what is due unto Him, and that is getting glory and praise. Now what is so hard about that? Nothing. You should be glad to give Him glory and praise. You should be glad to honor Him because the more you do that the higher He is going to raise you. God is not an unjust God. God is not an unfair God. "He is a rewarder of them that diligently seek him" (Hebrews 11:6). God has kept you alive, my friend, so rejoice, be glad about it, and give Him praise.

LIVE IN THE SPIRIT

My brothers and sisters, choose to live in the Spirit. Why? Because the Spirit is where God dwells. God does not dwell in the flesh, but in the Spirit. The Spirit is His habitation. The Spirit is His sanctuary. It's His place of rest. And by you living in the Spirit, you will be joining Him! My brothers and sisters, God wants you to join Him. He wants you to enjoy what He enjoys, the fruit of the Spirit which is love, joy, peace, longsuffering, gentleness, goodness, faith, meekness, and temperance (Galatians 5:22–23). He has it all waiting for you. Best of all, God will be well pleased with you if you live in the Spirit for you can not please Him living in the flesh because the flesh is the Spirit's enemy. They war against each other. They conflict with each other. Trust me, my brothers and sisters, being with God is where you want to be. "This I say then, Walk in the Spirit, and ye shall not fulfil the lust of the flesh" (Galatians 5:16).

LIVE THE WAY GOD WANTS YOU TO LIVE

My brothers and sisters, live the way God wants you to live. God's way is the right way. Not your way, but His way. Living your way will lead to a dead end. Living His way will lead you to life everlasting. Now do you like the sound of that? Of course you do. Anything that has life attached to it is good, especially when God, Jesus Christ, and the Holy Spirit are attached to it. You can't help but to have life when you are part of them. That is why I encourage you to live the way God wants you to live. You can't go wrong living His way. God will not bamboozle you. When He says you have life, you've got it. When He says He is going to bless you, He is going to do it. He is not a liar. But if you don't live His way, there is no blessing. Let me correct myself, there is a blessing that is from Satan. The other way of living is the way of the world, and that way is not of God, but of Satan. And of course, the world does bless its own, but it's only temporary, but with God, things are eternal. Live the way God wants you to live because living His way is blessed assurance and life.

LOVE JESUS

Don't hate Jesus, love Him. I don't understand why people hate Him. There is nothing hateful about Him. There is nothing about Him that makes you hate Him. Jesus is full of love, and He loves you more than anything for He is the Savior of love. He doesn't deliver bad to you; He delivers love. His beef is not with you; it's with Satan. All Jesus wants to do is love, bless, save, and take good care of you. He doesn't hate you. He is all that you need, so stop looking for love in the wrong places. When Jesus visits you, don't reject Him. He is not visiting you to destroy you but to deliver you from bondage. He wants to set you free from the lust of the world. The world has nothing good to offer you. The only thing the world has to offer you is death. What good is it to gain the world and lose your soul? But what Jesus has to offer you is life, and life more abundantly. That is something the world can't give. I already made my decision, and that is living with Jesus for all eternity. Love Jesus. Don't hate Him because He certainly does not hate you.

NOT A WASTE OF SKIN

Listen to me, my friend, you are not a waste of skin. You are a beautiful human being. God has you down here for a reason. All you have to do is go to Him, and He will reveal your purpose in life. You are destined to be down here. If you weren't, God would have not sent you down here. My friend, you are an important individual, so stop saying that you're not. Before you reach others, you have to reach yourself. Before you be a light to others, you have to be a light to yourself. You can't do either of those things if you are not doing it for yourself. When others see that you are making a positive impact on yourself, others will be influenced by it. You are not making a positive impact when you are having low self-esteem. Thinking or saying you are a waste of skin means you have low self-esteem. You have to speak good of yourself, and you have to begin to love yourself. It all begins with you. You are not a waste of skin, my friend, because the good Lord created you beautifully, and with a purpose and will to live. God doesn't make mistakes. He's perfect.

NOT ANGRY WITH YOU

What is your problem? God is not angry with you, so why are you acting as though He is? God is not angry with you. He loves you. Just because He is not moving the way that you want Him to move doesn't mean He is angry with you. Who are you to give Him orders? Who are you to tell Him when and how to move? You are not God. He is. He moves when He wants to move, and He moves how He wants to move. What you need to do is get a life and learn how to be patient. God is not upset with you. He has bigger things to think about. Believe me, if God was angry with you, you would know it. He is not someone you want to get upset. Continue to do what you are doing. Keep praying. Keep reading the Bible. And keep going to church. He has not forgotten about you. And as far as you thinking He is angry with you, that is ridiculous. Soon, very soon, He is going to bless you with what you have been praying and asking Him for, so give thanks and glory to His holy name. He is not angry with you. He is definitely not angry with you. Be in peace.

NOT LEFT YOU

What's wrong, my friend? What are you so down about? God has not left you. He is still with you. Okay, you've done something you had no business doing. Did you repent about it? Did you ask God to forgive you? God is waiting on you to confess it. He doesn't want you to be depressed. He wants you to be happy. Being depressed is not going to help the situation. You have to get out of your depression and go to God about it. He is waiting on you. Everyone has done wrong. Everyone has sinned, but it takes each individual to go to God and ask Him for forgiveness. I can't go for you, my friend. You have to go for yourself. I wasn't the one that committed the sin, you were. God wants to hear your voice. He wants you to come to Him with your burdens. What are you so afraid of? God is not going to beat you down. He is not going to condemn you. He is a wonderful, gracious, merciful, and forgiving God. He already knows you've done wrong, but He wants you to be humble and courageous enough to come unto Him. He wants you to come unto His throne of grace with boldness (Hebrews 4:16). God has not left you, my friend. If you will stop ignoring Him you will see that it is true.

NOT WORTHLESS

My friend, God is not worthless, so stop listening to those individuals who say that He is. They are the ones who are worthless. God is the most valuable being in the universe, meaning the most important.

A celebrity is not more valuable than He, nor is a wealthy person. God will put everybody to shame. I'm telling you, anything you ask of Him, He will provide. God is a God of His Word. If He says He is going to do something, believe me, He is going to do it. You will not be wasting your time serving Him. And you will not be wasting your time following Him. God loves you more than anyone. He loves you more than your family. And He will take care of you more than anyone. He holds the whole world in His hands. Who do you want to be most involved with, the people who live in the world or the one who holds it in His hands? If you want to go deeper, He holds the whole universe in His hands. Does that sound like someone who is worthless? I think not, because worthless is not who He is.

PRAY ABOUT IT

When someone acts shady toward you, don't curse about it, but pray about it. Cursing is not going to help the situation, but praying will. As long as you curse about it, the situation is going to stand, but when you pray about it, God is going to wash the situation away. What makes you think that God likes shady people? He doesn't like them; they despise Him. God doesn't like people who do mischievous things to His children. What God wants His children to do is better. He doesn't want us to curse people out. Don't give anyone that much power to make you sin. That's right, cursing someone out is a sin. You are better than that. You have to understand that everyone is not going to be for you. Everyone can not be trusted. You have to stay alert. Keep your eyes open. If you know someone is shady, don't try to develop a relationship with that individual. Keep your distance because people such as that will stab you in the back. Not everyone has your best interest at heart. Not everyone wants you to succeed. They can say good things about you from the outside, but inwardly, they can be filled with hatred and jealousy toward you. I love you, my friend, and remember, whenever you encounter wickedness, don't curse about it but pray about it. God will arrive.

SHARE YOUR TESTIMONIES

My brothers and sisters, share your testimonies. Why? Because your testimonies are what is going to draw souls unto God. You reach others through your testimonies. How are you going to encourage others to come to Christ if you don't have anything to share with them? You have to let others know how God brought you to salvation. You have to let others know how God brought you through your trials and tribulations. And also, when you share your testimonies with others it shows them that you can relate. Hearing your testimonies may be the answer to their problems. Your testimonies will be a big help pulling them through their hard times. Sharing your testimonies also lets others know how wonderful God is. It lets others know that God is a mighty God, and He will always be there for you in times of good and times of trouble. You see, my brothers and sisters, your testimonies are not all about you, but all about God and the many lives He wants you to touch. So share your testimonies and live a love-filled life.

SMILING INSIDE

Pal, you should be joyful! Why? Because God is smiling on the inside of you. And why He is smiling? He is smiling because He loves being in you. God loves you and would rather be nowhere else but inside of you. You are special to Him, and He wants to beautify you. He wants to enlighten you. Sometimes you wonder why you glow. I'm telling you, that is God smiling on the inside of you. He can't help but to smile for He is in a wonderful specimen. By God smiling in you that should let you know that you are unique. It should let you know that you are His sheep, and He's not ashamed to let His light shine through you. That is why your enemies scatter when they see you approach, because they know God is in you. They know the power that He contains, and they want no part of it. Walk with your head up high. Walk with confidence and be glad for God is inside of you, and He is most definitely smiling.

SOLID

My brothers and sisters, God's love for us is solid. There is nothing that can separate us from His love (Romans 8:39). There is nothing that can pluck us out of His hand (John 10:28) for His love for us is solid. God loves us so much that He made us joint heirs with Christ. God loves us so much that He has a magnificent place waiting for us when we depart from earth. God will never be finished with loving us. His love for us is for all eternity. It never ends! You should be excited that His love for us is solid. You should be praising, exalting, and worshipping His wonderful name for "Great is the Lord, and greatly to be praised in the city of our God, in the mountain of holiness" (Psalm 48:1). Meditate on the love that God has for you. Embrace it. Bask in it. "How excellent is thy lovingkindness, O God! therefore the children of men put their trust under the shadow of thy wings" (Psalm 36:7).

SOMEONE FOR YOU

My friend, continue to be patient for God has someone for you. He heard your prayers and knows that you need someone in your life. According to His will, He is going to send you that mate you have been asking Him for. Don't worry about when it's going to happen. Just know that it's going to happen. God is going to supply all your needs according to His riches and glory. He is not going to disappoint you. He knows what type of mate you need. He is going to send you someone that is going to love you the way that you are supposed to be loved. He is going to send you someone that is going to have your best interests at heart. The mate that God is going to send to you is made in His image. He is not going to send you a knucklehead. He is not going to send you a basket case. You have to trust Him. Be patient and wait because soon, very soon, your mate is going to be right beside you loving you and only you. Your mate is ordered by the Lord God. He does have someone for you.

STOP MISTREATING YOURSELF

My friend, stop mistreating yourself and begin to love yourself. Mistreating yourself is abusing yourself. You have to treat yourself with love. You have to treat yourself with goodness and kindness. Shower yourself with love. There is nothing wrong with that. How are you going to treat others right when you don't treat yourself right? My friend, besides God, Jesus Christ, and the Holy Spirit, you come first. You have to treat yourself well before you treat others well. You are not being fair to yourself if you are mistreating yourself. I encourage you to be good to yourself. I encourage you to please yourself. Take yourself out. Buy yourself some shoes and clothes. No, my friend, there is nothing wrong spending on yourself. In my opinion, we don't do that enough. We will spend for others before we would spend for ourselves. It is not a turnoff loving yourself; it is a turn-on, so stop mistreating yourself and begin to adore yourself.

STOP THINKING BAD ABOUT YOURSELF

My friend, stop thinking bad about yourself and begin to think good about yourself. As long as you think bad about yourself you are going to be in a state of slumber, also known as depression. My friend, you have to speak good about yourself. You have to let yourself know that you are somebody and that you love yourself. You are not some piece of trash in the garbage. You are someone special in the eyes of the Most High God, and knowing that means a lot. God doesn't want you thinking bad about yourself. He wants you thinking good. There is no need for you to think bad about yourself for you are His wonderful creation. You are unique. You are awesome. Put all those negative things aside. And if you are encamped around negative people, flee from them because they are not going to make you better, only worse. Be encamped around motivational people not bitter people because bitter people think badly about themselves as well. They are not going to feed you positive energy. Stop thinking bad about yourself. Embrace yourself. May peace be with you and God bless you.

SURPRISE

My brothers and sisters, God has a surprise waiting for us. If He tells us what it is, it won't be a surprise. Some things are worth waiting for. Some things are worth being kept a secret. God loves us that much to have a surprise waiting for us, and you know that it is going to be huge. All we have to do is keep seeking after His kingdom, His righteousness, and someday the surprise will be revealed unto us. I am highly anticipating His surprise. I want to know what it is just as much as you do, but I know whatever it is it is going to be spectacular because we serve a spectacular God. All of God's people know that when God does things, He does them big. He doesn't hold anything out on His people. He makes sure that they have the best. You are talking about a God who made us joint heirs with Christ. You are talking about a God who created the heavens and the earth. He holds all the riches. He holds the whole universe in the palm of His hand. "But as it is written, Eye hath not seen, nor ear heard, neither have entered into the heart of man, the things which God hath prepared for them that love him" (1 Corinthians 2:9).

TEST

My brothers and sisters, you have to test the Word. How do you know it works if you don't test it? God wants you to test the Word. That is how you show faith. It is how you find out that God is real, and that His Word is real. Many people are calling Him and His Word a lie. How are you going to call Him and His Word a lie if you never tried them? No, you are the liar. God never lied to me. And His Word never lied to me. When I test His Word, things get accomplished, blessings come through, and I gain power. You have to put the Word to the test. There is no sin in doing it. God is not going to punish you. What do you think the Hebrew boys did? They tested God's Word that He would never leave or forsake them when they got into the fiery furnace (Daniel 3). They could have avoided it by bowing down to the golden image that the king ordered everyone to do at a certain time, but they refused. They chose to have faith in God. They chose to put God's Word to action, and what was the result? The result was that God delivered them. No one better talk against the true and living God. Those Hebrew boys got promoted in the province of Babylon. Put God's Word to action. He showed up for the Hebrew boys, and

He will show up for you, not only in bad times, but good times as well.

THE EPITOME OF GODLINESS

Jesus Christ is the epitome of godliness. Everything about Him is righteous. And everything about Him is pure. Jesus never committed a sin (Hebrews 4:15). Jesus never served any other god besides His Father God. He never idolized. He never kneeled down to any statue. The only high power He kneeled down unto was His Father God. Everything about Jesus is godly. The way He walked was godly. The way He talked was godly. The way He preached and taught was godly. There is nothing worldly about Jesus. There is nothing fleshly about Him. And there is surely nothing sinful about Him. Jesus obeyed everything that God commanded. There was never a time He didn't hearken unto God's voice. Jesus Christ is the epitome of godliness, whether you agree with me or not.

TREAT YOURSELF

Hey! Stop being so hard on yourself and begin to treat yourself. For many years you worked your tail off, and now it's time for it to pay off. You see, living in mess will cause you to stress, and you don't deserve to live in grotesque. You earned the right to live in the best. Treat yourself with love, and like a dove, your spirit will fly high. Draw nigh to your inner self and you will be amazed by the power and strength it contains. And the minute you stop allowing your job and the world to dictate your life, you will see how it feels to be living in paradise. Let your mind, heart, and soul be at peace and rest because it is a crying shame to be stressed, overworked, and depressed. You are royalty, so treat yourself with loyalty. Don't be ashamed of treating yourself. Let the whole universe see it, for there is nothing else greater than honoring and rewarding oneself.

WINGS

My brothers and sisters, there is no need for you to worry because God has you under His wings. Being under His wings is tremendous, and being under His wings is awesome because there is nothing more beautiful than a Father protecting His children, and that is what God does so graciously, protect His children. Nothing can touch you, and nothing can harm you because you are under His mighty wings. You have all the protection you need. You have all the security you need. The word *fear* shouldn't even come out of your mouth because there is no need to fear. When demons hear the name of Jesus they tremble. Oh yeah, Jesus is also with you for He and God are one (John 10:22–30). I'm telling you, my brothers and sisters, you are living on high having God and Jesus in your life. I'm proud to be under His wings, and I love being under His wings because He takes care of my every need. I go to Him on a daily basis. Oh Lord, "I will abide in thy tabernacle for ever: I will trust in the covert of thy wings" (Psalm 61:4).

WORSHIP IN SPIRIT AND TRUTH

If you want to be blessed, one of the main things you have to do is worship God in spirit and truth. Spirit and truth is what He's about. God does not deal with the flesh. And He does not deal with liars. You can't come to Him being fleshly and expect to get blessed. You can't come to Him with lies and expect to get blessed. God knows every man's intentions. James said, "Ye ask, and receive not, because ye ask amiss, that ye may consume it upon your lusts" (James 4:3). That means that you ask God with wrong motives. Asking God in the flesh is most definitely a wrong motive. What is worshipping God in spirit and truth? Worshipping God in spirit and truth is seeking after His kingdom and all His righteousness. Worshipping God in spirit and truth is being honest with Him, your neighbors, and yourself. You get nothing positive accomplished by telling lies. The only thing you accomplish is telling lie after lie after lie, and soon, you are going to get caught up in them, which is going to lead to your destruction. Even a criminal hates a liar, and a criminal is a sinner. How do you think God feels about a liar? Proverbs 6:16–19 tells you how He feels. Worship God in spirit and truth, and His goodness and mercy shall follow you all the days of your life (Psalm 23:6).

YOU NEED

Listen to me, my friend, I know who you need in your life. You need Jesus in your life. Jesus will take your hurt away. Jesus will take your pain and worry away. He doesn't want you to suffer. He doesn't want you to be in pain. Stop listening to all those lies that others are telling you. Jesus does love you. He does want what's best for you. And I'm telling you if you get with Him, He will fulfill all the things that your heart desires according to His Father's (God) will. He is not here to bring destruction in your life. He is here to bring joy into it. Jesus will help you with all of your problems. He will not let you face them alone. You will see how much easier and relaxed your life will be if only you would invite Him into your heart. I lie to you not, Jesus will not break it. I know you are sick and tired of the stress in your life. I know you are sick and tired of the pressure. You get Jesus in your life, and He will ease the stress and the pressure. You need Him in your life, my friend, so go ahead and accept His offer of salvation.

YOUR ALL

My friend, for you to be complete in God, you've got to give Him your all. Just giving Him part of you is not enough. You've got to give Him your all. God doesn't want part of you, but all of you. You've got to be willing to give Him all of you. He is not going to force you, and He is not going to beg you to give Him your all. You should be thrilled to give Him your all for there is nothing greater than being complete in God. I'm talking about having His grace, favor, blessings, benefits, love, mercy, forgiveness, and protection. Let me not forget His strength and power. You would have all those things inside of you. And better yet, He will reveal His Son Jesus Christ inside of you. Now there is nothing on earth greater than that. It is a joy to have Jesus on the inside. It is a joy to have Jesus in your life. He is the greatest being that ever lived on the face of the earth. He is the one that walked on the sea (Mark 6:45–52). Now I know that you don't want to miss out on having Him, so give God your all so everything in this life, and your afterlife, can be fulfilled beautifully.

CHAPTER 6

APPLY THINE HEART

BE A DISCIPLE

Let me give you some great advice: be a disciple of Christ. Being a disciple of Christ is a great thing to be. It means you have the same power He has, the power to heal, deliver, and preach (Matthew 10).

You don't have to worry about a thing because Jesus is going to let you know everything that you have to do. He is going to teach you how to be a disciple. Jesus Christ taught me how to be a disciple. He taught me everything I know, and that is why I encourage you to be one. Believe me, you are not going to go wrong. Jesus Christ is the greatest teacher and leader in the universe. The wisdom He has He is going to give to you. Listen to every word that Jesus is going to tell you because He is going to lead you into the way of righteousness. When He leads you into the way of righteousness, He expects you to lead others into the way of righteousness.

Being a disciple of Christ also means that you are walking like Christ. It means that you are obedient to Him. It also means that you love Jesus with all of your mind, heart, body, and soul. You are willing to help people. You are willing to love and to save them. Jesus loves His disciples. He honors His disciples, and knowing that should motivate you to be one.

BE ABOUT JESUS

People, be about Jesus. Jesus is wonderful. Jesus is sensational. There is nothing bad about Him. There is nothing abusive about Him. Jesus is great, and He wants you to be great. How can you be great? Being about Jesus, that's how!

Jesus wants you to be about Him. He doesn't want you to follow anyone but Him. Jesus is not stuck up on Himself. He is not arrogant. He is not conceited, neither is He selfish. You have to understand that Jesus wants the best for you. You have to understand that Jesus has the best for you. He will provide you with the best, but you have to follow Him.

By you following Jesus, you will truly find out how much He loves you. You will see that Jesus was not lying when He said that He would take care of you. Jesus does not lie, nor does He deceive. He blesses and provides. He is a gracious provider.

Being about Jesus you will have no worries because your mind is focused on Him. Your mind is focused on serving and blessing Him. Jesus does not give your mind chaos, He gives your mind peace. With His peace, He keeps your mind stable. Jesus was the one that brought my mind peace when it was out of order. He was the one that got rid of the strongholds that I had. I am not blowing smoke, my brothers and sisters. I am telling the truth.

With Jesus in your mind, there is no confusion. Jesus is balance not unbalance. He is not double-minded. He is absolutely level. Jesus wants your mind to be level. He does not want it to be out of order, but in order. Be about Jesus, and I promise you He will never be ashamed of you.

BE FRIENDLY

My brothers and sisters, this is a hard world to live in. You have to deal with sin and evil people, but I have a solution that will help you deal with those that are evil: be friendly. Be friendly to those that are evil. Jesus Christ said, "Love your enemies, do good to them which hate you, Bless them that curse you, and pray for them which despitefully use you" (Luke 6:27–28). Love your enemies and pray for those that despitefully use you because that shows you are obeying Jesus Christ. Some people do not know how to be loved. Some have not experienced it. We as the followers of Christ have to show them love. We as the followers of Christ have to be friendly and peaceful.

"Be not overcome of evil, but overcome evil with good" (Romans 12:21). If someone curses you, hold your peace. Do not be ignorant because that person is ignorant. You are a follower of Christ, and being a follower of Christ you've got to have class. You can not be a thug. The only way that you can overcome evil is with good. You can not overcome evil with evil. Love conquers all. With love, evil will be defeated.

My brothers and sisters, treat each other with kindness. Love and embrace each other. Jesus Christ died for all of our sins, which means He loves all of us. He did not die for any particular people. He died for all people, meaning all races. Keep this in your hearts and minds, "Love ye your enemies, and do good, and lend, hoping for nothing again; and your reward shall be great, and ye shall be the children of the Highest: for he [God] is kind unto the unthankful and to the evil" (Luke 6:35). And on that note, my brothers and sisters, be friendly.

BE GOOD TO OTHERS

My brothers and sisters, be good to others. It's a wonderful thing to be good to others because it shows that you have the love of Christ. You are made in the image of Christ, and you are showing it by being good to others. You are following His example. Christ was good to others. He was not evil or hateful to others. He showed others love and respect. He was great to others, and He wants you to be great to others.

Jesus disciplined you to be good to others. He trained you to be good to others, so there is no excuse for you not to be good to others. If someone disrespected you or was rude to you, forgive that person and pray for him or her. You don't return evil for evil. Many people don't have the love of Christ, so it is up to us to show it to them. Many people were not raised in church. Many people didn't have good upbringing. We have to be good to those individuals. We have to show them love.

When you are being good to others, they open up to you. They thank you. They think about how good you were to them. It makes them happy that you were good to them. It shows that someone cares about them. It shows that everyone in the world is not evil. It also makes Jesus happy. It makes Jesus happy because His work was not done in vain. It makes Him happy that you are obeying His Father's (God) commandment, "thou shalt love thy neighbour as thyself" (Matthew 22:39). My brothers and sisters, be good to others for it shows that you don't want to disappoint Christ, and you love others.

BE HOLY

My brothers and sisters, be holy. Being holy is the only way that you can see God. How do you become holy? You become holy through Jesus Christ. Jesus Christ is holy, and if you get a relationship with Him, you too will become holy.

Being with Jesus you have no choice but to become holy for He is holy. His holiness is going to rub off on you. His righteousness is going to rub off on you. Things that you used to do you will no longer do for you have become a new creature. "Therefore if any man be in Christ, he is a new creature: old things are passed away; behold, all things are become new" (2 Corinthians 5:17). Jesus has made you new and improved.

Being holy is great for it shows that you have a relationship with Christ. It shows that Christ has transformed you from a sinner to a saint. Paul the apostle was not always a saint. He considered himself chief among sinners (1 Timothy 1:15), but once Christ transformed him, he became a holy and powerful saint (Acts 22:6–16). He wrote some of the manuscripts that are in the New Testament. If you do not believe me, scroll through the New Testament and you will see that I'm not deceiving you.

Just like Christ made Paul holy, He wants to make you holy. He wants the two of you to be best friends. He wants to show you what real love is all about. Jesus Christ also wants you to see God, so accept Him as your personal Savior to be holy as He is holy.

BE HOOKED

People, don't be hooked on drugs and alcohol, but be hooked on Jesus. The high that Jesus gives is greater than the high that drugs and alcohol gives. The high that Jesus gives does not lead you to death, it leads you to abundant life. The high that Jesus gives will not destroy your mind and body, but will enhance it for it gives you love, peace, power, strength, joy, and comfort. Jesus' high does not make you crazy. It makes you awesome.

Being hooked on Jesus is also wonderful. It is wonderful because Jesus is full of love and joy. There is not an ounce of hate or depression in Him. He is too good to be hateful. He is too happy to be depressed. You never heard anything about Jesus walking around spitting on people. You never heard anything about Jesus walking around giving people a sad spirit. Jesus does not give people the spirit of sadness. He gives them the spirit of love and joy. That's why I'm encouraging you to be hooked on Him.

Moreover, being hooked on Jesus is outstanding. Anything you ask of Him, He will grant it to you (John 15:7). When you are hooked on Jesus, you are hooked on success. When you are hooked on Jesus, you are hooked on love, joy, and peace. I know that you are sick and tired of being empty on the inside. I know that you are sick and tired of being sad, lonely, and angry. Get hooked on Jesus!

Let me ask you some questions. Do you think drugs can put you into heaven? Do you think alcohol can give you eternal life? The only places that drugs and alcohol can put you in are jail, the hospital, and the grave. Is that what you want? Is that what you want to be hooked up with? Jesus will not put you into those places. Jesus will not kill or murder you. He wants what's best for you, so be hooked up with Him, and feel the spiritual high.

BE KIND

My brothers and sisters, we serve a loving Savior. Jesus Christ's love for us is eternal, which means that He will not stop loving us. Season after season, He proves to us He loves us. My brothers and sisters, we need to be kind unto Him.

Everything that we have, Jesus Christ was the one that blessed us with it. The beautiful spirit that we have, Jesus Christ blessed us with it. He is the reason that the Bible is holy. He is the reason that we are not in bondage. He promoted you to that high spiritual level that you are on. He blessed you to get a good-paying job. He blessed you to have a fancy car.

Jesus Christ made a way for us not to go to hell. His mission was to keep us from going there. Jesus Christ delivered us from sin and cleansed our souls from the pollution of it. There is no way that any of us would go to heaven with sin remaining in us. God will not let anyone enter into the kingdom of heaven with traces of sin remaining in him or her. It is because of Jesus that you are holy. Jesus saved us from roasting in hell for all eternity.

My brothers and sisters, Jesus Christ adores us. There is no one or anything that will stop Him from adoring us. Sinners, repent from all of your sins and follow Jesus. Christian saints, continue to follow Jesus. Jesus is love and the definition of it. Be kind to Jesus because He is surely kind to you.

BE LIKE

Christian saints and friends, be like Jesus. I know that it's hard to be like Him because of the world that we live in. Not everyone wants to do right. Not everyone wants to serve the true and living God. The lust of the world controls those individuals who do not want to do right and do not want to serve God.

Moreover, the world hates Jesus, and the world hates you because you are made of Him (John 15:18–20). The world hates love. The world rejects love, so don't feel bad when you are rejected. I know that you want to curse others sometimes. I know that you want to fight sometimes, but don't do it because it's not being like Christ. Sometimes I want to curse and fight others, but I find a way to keep myself in peace.

Jesus Christ is peace. He is the Prince of Peace, and I gladly serve Him. I'm doing my best to be like Him. It's hard, but I'm trying. I'm not going to write to you and tell you that it's not hard. It is hard being like Jesus. It's not easy. You have to deal with sin and people that are hateful. You have to deal with jealous people. Everything that Christ went through, you have to go through. You have to go through trials and tribulations, and Satan is going to tempt you to sin.

Christian saints and friends, walk like Jesus because He walked in peace. He also walked in power and confidence. Talk like Jesus because His Words are positive, pure, truthful, peaceful, joyful, and powerful. Love like Jesus because He loved everyone. He did not love only a few, but loved everyone. Though He was hurt by many, He continued to love and to forgive them. Jesus did not let anyone take the love out of His heart. His heart was full of love. Be like Jesus because He is the most caring role model in the universe.

BE PEACEFUL

My brothers and sisters, be peaceful. Being peaceful is the only way that you are going to defeat destruction. Violence is destruction. Being peaceful is the only way that you are going to defeat violence. Violence versus violence equals more violence. Peace overcomes violence. Peace overcomes hate.

Violence is not only when someone raises his or her hand against you, it is also violence when someone speaks badly to you. When someone speaks badly to you, you speak kindly to that person. Be peaceful to that person. It doesn't make things better by you responding negatively to that person. Just because that person chooses to be ignorant, it doesn't mean that you have to be ignorant. The only way that you are going to defeat that person's violent attitude is by being peaceful. Two wrongs don't make a right.

Moreover, it doesn't make you a punk just because you refuse to fight someone. It doesn't make you soft just because you speak kind words to people. It makes you peaceful. There are too many people in the world that want to be evil. There are too many people in the world that want to be violent. They think being peaceful is weak. Being peaceful is not weak because it takes a courageous person to be peaceful. Anybody can be evil, and anybody can be violent, but it takes a strong person to be peaceful.

My brothers and sisters, be peaceful. Don't walk in hate, but walk in peace. When others see you walk in peace, it encourages them to walk in peace. When others see you walk in love, it encourages them to walk in love. Martin Luther King Jr. walked in peace. Our Leader and Savior Jesus Christ walked in peace. Be peaceful because it shows that you are made in the image of Christ. Be peaceful because it shows that you love your neighbor as you love thyself. Be peaceful because it overcomes violence, hatred, and bad behavior.

BE PROUD TO SERVE JESUS

What's up? What's going on in your life? Is your family doing well? At this point in my life, I'm doing fine. I'm doing fine because I serve Jesus. You know in life you are going to have rough times, especially when you are serving Jesus because the enemy is going to attack you in every area of your life. Despite his attacks, still serve Jesus, and be proud to serve Him.

Don't let anyone stop you from serving Jesus. I don't care if it's your friend or a family member. They did not die on a cross for you. Jesus died on a cross for you (Matthew 27:31–66). He sacrificed His life so you can have life. When someone made you angry, Jesus made you happy. When someone called you ugly, Jesus was the one that said, "Dry your tears because you are beautiful."

Be proud to serve Jesus. Honor and adore Him. Jesus' love for you is more than outstanding. Words can not describe how beautiful the place is that He prepared for you. You are not serving Jesus in vain. You are not wasting your time. I know that there are people telling you to give it up. I know that there are people telling you to curse your God and die. I know that there are people telling you that God does not exist. Do not worry about what people have to say about you. Continue to serve Jesus and be proud to serve Him for He is going to be proud to open the gates to the kingdom of heaven for you.

BE REAL WITH JESUS

Church people, be real with Jesus. Jesus wants you to be real. He wants you to be straight-up and honest with Him. If you want a house, ask Him for a house. If you want a car, ask Him for a car. If you want a job, ask Him for a job. Jesus wants you to have things. He wants you to get married.

What makes you think that Jesus does not want you to have things? What makes you think that Jesus does not want you to enjoy life? Jesus knows that you've got to have a place to stay. He knows that you've got to have transportation. He knows that you've got to have money. Jesus is not ignorant.

"If ye abide in me, and my words abide in you, ye shall ask what ye will, and it shall be done unto you" (John 15:7). That is what Jesus said. It is not a sin to ask Jesus for what you desire. He will give you what your heart desires. He just does not want you to be caught up on material things. He does not want you to be consumed by things. He does not want you to forget about Him, that He is the one that provides and blesses.

You have to acknowledge Jesus and respect Him. You have to remember that the Lord is God. Many people get blessings from Jesus, and then they forget about Him. They get what they want from Jesus, and then they ditch Him. They are not concerned about blessing Jesus. They are only concerned about pleasing their own selves. Jesus does not want you to be that way. He does not want you to be selfish. He does not want you to be in the church game just to get what you want to get out of Him. He wants you to be in the church game to love, worship, adore, follow, and acknowledge Him. Jesus will reward you for your faithfulness. He will reward you for your unselfishness. Remember to be real with Him, ask what ye will, and don't forget about Him.

BE ROOTED IN JESUS CHRIST

My brothers and sisters, be rooted in Jesus Christ. Jesus Christ is a strong foundation. Once you are rooted in Him, you will not be uprooted. You shall not be uprooted. You are a tree planted by the rivers of water (Psalm 1:3). At times you are going to be shaken by the many winds that blow, but the winds will not prevail against you. The winds are demonic spirits that seek to destroy you. Their mission is to destroy you.

Jesus Christ is the one that keeps you standing. He is the one that is able to keep you from falling (Jude 24). Who do you think is the one that keeps you from losing your mind? Who do you think is the one that keeps you from being destroyed? Jesus is the one that keeps you from losing your mind and being destroyed. He is a solid foundation.

Christ keeps His promises. When Jesus says He is going to protect you, He does it. When He says that He is going to bless you, He does it. It is you that have to walk in faith. It is you that have to be strong in the Lord and the power of His might, so be rooted in Jesus because He is a foundation that will never fall.

BE UPLIFTED

My brothers and sisters, be uplifted. Jesus does not want you to walk in sorrow. Jesus does not want you to walk in bitterness. He wants you to walk in happiness. He wants you to walk in joy. He knows living in this world is rough. He knows living in this world can easily depress you, and that's why He wants you to be uplifted, so you will not get depressed.

Depression will find a home in you if you allow it to. It will find a place to dwell in you. It is waiting for you to fall. It wants you to fall. Do not let the cares of this world get you down. Do not let the cares of this world stress you. Be strong and be encouraged. Whenever you see yourself getting a little depressed, begin to rejoice in the Lord.

Always rejoice in the Lord because rejoicing in the Lord gives you strength. Rejoicing in the Lord gives you hope and confidence that everything is going to be all right and that everything is going to work out for you. Sometimes I know you feel that there is no hope, but remember that in Jesus there is always hope. Have faith and rely on Him.

Jesus never fails. He always accomplishes His task. You are a big part of Jesus. You are important to Him. Jesus wants you to have the best in life. He wants you to enjoy life. He is not here to stop you from enjoying yourself. Many people get Jesus all wrong. They say living in Him there is no fun. Well, I'm here to correct them. Living in Jesus is fun. There is happiness living in Him. There is no condemnation living in Him (Romans 8:1). There is no guilt. Living in Jesus you do not worry about going to hell because you know that you are going to heaven. You know that your name is written in the book of life.

If you sin, Jesus will forgive you. He knows that you are not perfect. Jesus is not going to kill you for doing wrong. He is going to love and forgive you. I know that I'm going to enjoy life on earth. I know I'm going to have fun. I am going to be uplifted. You too should be uplifted because you are living in Christ, and in Christ you are not only going to enjoy earthly life, but eternal life. Be uplifted!

BELIEVE IN JESUS

Many of us have a hard time believing in things. We do not know who or what to believe in. Some of us create things to believe in, but I know someone that we all can believe in, and that someone is Jesus Christ.

My brothers and sisters, Jesus wants us to believe in Him. All of your blessings come through belief. Believing in Jesus heals you. Believing in Jesus saves and delivers you. It is for your own good and benefit. Jesus has all that is good waiting for you, but you have to believe.

Moreover, you can't see Jesus, but you can get in contact with Him. You can get in contact with Him by praying, going to church, and reading the Bible. Going to church helps you to believe in Jesus because you see more people striving to do the same thing that you are doing. Praying and reading the Bible strengthens your spirit and faith to believe in Jesus. There is nothing wrong believing in Him. It does not make you a fool because you believe in Him.

Furthermore, don't worry about what people have to say about you. Don't worry about people laughing at you. You just believe in Jesus and you shall have the last laugh. While they are laughing at you, Jesus is preparing a wonderful place for you. While they are persecuting you, He is supplying all of your needs. He does not supply you with just some needs. He supplies you with all needs. Continue to believe in Jesus, and He will not stop blessing you.

People, I know that you are asking, "How can I believe in someone that I can not or do not see?" That is the purpose of believing. That is the purpose of having faith. You have to believe in things that you can't see (Hebrews 11:1). You've got to have faith in things that you can't see. I know it may sound crazy, but it's not. What's so crazy about salvation? What's so crazy about being prosperous? What's so crazy about going to heaven? Nothing is crazy about it. Jesus is not crazy. He has plenty of sense. If He were crazy, He would not be sitting on the right-hand side of God. Jesus loves you, and He wants you to love Him by believing in Him.

CHRIST IS THE HEAD OVER EVERYTHING

Christ is the head over everything (Hebrews 1). God gave Him the power and authority to be the head over everything. Christ has the right to be the head over everything. He earned that right. He left His wonderful place in heaven to come to this sinful earth and die for everyone's sins. He is unselfish and courageous.

First of all, Jesus is unselfish. He could have told God, "Don't worry about saving earth." He could have told God, "Let everyone die in his or her sins." He could have told God, "Let everyone go to hell." Instead, Jesus said, "Send me to earth so I can make a way for the people to go to heaven. Send me to earth so I can be the ultimate sacrifice for their sins. I want the people to dwell with us. I want the people to go to heaven for all eternity."

Moreover, Jesus is courageous. He went through many trials and tribulations to be the head over everything. He had to go through people plotting against Him. He had to go through demons trying to attack Him. He had to go through Satan tempting Him to bow down and serve him (Matthew 4:1–11), but Jesus did not do it. He overcame all of His enemies with the help and power of God.

My brothers and sisters, the road was not easy for Jesus, but He succeeded. He succeeded in saving you from your sins by dying on a cross. He succeeded in defeating death by resurrecting from His grave. Sin and death are no match for Jesus, and that is why God appointed Him to be the head over everything, because Jesus saved the world by defeating them both.

DINE

My brothers and sisters, get ready to dine with Jesus. When you dine with Jesus, be yourself. He wants you to be yourself. He wants to dine with the real you. You are the guest of honor. Jesus wants to honor you. He gave you the invitation to dine with Him and His Father (God), not just for one night, but for all eternity.

Jesus is getting everything prepared for you. He's waiting to see you. He wants everything to be special for you. He introduced you to His Father, and God told Him that He loves you. God told Jesus that He wants Him to spend the rest of His life with you. He wants Jesus to marry you. He wants you to be His bride. The dining is after the marriage, and the heavenly angels are the host.

God is getting you ready to meet His Son for marriage. He is getting your spirit right so you can be fit for His Son. He does not want His Son to be tied with the wrong spirit. He wants His Son to be tied with the right spirit. God knows that I'm ready for the dinner because I am part of the body of Christ which is the bride of Jesus. Rebuke not the chastisement of God. Give Him reverence. Get excited to dine with His Son. Be happy to dine with His Son because He is the greatest husband in the universe.

DON'T BE AFRAID TO TAKE A RISK

People, don't be afraid to take a risk. I'm talking about a positive risk. I'm not telling you to jump off a cliff. Oh no! I'm saying when it comes to doing things for God, don't be afraid to take a risk. Jesus Christ took the risk to leave His glorious throne to come to this sinful world to save us from all of our sins. Jesus Christ could have refused to do it, but He didn't.

When it comes to paying tithes and offerings, many of us are afraid to take risks. We are afraid that we may not have enough money to pay our bills. I just would like to tell you that paying your tithes and offerings is more important than paying your bills. A poor widow gave God the little that she had to honor Him (Mark 12:41–44). You've got money to buy clothes and to get your hair fix. Why you don't have money to pay your tithes? I can not lie to you, my brothers and sisters, I used to feel the same way you feel, but I had to put my faith and trust in God that He would make a way for me to pay my bills due to me paying my tithes and offerings. God comes first.

By you paying your tithes, God will increase your finances. He will help you build your bank account. He will fill your purse or wallet. God will help you pay your bills. He will not leave you hanging. He will not allow you to get evicted. He is the reason why you have a car, a house, and clothes to wear, and if you don't have those things, He will bless you with them. Why do you choose to be stingy toward Him?

Furthermore, don't be afraid to take risks when it comes to following Christ. Are you afraid that you are not going to have fun if you follow Christ? My brothers and sisters, following Christ is when the real fun begins. In Christ you don't have to drink alcoholic beverages or smoke to have fun. You don't have to go to clubs to have fun. That is amazing! When you follow Christ, you don't come home with a hangover. You don't need a designated driver. Your mind, body, and soul feel good. Jesus will make sure that you don't get bored. He will find something fun for you to do. Take the risk to pay your tithes and offerings, and take the risk to follow Christ and you will see how great God will reward you (Deuteronomy 12:5–12).

DON'T BE HARDHEADED

My brothers and sisters, don't be hardheaded. When Jesus Christ tells you to do something, do it. Though it may be or sound crazy, still do it. Do not be disobedient. Do not hesitate to be obedient. You may not understand why Jesus wants you to do something, but still do what He says. You are not going to understand everything. Some things are not meant for you to understand. You are not going to always know why He wants you do something. The important thing is that Jesus knows why, and He understands. Just do what He says and receive your blessings through obedience.

A hardheaded person does not receive anything from the Lord. The Lord does not associate with disobedience, He associates with obedience. He associates with those who love and obey Him. Why should the Lord associate with a hardheaded person? A hardheaded person does not listen. A hardheaded person is stubborn in all of his or her ways. The Lord is not going to force you to obey Him. The Lord is not going to force you to listen to Him.

Furthermore, the Lord didn't give you any reason to be hardheaded. He never lied to you. As a matter of fact, He never lies (Numbers 23:19). He never disappointed you, and He will never disappoint you. It is you that have to trust and obey Him. It is you that have to follow Him. Jesus did His job. He obeyed God. He was not hardheaded. How can the Lord bless you if you are hardheaded? Something's got to give. Give your love to Christ. Respect and acknowledge Him. Honor Him and don't be hardheaded because Jesus is going to greatly reward you. Just wait you'll see.

DON'T BE HATEFUL

My wonderful brothers and sisters, don't be hateful. Being hateful is not good for the soul or your character. Jesus Christ did not die for you to be hateful. He died for you to be full of God, which means complete in His love. By Him dying on the cross, He gives you a chance to be full of God. He defeated the nature of hate, which is sin. He does not want you to be hateful. He wants you to be kind. He wants you to love others (Matthew 19:19).

Besides, what does being hateful solve? Being hateful doesn't solve a thing. All it does is prove that you are a bitter person. It proves that you are an angry person. It's not cute to be hateful. It's not healthy to be hateful. It slowly destroys the spirit. I can see the darkness of a person when he or she is hateful. It comes from the inside, and therefore, is shown on the outside.

When you are hateful, it pushes people away from you. People do not want to be in the presence of a hateful person. People do not want to deal with a hateful person. I know that I don't want to. I feel the bad vibes of a hateful person.

When you are hateful, you are a selfish person. You don't want to do anything for anyone but yourself. You are too caught up on yourself. You don't care about others. My wonderful brothers and sisters, don't walk in hate, don't live in hate, don't accept hate, and don't be hateful, for Christ is not hateful.

DON'T DOUBT JESUS

My brothers and sisters, don't doubt Jesus. There is nothing too impossible that He can not do. There is no obstacle that He can not overcome. Jesus Christ walked on the sea (Mark 6:45–52). He healed the Syrophenician woman's daughter without being in the daughter's presence (Mark 7:24–30). He healed a centurion's servant without being in the servant's presence (Matthew 8:5–13). And He healed a deaf and dumb man (Mark 7:31–37).

Jesus Christ is the best of the best. Jesus Christ fed over a thousand people (Mark 6:30–44, 8:1–10). He healed millions of people. He brought a man back from the dead (Lazarus) (John 11:30–46). Why would, and how could, you doubt Jesus? He defeated death by resurrecting from His grave (Mark 16:6–7).

Believe in Jesus Christ, my brothers and sisters. Have faith in Him. Jesus Christ is still the same as He was two thousand years ago. He will not run out of power. He will not let you down. He will not disappoint you. You have to do your part, and that is to have faith. Have faith in Jesus, my brothers and sisters, and don't doubt Him because He will not leave you comfortless.

DON'T HAVE A

Do not have a "don't care" attitude. There are too many people that have that type of attitude. They don't care about a thing. They don't care about anyone. The only thing that they may care about is themselves or making money. They don't care about when others get hurt. They don't care about when others get abused. That is the wrong type of attitude to have. That attitude is not godly.

God blessed us with a heart to care about others. He blessed us with a mind to think about, and be concerned about, others' well-being. Why do some of us choose to be hateful? Why do some of us choose to not care? Love is deep down in all of us. Some of us may have to pull deeper to get hooked to it, but love is in us.

Jesus Christ did not die so we can have that type of attitude. He does not want us to have that type of attitude. He wants us to love and care for each other. No matter how bad people may have hurt us, He still wants us to care for people. Don't be a fool for people, but love them.

If Jesus Christ had a "don't care" attitude, we would all be in hell. He was rejected, persecuted, and crucified for us. He could have said, "I don't care anymore; forget everyone," but He didn't. He continued to move on with a caring attitude. What I'm simply saying is do not have a "don't care" attitude because the world can do a great deal better without a selfish attitude.

DON'T LAUGH YOUR WAY

Don't laugh your way to hell. Get a relationship with Jesus Christ. It's not funny going to hell. It's not humorous going there. Hell is not a playground. Hell is not a carnival. It is a place of torment.

Some people are ignorant. For example, one person told me that I was gay because I don't have a girlfriend. He told me that I was gay because I'm not having sex. I told him that you have to be patient and wait on God. God will send you a mate. He asked me what I do when my body is craving for sex. I told him that I pray and ask God for help.

What shocked me was that this was a person who said that he believed in God. This man believes in God, but he's ignorant. I told him that God wants you to have sex when you are married. Marriage is respectable to God. He told me that it is okay to have sex before marriage. He told me that you could have sex with the person that you are going to marry. When you have sex with the person that you are going to marry, it is still a sin because you all are not married yet. Surely God gave us the gift of sex, but He does not want us to abuse it. He wants it to be honorable, and that is found in marriage (Hebrews 13:4).

Listen to me, I'm not judging anyone. I'm just telling the truth. I'm not perfect. I have sinned just like everybody else. How can you say you believe in God but don't know Him? How can you believe in God but don't have any knowledge of Him? That person was ignorant that told me that I was gay because I don't have a girlfriend and I'm not having sex. I told him that he is ignorant, and he laughed about it. I told him that he needs to read the Bible and he still laughed.

How can you say that you believe in God and laugh about reading the Bible? Reading the Bible gives you knowledge of God. Reading the Bible gives you knowledge of Christ. It teaches you the correct way to live. It teaches you how to live godly.

Jesus Christ will save you from going to hell. He will keep you from going there, and that is His purpose and mission. Do not be ignorant like that person that told me that I was gay. My brothers and sisters, I'm far from gay. Get a relationship with Jesus and get knowledge of God because with them, you will not be laughing your way to hell, but heaven.

DON'T MISS OUT

People, don't miss out on going to heaven. Get saved today. Hearken unto God and get a relationship with Jesus Christ. Confess to Jesus, acknowledging to Him that you are a sinner and you want to accept Him as your Lord and Savior. That you believe He resurrected from the grave on the third day of His death. That you want to give up living a sinful life and want to serve and follow Him (Romans 10).

Jesus will hear your confession, and He will save you. His purpose is to save you, but you have to believe in Him. His purpose is to set you free and to heal your broken heart (Luke 4:18–19). Jesus does not want you to walk in hurt. He does not want you to live in sin. He does not want you to go to hell. You have to make the choice to get saved. You have to be willing to follow Christ and serve Him. You've got to be willing to have eternal life in the glorious kingdom of heaven.

Heaven does not care how rich or poor you are. It does not care how handsome or beautiful you are. If you are not saved, you are not going to set your feet inside of it, point-blank. Heaven will love to have you, but you've got to have a relationship with Jesus Christ. You've got to know Christ. You've got to be cleansed from your sins and be holy.

Jesus is the key for you to be saved, cleansed from your sins, and to be made holy. He is your key to seeing God. Heaven is filled with love, peace, happiness, joy, and laughter. Heaven is beautiful, so get in contact with Jesus and don't miss out on going because you are going to wish that you didn't. Read John 11:25–26.

FOLLOW JESUS AND LOVE HIM

Follow Jesus and love Him. Why? Because He paved the way for you to see God's glorious face. Jesus humbled Himself to die for us. Jesus sacrificed Himself to die for us. He was the ultimate sacrifice for our salvation. His destiny was to die on a cross for us. He died for all of our sins. That's how much He loves us! If it weren't for Jesus dying for our sins we would all be on our way to hell.

Jesus is the Son of God. He endured a lot of punishment such as abuse, persecution, rejection, denial, and betrayal. He endured all of that punishment for us. He could have stayed in heaven where there is peace, joy, love, and life. He could have stayed in heaven where He was being worshipped by angels. Instead, He came to this sinful world and took abuse. He went from being worshipped and praised to being abused and tortured.

Jesus did what no other man would do or could do. He defeated death. He wasn't afraid of death. Death could not hold Him captive. He went down to hell and ministered the Gospel. Jesus resurrected from His grave and took His position as God's right-hand man.

Get on your knees and ask Jesus for forgiveness. Give Him thanks for dying for your sins. It was supposed to be us on that cross, not Jesus. Submit yourself and commit yourself unto following Jesus. Obey and love Him. Put no other god before His Father God. Jesus doesn't ask for much, but I'm asking you to follow Him and love Him because Jesus is what love is all about.

GIVE YOUR LIFE TO JESUS

Jesus, before I write these words, I want to ask you for your forgiveness. Forgive me for the bad attitude that I had today. I was not myself today, so please forgive me. My brothers and sisters, give your life to Jesus. Jesus will not destroy your life. He will not lead you astray. He will not deceive or abuse you. He loves you.

You think you are free, but you are really not. You are not free until you accept Jesus Christ into your life. Jesus Christ will free you from sin and bondage. He will also free you from the second death. Those who are going to heaven are only going to die once, and that's on earth. Those who are going to die the second death are going to hell. They are not only going to die on earth, but also in hell. Hell is the second death for the unsaved (Revelation 20:14–15). The unsaved are the ones who refuse to accept Jesus Christ as their personal Savior and are those who are not found in the book of life.

My brothers and sisters, Jesus does not want you to go to hell. He wants you to go to heaven. Jesus wants you to have fun. He wants you to enjoy yourself. He wants you to enjoy life. With Jesus in your life, you don't have to please people. The only one you have to please is His Father God. You don't have to use drugs, drink alcoholic beverages, go to clubs, or smoke. All you have to do is believe and have faith in God. Jesus Christ will wipe fear away from you. You will not fear death. Jesus defeated death. Give your life to Jesus. What else can I say, but Jesus is amazing!

GREAT

Hello, my brothers, and hello, my sisters. When I see you all, I see greatness. I see greatness because we serve a great master, and that is Jesus Christ. Jesus is the reason why we are great. If it weren't for Him, we would not be great. He ordained us to be great. He anointed us with His power so we can be great.

That is what I love about Jesus. Instead of keeping His power to Himself, He shares it. He gives His power to His followers. His gives His power to His people. He knows that we need it. He knows that we can not survive without it. The world would rip us apart if we didn't have His power.

Jesus is so considerate. He is always thinking about feeding His people. He is always thinking about clothing His people. When His people get weak, He strengthens them. When His people get depressed, He motivates and encourages them.

When His servants do something outside of His will, He forgives them. He does not come down hard on His servants because He knows that they are not perfect. He knows that they are going to make mistakes. Jesus does not condemn His people. He loves and encourages them. He keeps His people strong and uplifted.

Jesus is a great shepherd. He keeps His sheep lined up and in order. And if one of His sheep gets out of order, He kindly puts him or her back in order. Jesus is great, and I thank God that He is great because He is the reason for our greatness. May peace always be with Him.

HE STILL LOVES YOU

Heaven is a glorious place. It's where the Holy Trinity dwells. The Holy Trinity is the unity of God, Jesus Christ, and the Holy Spirit. My brothers and sisters, I just want you to know that no matter what you do, God still loves you. He operates off of love. My brothers and sisters, don't be too hard on yourselves. God knows that you want the best for yourselves. After you make a mistake, know in your heart that it's okay and God loves you. After you fall, know that God still loves you. When you sin, know that God still loves you. The enemy wants you to feel bad. The enemy wants you to condemn yourself, but know that "There is therefore now no condemnation to them which are in Christ Jesus, who walk not after the flesh, but after the spirit" (Romans 8:1).

The great and loving Jesus Christ doesn't hate you. He doesn't want you to feel bad about anything. Know that Jesus Christ will forgive you of all your sins. As a matter of fact, He has *already* forgiven you for all of your sins. There is nothing that will stop Him from loving and forgiving you. He knows you are going to make mistakes. He knows there are going to be times that you are going to be disobedient. He knows you are not perfect. When you fall, get up, keep your head up, and keep pressing on. It doesn't matter what people say. People will tell you anything to keep you down. People will say anything to stop you.

My brothers and sisters, don't let anyone one bring you down. Know that you can't be stopped. You have a higher power that is strengthening you. Don't let your life be in vain. Listen to the people that God appoints over you, and if they are not right, God will get them. You are precious to God, and He will do anything for you according to His will. So praise God, my brothers and sisters, for you know no matter how many times that you may fall or sin, God still loves you.

P.S. Just because you know that God will forgive you doesn't mean that you continue to sin. There are people out there in the world that say, "Go ahead and do it, man. God will forgive you." In a case like that, you don't listen to that person. Continue to serve God and be strong and know that He has a great reward for you.

HOLD THY PEACE

Some people need to learn how to hold their peace. They talk too much. They run their mouths too much. If Jesus would have run His mouth during the trial instead of holding His peace, none of us would be here. It was meant for Him to hold His peace (Matthew 27:12–14). He had to hold it. Jesus was a man of innocence and integrity that never sinned, and at the right times, He always held His peace.

There is a time to speak, and there is a time to hold thy peace. Many people do not know that. They think that every time is the time to speak instead of listening and holding their peace. They just keep on talking. You can not tell them anything because they are flapping their gums all the time. They do not know how to listen.

Many people today do not know how to hold their peace. They just keep running their mouths. They think that they know more than God does. They think that they know more than their parents do. And they think that they know more than their elders do. That is why they get into trouble due to their uncontrollable tongues. And that is why many people are in their graves due to their mouthpiece.

People, there's nothing wrong speaking. But you have to learn when to speak. You have to learn when it's the right time to speak, so when it's the time to speak you will know. You will get yourself into deep trouble by running your mouths at the wrong time. You gain wisdom by listening and holding your peace. You need self-control. Hold thy peace, and keep thy peace because you will go a long way in life if you do.

HONOR JESUS

Jesus Christ is tremendous. Day after day He strengthens His followers to do the right things in life. Jesus knows that it is easy to do evil. That is why He is always there to remind His sheep to do well. Jesus is a true leader, and you know what? We need to honor Him.

We need to honor Jesus for being our guide. Jesus is our guide to getting to God. He is our guide to going to heaven. He never tells us to do immoral things. He tells us to do moral things. Jesus is a guide of righteousness. He is a guide of true and holy living. He is a guide that will never wash away. And He is a guide that will never run out.

We need to honor Jesus for being our teacher. Jesus taught us how to pray (Matthew 6:5–13). He taught us how to live godly. He never taught us how to live wickedly. He never taught us how to abuse people. There are many teachers out in the world deceiving people. There are many teachers out in the world guiding people down the wrong path, but Jesus is guiding His sheep down the right path. He teaches with authority, truth, and power.

We need to honor Jesus for being our protector. Jesus doesn't let any evil harm us. He is there to shield and protect us from all wickedness. Jesus is a spiritual wall that keeps evil from trying to get inside of us. He is an armor that blocks the fiery darts that the enemy shoots at us. He is a present help in time of trouble.

My brothers and sisters, Jesus deserves all of our attention. He deserves acknowledgment. He did billions of wonderful things for us. The greatest thing that He did for us was to die for our sins. Then He defeated death by resurrecting from His grave. After His resurrection, He ascended to heaven and prepared a place for us. Honor

Jesus for His love. Honor Jesus for His kindness. Honor Jesus for His magnificence. Last, but not least, honor Jesus for His great Father the Almighty God.

IMPROVE YOUR CHARACTER

Improve your character. And how do you improve your character? You improve your character by praying and asking Jesus to help you improve it. Jesus will be delighted to help you improve your character. He will be honored to help you improve your character. That is what He is here for.

Drop that ego and ask Jesus for help. Drop that pride. You can not improve all by yourself. If you do improve all by yourself, you are not going to do anything but fall back to the way that you were before you improved. Then you would be mad at yourself and have to start all over.

With Jesus' help, you do not have to start all over. He will not let you go back to the way that you used to be. The only way that you would go back to the way that you used to be is if you forsake Jesus. It will be your fault, not His, so you can not blame Him. You can only blame yourself. Jesus did not forsake you. You forsook Him.

My brothers and sisters, there is always room for improvement. Jesus wants you to improve. He does not want you to be complacent. On the journey to excellence, you have to constantly improve your character. You can not have an excellent spirit without improving your character.

Improving your character is a continuing process. It is an excellent thing. You should never stop improving it. Others will notice your change. They will be amazed about it. They will compliment you about your change. And I can see you giving thanks to Jesus because He helped you improve your character to a complete human being in God's love.

JESUS CHRIST IS HAPPY

Hello, my brothers and sisters. I don't care what color you are because you are still my brothers and sisters. Like the majority of times in my life, I'm doing fine. I just want to let you know that Jesus Christ is happy.

First of all, Jesus Christ is happy because He died for your sins. Jesus Christ was bold enough to do that. Jesus Christ loves you so much that He died for your sins. By Jesus dying for your sins it gives you an opportunity to dwell with Him for all eternity, and that is what He wants for you. That is why He is happy that He died for you.

Moreover, Jesus is happy because you chose Him as your personal Savior. By you choosing Him as your personal Savior, it gives Him a chance to adore you. It gives Him a chance to wash you whiter than snow. Before you chose Jesus as your personal Savior, your soul was filled with pollution. Now that you chosen Him to be the Lord of your life, He is going to get rid of that pollution that is inside of you. Jesus Christ's goal is to make you holy. He wants to make you holy because that is the only way that you can see God. Without Jesus, you are not going to see God. He loves you, and by you choosing Him as your personal Savior, you are going to experience His love, and believe me, it is going to blow you away.

Furthermore, Jesus is happy because you chose to follow Him. When you chose to follow Jesus, you spit in Satan's face. By following Jesus, it lets Him know that you appreciate Him for dying for your sins. It lets Him know that He did not die in vain. Jesus loves you for making that sacrifice because you could have chosen other things to do in the world, but you chose to follow Him.

My brothers and sisters, you are extraordinary people. God knows it, and Jesus knows it, and if you are extraordinary, what does that make God, Jesus Christ, and the Holy Spirit? They were the ones who created you and me. They knew that you were extraordinary before they created us. We are made in their image. Know that Jesus Christ is happy because He has no choice but to be, for He created extraordinary people that are beautiful.

JESUS IS NOT A LIAR

Jesus is not a liar, so you need to slow your roll. Anyone who says that Jesus is a liar, he or she is a liar. Jesus never told a lie. He never had been dishonest. His loins are girded in truth.

Everything that Jesus said came to pass. When Jesus said that He was going to die for our sins, He did it. When Jesus said after the third day of His death He was going to rise from His grave, He did it. When Jesus said He was going to sit on the right-hand side of God, guess what? He is there right now. Read the book of Matthew and Hebrew, and you will see that it is true.

What you need to do is stop denying that Jesus is real. Stop denying that Jesus is the truth and the life. Jesus worshipped God in spirit and in truth. He obeyed God by telling the truth and being honest with others. When did Jesus ever deceive anyone? When did Jesus ever mislead anyone? He never did those things, and He is not going to do those things, so stop deceiving yourself because Jesus is not a liar.

JESUS IS NOT THE BAD GUY

Jesus is not the bad guy. He is the good guy. Satan is the bad guy. He is the cause of the evil in this world. God had to kick him out of heaven because he caused trouble. Now he is causing trouble on earth. That is why Jesus, the good guy, had to come to earth to deliver us from the evil one, which is Satan.

Just like His Father, He had to get rid of the same bad guy. There is only one place that God has reserved for Satan, and that place is hell. While the people of God are going to be in heaven getting their party and praise on, Satan is going to be in hell getting his burn on. He better not ask me for any water to cool his tongue because my answer is going to be an emphatic no, and may I add, *hell no!*

I care about the good guy, and that is Jesus Christ. I will not go behind His back and betray Him. Jesus has done so much for me. He changed my life. He saved me from destruction. Jesus loves me, and I love Him. I'm going to continue to serve Him. I'm going to continue to bless Him.

People, Jesus is not the cause of the world being hateful. Jesus does not hate the world, He loves it. He came from His throne to save the world. When Jesus returns, He is going to show the world what real peace is all about because He is not the bad guy, but the good guy that truly hates evil.

JOURNEY TO HEAVEN

How are you doing, my brothers and sisters? I hope you are doing great. Today is a lovely day. Today is a beautiful day. Today is a blessed day. I thank God for blessing you to see this lovely, beautiful, and blessed day. Oh, I forgot to tell you how I'm doing. I'm doing excellent. I'm doing excellent because I have wonderful brothers and sisters like you. I want you to know that I love you, and I'm going to keep on writing to encourage you on your journey to heaven.

First of all, I want to encourage you to stay focused on your destiny, which is heaven. Stay focused on your destiny that is in Jesus Christ. He is the beginner and finisher of your destiny. He knows your destiny and the outcome of it, so stay focused on Him. Jesus is going to help you reach your destiny. He is going to help you fight the good fight of faith. He is going to help you through your struggles. Through good times and bad times He is going to be with you. He knows that you desire to touch others' lives. He knows that you desire to be an inspiration to others, and He loves and respects you for that because you are willing to sacrifice yourself to others and for righteousness' sake.

My brothers and sisters, there is nothing wrong with being righteous. I'm not talking about self-righteous. I'm talking about righteous in Christ, and through Him. By Christ you are righteous. He died so you can be righteous. You are His joint heir in the kingdom of heaven. Jesus loves you. He appreciates you. He sees and notices what you are doing. He sees that you are blessing people with a caring heart. He sees that you are giving with a cheerful heart. You just don't know how much you amaze Him. You excite Him with your wonderful spirit. You please Him by your faith. Stay strong. Continue to pursue greatness. Continue to stay focused on your destiny and continue to reach out and love others because you are what a follower of Christ is all about. I love you.

KEEP YOUR HEART

My brothers and sisters, keep your heart open to Jesus. Jesus can not operate in a closed heart. Your heart has to be open to Him. How can He heal your broken heart if it's closed? He can't. You've got to have your heart open to Him. He is not going to force His healing on you. He is not going to force His love on you. You've got to invite Him in. With your heart being open, He's welcome anytime.

Don't reject His love, accept His love. The only thing you should reject is evil. The only thing you should have your heart closed to is evil. Evil doesn't care about you or what you do, but Jesus cares about you.

Jesus is not evil. He loves you. As long as you keep your heart open to Him, He will purify it with love. He will purify it with peace, joy, and happiness. Jesus' well never runs dry. He will flood your heart with all those wonderful blessings. Jesus wants you to be perfect in His love, which means complete. He will not leave you comfortless. He will not leave you alone, so keep your heart open to Him because it will always be safe with His loving protection.

KNEEL

People, kneel to Jesus. Jesus is the King of kings and Lord of lords. He is worthy to be praised. He is worthy to be honored. He earned the right to be praised. He earned the right to be honored. God promoted Jesus to be the head of everything. He raised Jesus to be the head of everything, so kneel to Him (Philippians 2:9–10).

If you don't kneel to Jesus and honor Him, you are selfish, pathetic, and don't deserve to see Him. Jesus was bold enough to die for you. He was kind enough to die for you. He got on that cross and died for you. Jesus suffered for you, and here you are too stubborn to kneel to Him. People like you make me sick.

Jesus loves us more than life itself. He gave up His life so we can have abundant and eternal life. Jesus made Himself "of no reputation, and took upon him the form of a servant, and was made in the likeness of men" (Philippians 2:7). And He did that for you and me. He humbled Himself to die on a cross for us. Jesus left His throne to save us. He left His place of royalty to save us.

My brothers and sisters, I mean what I say. I will not apologize for the way I talk. I will not apologize for telling the truth. The world is corrupted because people don't want to hear the truth. People want the children of God to sugarcoat the truth about the Bible. People want the children of God to sugarcoat the truth about Jesus Christ. My brothers and sisters, Jesus is real, so kneel to Him because He is your King.

LEAVE IT IN THE PAST

Check this out, my brothers and sisters. Why do we continue to mention our past troubles or mishappenings? It's okay to mention it for the glory of God in testimony on how He brought you out, but don't mention it so you can stay down in a pit. God wants you to press forward. He doesn't want you to linger in the past. God wants you to keep going toward the prosperous future that He has for you. I have to press forward. We all have to. Even when Jesus Christ died, He pressed forward. Jesus really loves us.

My brothers and sisters, continue to endure. Show God that you appreciate the grace that He has given to you. We are all blessed. I love Jesus Christ, and I appreciate the great job that He did for us. He put His life on the line for us. Surely we need to pick ourselves up and move forward. Surely we need to touch the hem of His garment and be made whole.

The future that God has waiting for us should motivate each of us to move forward. In the future there is more love, peace, joy, understanding, maturity, hope, patience, prosperity, and all the other wonderful blessings that God has waiting for us. My brothers and sisters, pick up your cross and follow Jesus Christ. Thank Jesus Christ, and leave all of your troubles in the past.

LET JESUS BE YOUR VALENTINE

My brothers and sisters, let Jesus be your valentine. With Jesus, Valentine's Day is *every* day. Jesus does not have to be shot by a Cupid to give you love. He is love, and the ruler of it. With Jesus as your valentine there is comfort. With Jesus as your valentine there is compassion. With Jesus, love is in the air every day, and the people that walk by you will notice it.

Christ will not break your heart. He will not stand you up on a date. He is a true lover. Jesus Christ knows that you are precious. He knows that you are a jewel that shines, blings, and sparkles. He wants to have a great relationship with you. He will never dump you. He will not forget about you all's anniversary.

Moreover, the Prince of Peace knows that you have been hurt in your previous relationship. He knows that you have been cheated and lied on. I'm here to tell you that Jesus will never do those ungodly things to you. He will not take His relationship with you as a joke. He will not take you for granted. He will not take advantage of your kindness, so let Jesus be your valentine, and you will see that He is what a true valentine is all about.

LET JESUS TOUCH YOUR HEART

What's up? Some of us need a spiritual healing instead of a sexual healing. My brothers and sisters, let Jesus touch your heart. When Jesus touches your heart, I guarantee that your heart will not have any problems. Jesus does not give your heart problems. He gives it comfort. He gives it power, strength, and protection. Once Jesus touches your heart, it will not have any bad conditions. Your heart will be clean and free from sin.

Believe me because my heart was polluted and full of sin. Jesus cleaned my heart and freed it from sin. Sin no longer controls me because of Jesus' touching power. Jesus will do the same for you. You have to allow Him too. You have to go to Jesus. You have to make the decision of letting Jesus touch your heart.

Jesus does not have a filthy heart. Jesus does not have sin or problems with His heart. We are the ones with sin and pollution in our hearts. Until we come to Jesus and allow Him to touch our heart, sin and pollution are going to remain in it. Sin is not going anywhere until you get rid of it. The only way that you can get rid of sin is by going to Jesus.

Jesus is waiting for you to come to Him. He wants you to come to Him. He does not want your heart to be full of sin. He does not want you to be destroyed by sin. He does not want your heart to be contaminated. He wants your heart to be clean. Let Jesus touch your heart so you can have a wonderful heart like His.

LORD OF FORGIVENESS

Jesus is the Lord of forgiveness. If you sin, He will forgive you. All you have to do is ask Him for forgiveness. It does not take Jesus a long time to forgive you. He will forgive you as soon as you ask Him to. There is nothing that will stop Jesus from forgiving you.

By you asking Jesus for forgiveness, it shows that you acknowledge and respect Him. It shows Him that you believe in Him. It shows Jesus that you are willing to clean up your life. It shows Jesus that you are kind enough to humble yourself unto Him.

Jesus loves you. He knows that you are not perfect. He knows that you are going to sin. He knows that the world is full of lust. It means a lot to Jesus that you ask Him for forgiveness. It shows Jesus that He did not die in vain. It shows Him that He did not waste His time dying for you.

When you ask Jesus for forgiveness, it makes Him happy that He died for you. It makes Him happy to forgive you. It shows Jesus that you recognize Him as your Lord and Savior. It shows Jesus that you have faith in Him. Some people sin on purpose. Some people sin and don't ask Jesus for forgiveness. They sin continually. They don't care about being forgiven. They don't care about being righteous. They don't care about being holy.

Jesus does not want you to be that way. He did not die so you can be that way. That way is evil and selfish. That way is disorderly and rebellious. Continue to strive for excellence. Continue to strive for success. Continue to stay on the righteous pathway, and remember, when you sin, ask Jesus for forgiveness, and He will forgive you because He is the Lord of forgiveness.

MAGNIFY THE LORD

Jesus Christ is the boldest soldier in the universe. He did what He had to do to save everyone from his or her sins. Jesus withstood pain by dying on a cross for us. He had nails driven into His flesh. We need to show Jesus Christ appreciation by magnifying Him.

Jesus is Lord of everything. He was anointed by God to heal many people. He was the most perfect soul on earth. Jesus never committed a sin. Jesus was perfect in God's eyes. He made God so proud of Him. Anything that God told Him to do, He did it. Jesus never disobeyed God.

What was so great about Jesus was that He was willing to do God's work. You never heard Jesus complaining about anything. Some of us cry like we go through hard times, but we really don't go through them. I'm talking about a man who endured twice as much of what we go through. We all need to do is to follow in Jesus Christ's footsteps. He is the key to getting closer to God. Jesus is God's right-hand man. Jesus is the true vine, and we are His branches, so magnify Him because He is Lord of lords.

NO ONE IS GREATER THAN JESUS

Rise, shine, and give the Son of God the glory. I did not say give people the glory, I said give Jesus Christ the glory. The glory belongs to Jesus. The glory is Jesus. He worked hard and earned it. He defeated sin, death, and the evil one to claim the rights of glorification. There is no one greater than He is. If there were anyone greater than He, he or she would be sitting on the right-hand side of God, and not Jesus.

One thing that is so great about Jesus was that He was humble. He was humble to God. He did anything that God told Him to do. He was obedient to Him. How many people you know are obedient to God? Jesus always obeyed His Father. From the beginning of time Jesus was obedient to God. He hearkened unto His voice and respected it.

There is no one greater than Jesus. No one's love is greater than Jesus'. No one's spirit or heart is greater than His. His love conquers all things! I know that I'm not greater than Jesus. I serve and follow Him.

He is my master, and no servant is greater than his master (Matthew 10:24). Get off your high horses and glorify Jesus. Stop being so arrogant and stop being so stubborn! Jesus is the greatest King that ever lived, and no one is greater than He is!

NOT A BEGGAR

Let me tell you all something, my brothers and sisters. Jesus is not a beggar. You've got yourself all wrong if you think Jesus is going to beg you to follow Him. You've got yourself all wrong if you think Jesus is going to beg you to invite Him into your heart. Jesus does not beg anyone for anything. When Jesus chose a disciple, He simply told him to follow Him. The disciple did not ask any questions. He dropped everything he had and followed Jesus. Jesus did not beg him. The man did what Jesus told him to do (Matthew 9:9).

As a matter of fact, Jesus does not want you to be a beggar. He does not want you to beg Him for a thing. What did Jesus say in Matthew? He said ask and you shall receive (Matthew 7:7–8). He did not say beg and you shall receive. He said ask and you shall receive. If Jesus is telling you not to be a beggar, do you think that He's going to be one? Heck no! Jesus is not a beggar, and He does not want you to be one.

You should be eager to serve Jesus. You should be eager to invite Him in. What did Jesus tell His disciples? He told His disciples if anyone does not invite them into their home, kick the dust off their feet and move on (Matthew 10:14). He did not say stand there and beg. He told them to move on.

Jesus is not going to lose His mind if you don't invite Him in your heart. You are the one that needs Him. Open your spiritual eyes and see that He is here for you. Open your spiritual eyes and see that He loves you. Jesus is not going to force or beg you to do a thing because He is not a beggar. Being a beggar is not His type of party.

PAY ATTENTION

What's up, my brothers and sisters? What's going on? I appreciate your prayers. Your prayers bless me to stay strong and to continue to move forward. I love and appreciate you for that. What I want to tell you today is to pay attention. Pay attention to Jesus Christ. He does not teach false information. He teaches true information, so listen to every word He says. Don't leave a word out because every word is important, no matter how big or small, long or short.

Jesus is the way, the truth, and the life. He will never misguide you. He will never mislead or deceive you. He will never tell you a lie. That is why God told Him that it was all right for Him to come to earth because He knew Jesus was not going to deceive us. God trusts Jesus. He knows that Jesus is a man of His word, and a man of action.

Furthermore, Jesus knows God. He knows everything about God. He gave us the knowledge about God. Jesus knows everything about heaven. He is the one that is going to take us there. He is leading us there. We have to pay attention to Him. Jesus does not talk to waste His breath. He talks to bring souls out of captivity. He talks to bring understanding, to give knowledge, so we will no longer be spiritually blind or spiritually enslaved. He talks to teach, preach, and to empower His people.

People, forget about everything else and focus on Jesus Christ. Don't let what Jesus says go into one ear and out the next. Whatever He says, take it in, and leave it in. Live by His sayings. They that love Him keep His commandments and teachings in their hearts (John 15:10). Pay attention to Jesus, and I guarantee that your life will not be ignorant.

PRINCE OF PEACE

Jesus Christ is a wonderful Savior. He is the best friend that you can ever have. Whenever you need Him, He will be there to talk to you and comfort you. No matter what trials or tribulations that you may go through, never give up hope on Him. Jesus is Lord; He sits right beside God in the kingdom of heaven. What I love about Jesus the most is that He will grant you peace. "And the peace of God, which passeth all understanding, shall keep your hearts and minds through Christ Jesus" (Philippians 4:7).

First of all, Jesus will bless you with peace of mind. Many of us have wars in our minds because we don't have peace. You can describe the difference between a person who has peace of mind and one who doesn't. A person who has peace of mind is prestigious, graceful, caring, faithful, trustworthy, and God-fearing. A person who doesn't have peace of mind is weak, foolish, conniving, a liar, unstable, and carries anger in his or her heart. "Make no friendship with an angry man; and with a furious man thou shalt not go" (Proverbs 22:24).

Moreover, Jesus will bless your home with peace. He will fulfill your home with so much peace that when people walk in it, they can't help but to feel it. You know your home is filled with peace because people don't want to leave it. "And my people shall dwell in a peaceable habitation, and in sure dwellings, and in quiet resting places" (Isaiah 32:18). If you don't have peace in your home, ask for it and you shall receive it. God is not selfish. He will bless you with whatever you desire.

Furthermore, Jesus will bless you with peace in your heart. All you have to do is invite Him in. Jesus is not hard to find. Some of us just don't want to look for Him. Many of us cry to God asking Him, why don't people want to be around us? People don't want to be around you because you raise hell all the time, and you run your mouth too much. Jesus will fill your heart with so much peace that when people walk by you, they will know that you are blessed by the grace of God. "Peace I leave with you, my peace I give unto you: not as the world giveth, give I unto you. Let not your heart be troubled, neither let it be afraid" (John 14:27). After the Lord blesses your mind, home, and heart with peace, then you will know that He's the Prince of Peace.

RESPECT YOUR ELDERS

My brothers and sisters, respect your elders. Respect your elders because they are the ones who Christ appointed over you. Your elders know more. They have more experience than you. They know more about life. They have wisdom and can surely teach you some things. Pay attention to them because they are full of knowledge. They want to give the knowledge. They must give the knowledge to the next generation.

We must respect and honor our elders. Many people do not respect their elders. They do not know the meaning of respect. They treat their elders like animals. They abuse them. They are unpleasant to them.

Jesus does not like that type of behavior. He is going to punish those that do not respect their elders. They are going to greatly pay for their bad behavior. Jesus wants us to honor those who are older than we. He wants us to show them kindness. We have to give them love.

I know some of us may have stubborn elders, but we still have to respect them. We have to let them know that we appreciate them. We have to show them appreciation. Our elders are a delight to us. They let us know how to handle some situations. They let us know who to be friends with, and who not to be friends with. We must love our elders. We must honor our elders. We must respect our elders because that is what Christ commands us to do. "Let the elders that rule well be counted worthy of double honour, especially they who labour in the word and doctrine" (1 Timothy 5:17).

SO ASTONISHING

Before I tell you who's so astonishing, I want to get something off my chest. My brothers and sisters, no one has the right to judge you. Only God can judge you. A man or a woman can not judge you. Only God can judge you. Neither man nor woman created you. God created you, and only He has the right to judge you. No one is perfect but God and Jesus Christ. And speaking of Jesus Christ, He is so astonishing.

When Jesus Christ was on earth, He didn't judge anyone. Jesus mainly minded His own business. It was the Pharisees and Sadducees harassing Jesus. It was the Pharisees and Sadducees questioning Jesus about His teachings, but you know what? Jesus kept His cool. Jesus knows that He is astonishing. He does not have to prove it to religious people. He is above religious people.

Jesus teaches and preaches realness and truth. He does not preach and teach to put people in bondage. He preaches and teaches to set people free. To open their eyes, so they can see the light. The way that

He heals people is so astonishing. The way that He loves people is so astonishing. He never rejected a child. He never rejected anyone.

There is no one astonishing like Him. You have people that say if they were Jesus, they would have stayed in heaven and not come down here and died for everyone's sins. People like those are selfish. That is why I said that Jesus Christ's love is astonishing because He came down to earth and died for your sins. He's in heaven this very moment doing intercessory prayer for you. He never stops praying for you. Jesus Christ is so astonishing. Believe me because it's true.

P.S. God knows that His Son is so astonishing.

SO KIND

Thank you, Jesus Christ, for your invitation. I gladly appreciate it, and I will surely be there to dine with you. Jesus, you are so kind. You thought about me to dine with you. You thought about me to send an invitation.

After your resurrection, you went to heaven and prepared a place for your followers. I'm proud to say that I'm among them. You are always thinking about us. Everything that you do is for our sake. You don't want to see anyone burn in hell but Satan.

Jesus, you are full of kindness. It had to take someone full of kindness to do what you did for us. Jesus, you want us to be full of kindness. You want us to put God first and to love our neighbors. You are the mediator of the new covenant. We no longer have to sacrifice animals, because you were the ultimate sacrifice. With your blood, we are cleansed of our sins, and you were kind enough to offer your blood. With your blood, God is satisfied because it is pure. Your blood is not contaminated or polluted.

Jesus, we thank you for your kindness. We love you for your kindness. Every day, we are working on our kindness, so we can be just like you. You are our leader. You are our provider. Thank you so much because you are so kind.

STAY IN

My brothers and sisters, stay in the Word. The Word is the Holy Bible. Jesus wants you to stay in the Word so you can gain more knowledge about God, the Holy Spirit, and He. He wants you to stay in the Word so you won't be deceived by the enemy, for many false prophets are gone out into the world (1 John 4). The Holy Bible gives you knowledge of who the enemy is.

Jesus wants you to be attracted to the Bible, and He wants you to stay attracted to it. Get to know the Bible, and God, Jesus Christ, and the Holy Spirit will get to know you. What does it say in 2 Timothy 2:15? It says study to show thyself approved unto God, a workman that needs not to be ashamed, rightly dividing the word of truth. It is your duty to stay in the Word. It is your duty to study the Word. It is your duty to get closer to God, and may I add, it is a wonderful thing to be approved of Him. That is why Jesus wants you to stay in the Word, so you can get closer to God and be approved of Him.

Let me tell you more good news. Jesus is the Word. He is the Word made flesh (John 1:14). The Word became as man, which is Jesus. Open your eyes and see what the Bible is telling you about. Open your eyes and see what I'm talking about. I am not trying to confuse you. I am not trying to deceive you. I know I told you earlier that the Holy Bible is the Word, and that is true, but Jesus is the Word, which is the Holy Bible made flesh. Let's go back to 2 Timothy 2:15 when Paul said study to show thyself approved unto God. Studying Jesus and having a relationship with Him is the only way God will approve of you. How are you going to get to know God without knowing Jesus? How are you going to see God without knowing Jesus? You can't. Jesus said that He is the way, the truth, and the life, and no man can come unto the Father (God) but by Him (John 14:6).

My brothers and sisters, you've got to know and have a relationship with Jesus. Jesus is your guide to God. He is your Savior. He will not deceive you. He will not lead you astray. When Jesus ascended to heaven, what did He do for you? He sent His partner down from heaven, which is the Holy Spirit, to comfort you because He is the spirit of truth. Stay in the Word and get acquainted with it because it is your guide to everlasting peace, love, harmony, and most of all, eternal life.

STOP BEING SO HARD

My brothers and sisters, stop being so hard on yourselves. Stop abusing yourselves. You are doing a wonderful job serving Christ. You are doing a great job serving Him. Jesus is proud of you. He is going to reward you.

You can not save everybody because everybody does not want to be saved. Some people just want to live the way of the world. They enjoy the pleasures of the world. They love what the world gives to them. You can not stress yourselves over people like them. If they want to perish, let them perish. It will not be your fault. It will be theirs.

You did the best that you could to bring them to Christ. You prayed for them and poured your heart out to them, but they still went on to live their worldly lives. Jesus does not want you to worry about people. You can love them, but don't worry about them. People are going to do whatever they want to do anyway. You have to keep your peace in Christ, and move on.

My brothers and sisters, as long as you are serving and obeying Christ you have nothing to worry about. If no one else is worried about his or her salvation, why should you worry? People make their own decisions. You can not make it for them. Either they want to serve Christ or not. Either they want to be saved or not. You keep preaching the Gospel and keep serving Christ. And remember, stop being so hard on yourselves.

STOP LIVING IN FEAR

Let me tell you all something, my brothers and sisters. Fear is not of God. So why are some of us living in fear? Stop living in fear and serve Jesus Christ. Stand face-to-face to fear, and let it know that you will no longer be afraid. Tell fear that Jesus Christ gave you the power to overcome it. Tell fear that Jesus Christ is on your side, and He will not let you be defeated. That Jesus Christ will not forsake you.

With God, Jesus Christ, and the Holy Spirit working together, fear does not stand a chance against you. It will be a no contest. Fear will forfeit. Fear is afraid of Jesus Christ. It knows that it doesn't stand a chance against the power of Christ. Jesus Christ punked fear and died on a cross for you and me. He made fear look like a wimp. Fear is a wimp when it comes to Jesus. That is why I'm telling you to stop living in fear and serve Jesus Christ.

You better tell fear that it no longer has any control over you. You better tell fear that you serve the mighty Jesus Christ. You can not defeat fear without the power of Christ. You have to proclaim the name of Jesus, and like the coward that it is, fear will flee. Fear hates the name of Jesus. It is afraid of that name. It remembers what Jesus did to its ancestors. It heard of the beating that Jesus Christ gave to death. Go after your hopes and dreams without fear. Go after your destiny. Proclaim the name of Jesus and stop living in fear because Jesus does not want you to live in fear, but power (2 Timothy 1:7).

STOP PUTTING YOURSELVES DOWN

My brothers and sisters, stop putting yourselves down. Stop discouraging yourselves. Putting yourselves down hinders you from reaching your goals. It hinders you from growing and maturing. It delays your destiny.

Downing yourself also hinders the Spirit. It angers the Spirit. Yes, it does because the Holy Spirit is a person and has emotions. He does not want you to be discouraged; He wants you to be encouraged. He does not want you to down yourself. He wants you to motivate yourself. The Holy Spirit works better when you are encouraged.

Furthermore, downing yourself does not help you, it hurts you. It drowns you into a sad pit. Downing yourself shows that you don't have much confidence in yourself. It shows that you don't have much belief. It also shows that you are constantly disappointed in yourself, and you believe that you can't do a thing. You believe that you can't be successful.

In life we are going to face challenges. We are going to face obstacles, but it does not mean that we should down ourselves. It does not mean that we are going to faint. We have to believe in ourselves. We've got to have confidence in ourselves. We have to love ourselves enough to keep pushing toward our destiny. It is worth it.

Believe in yourselves and have confidence in yourselves because we are made in the image of Christ. Christ wants us to believe in ourselves. He wants us to have faith and confidence in ourselves the way that He had confidence in Himself. And if Christ wants us to be that way, we should strive to be that way. So stop putting yourselves down.

THE GOOD SHEPHERD

"I am the good shepherd: the good shepherd giveth his life for the sheep" (John 10:11). That's right, Jesus, you are the good shepherd. You are a fascinating shepherd that loves His sheep. Jesus, you are the highest ranking of shepherds.

First of all, you are the good shepherd because you came down on earth and died for our sins. Jesus, you got on a cross, suffered, and died for us. You took our death and punishment. You spit in the enemy's face and defeated death like the powerful soldier you are. Jesus, you sacrificed your life for us and gave us life more abundantly.

Moreover, you made a way for us to see God. In heaven, you asked God if we can be your brothers and sisters. In heaven, you asked God if we can be adopted into the heavenly family. You made a way for us to be adopted into the family. Jesus, you are the good shepherd.

Furthermore, you prepared a place for us. After your resurrection, you ascended to heaven and prepared that place for us. You know how you want us to live when we leave this planet. You don't want us to be bored. You want us to have fun and to be happy. The place that you have prepared for us is freedom from being mad, sad, depressed, discouraged, sinning, and angry. Jesus, you are not selfish. You are always thinking about us.

Jesus, we appreciate everything that you have done, and are still doing for us. We thank you for the love that you have for us. We love and adore you. Jesus, we thank you for being our shield and protector, for you are the good shepherd that always tends to His sheep.

THE PERFECT ONE

The perfect one to be in a relationship with is Jesus. He is the perfect one for everyone. He wants to have a relationship with everyone. Jesus does not exclude anyone; He includes everyone, but you have to be perfect for Him.

For you to be perfect for Him, you have to believe, trust, love, and have faith in Him. Why should Jesus want to be in a relationship with anyone who does not believe, trust, love, or have faith in Him? That goes for anyone. I don't want to be in a relationship with anyone who does not love or trust me. I know you don't either. You can not have a solid relationship without love or trust. You are only fooling yourself if you think that you can. That is why many relationships today do not last due to a lack of trust.

I'm telling you if you get with Jesus, you will never lack in getting love. Your husband, wife, boyfriend, or girlfriend do not or will not love you more than Jesus. It is impossible. Jesus' love for you is bigger than the universe. His love for you stretches farther than any galaxy. He wants you to experience and absorb His love. He wants to get to know you. He wants to make a big impact in your life. Get with Jesus and you will see that He's the perfect one to have a relationship with. And the relationship will not be temporary; it will be eternal, meaning . . . everlasting.

THE WORLD DID NOT ACCEPT

The world did not accept Jesus Christ, so don't get upset if it doesn't accept you. The world hates you just like it hated Jesus Christ. The world does not want to get along with Jesus Christ or His followers. The world is His enemy. If I had a penny for the many times I've been rejected, I'd be a billionaire.

Don't stress yourself trying to save someone that doesn't want to be saved. Don't force anyone to get saved. Don't force anyone to go to church. You just do your job and tell them about Jesus Christ, and it is up to them to listen or not listen. Don't get upset with people. Don't get angry with people if they don't listen. They are not hurting you, they are only hurting themselves. You have your salvation. You have your place in heaven, so don't worry about anyone not accepting Jesus.

If people don't want to accept Jesus, they are hurting their souls. If they don't want to get saved, fine. You just continue to serve Jesus Christ. You continue to walk that walk of faith. People make their own decisions. I made the decision to follow Jesus, and just because I made the decision to follow Jesus, it doesn't mean that other people are going to make that same decision.

On the day of judgment, Jesus is not going to be upset with you because you tried your best to get people saved. You did what He told you to do. You went out into the world and told people about Christ. You preached the Gospel. You were a great disciple, and those that rejected Christ are going to pay for it eternally. They have no excuses. Jesus knows how the world operates. The world did not accept Him, so don't cry if the world doesn't accept you. Read John 15:18–27.

THERE IS NOTHING WRONG WITH LOVING JESUS

There is nothing wrong with loving Jesus, so go ahead and do it. Jesus is the one that blessed you with a beautiful smile. Jesus is the one who truly loves you. His love for you is eternal. His love for you is unconditional. Each day you are on His mind. Tell Jesus that you love Him. Prove to Jesus that you love Him. Don't worry about the negative things that people are going to say about you. They are just jealous because you have a good relationship with Jesus.

A relationship with Jesus is a good one. Go to church, read your Bible, pray, meditate, and listen to Gospel music. Sing songs of praise, worship, and commune with Jesus in your heart. Don't be ashamed to fellowship with Jesus. Jesus is excellent. Jesus is your Savior. He is remarkable. He is the best. He is the one that is sitting right beside God in the kingdom of heaven.

Everything about Jesus is right. The way that He talks is right. The way that He walks is right. His love is right. If there were something wrong with loving Jesus, you would not be going to heaven. Jesus would have not died for you. Love Jesus, my brothers and sisters, and remember, there is nothing wrong doing it.

WE NEED JESUS

One phenomenon that we all need is Jesus. The people of God can not survive without Him. Without Jesus in our lives, the enemy would destroy us all. There are people walking around saying that they can survive without Jesus. They are saying that they don't need Him. There are people that do not believe in Him.

The people of God can not be ignorant. We will not be ignorant. We shall not be ignorant. We know that Jesus is the Son of God. We know that we need Him. Jesus is our Savior. He is our Leader. He is our Provider.

We as the people of God have to continue to follow Jesus. We as the people of God have to continue to love, trust, and obey Him. We have to continue to believe in Him. When we are hungry, Jesus is the one that feeds us. When we are weak, Jesus is the one that strengthens us. When the enemy is trying to destroy us, He is there to protect us. We need Jesus to protect us. We need Him to comfort us. We need Him to supply our needs. Saying that we don't need Jesus is a lie. People, we all need Jesus, so don't deny it because you know it's true.

WORK FOR JESUS

I know a great master that you should work for, and that is Jesus. Jesus rewards those who work for Him. He blesses those who work for Him. He does not treat His servants unfairly. He does not abuse His power over them.

Jesus' workers are precious to Him. He is concerned about each of their well-being. Jesus does not overwork His staff. He makes sure they get the proper rest they need. He appreciates His workers because He knows the work they do is not easy. He loves when His workers go the extra mile, because it lets Him know that they are willing to work. It lets Him know that they care. It also lets Him know that they love Him.

Unlike man or Satan, Jesus will not punish His servants if they make a mistake. He knows that they are not perfect. He knows that there are going to be times that they are going to get weary. I didn't mention that Jesus' workers have the hardest job in the world, and

He knows that they do. When they make a mistake, He corrects it. Jesus does not curse them. He does not yell at them. Jesus is not about discouragement; He is about encouragement. He motivates and encourages His workers. That is why they love working for Him. He looks out for them. He takes care of them.

Jesus wants you to work for Him. There is always room available to work for Him. Jesus has more than enough space for everyone to work for Him. He is always hiring. You do not need to bring a résumé. Jesus knows everything about you. He knows what kind of worker that you are going to be. He will not interview you. He is waiting for you. All He wants you to do is show up, and He will handle the rest. Work for Jesus because with Him, you will absolutely have benefits.

#1 FAN

Who's your #1 fan? Jesus is your #1 fan. He is cheering you on to victory. He knows that the enemy doesn't stand a chance against you. He knows that you are going to prevail. He has faith in you. He trusts you to do the right things in life. Every time you bless someone, He cheers for you. Every time you overcome temptation, He leaps with joy. Jesus has an enormous cheering section for you. He is a great cheerleader. He brags about you. He lets all His angels know that He's your #1 fan. Jesus can't stop talking about you. You just don't know how He feels when you resist the devil. He feels great! Jesus knows that you are strong. He knows that you are not going to disappoint Him. You are a true person. You are a faithful person. Jesus just can't stop talking about when you accepted Him into your heart. You did not reject Him, and He appreciates the fact that you did not reject Him. Continue to be uplifted. Continue to praise God. Continue to do what is right because you have someone very special cheering for you, and that is Jesus Christ, your #1 fan.

A BEAUTIFUL SAVIOR

Hear me! There is nothing ugly about Jesus Christ. There is nothing corrupted, bad, or evil about Him. Jesus is a beautiful Savior. He is the only beautiful Savior that I know. Jesus never mistreated anyone during His days on earth. He never turned anyone down. When children came unto Him, He blessed them (Mark 10:13–16). Jesus did everything in love. He healed people in love. He delivered people in love. He taught, preached, and blessed people in love. There is nothing wicked about Him. He never talked behind anyone's back. He never plotted against anyone. Jesus never cursed anyone, and He never sought to kill anyone. Jesus walked and talked with grace. Everything that came out of His mouth was filled with love, peace, and authority. He never forced anyone to do a thing. He never demanded anyone to do a thing. He allowed people to do things according to their own will. Jesus was not a terrorist. He was not a slave master. These days you don't have too many beautiful people. There are people who are only just looking out for themselves. I mean that is wrong and selfish. I am happy and glad to serve Jesus. I am joyful to serve Him because He is a beautiful Savior that is kind to everyone.

A MAGNIFICENT SAVIOR

Jesus Christ is a magnificent Savior. He is larger than life. Anything you ask of Him, He gives it to you. He will not hesitate to bless or save you. As soon as you ask Him to forgive you of your sins and save you, He does it immediately. Jesus Christ is a protecting Savior. He will not let anything destroy you. Jesus Christ is here to give you life (John 10:10). He sacrificed Himself, so you could have life. Jesus Christ is the author of love, and His book never needs editing because it doesn't have any errors or mistakes. Jesus Christ is awesome, and He will surely prove it to you. He doesn't play any games. A demon even knows when He is approaching. Jesus Christ is the light of life, and in Him there is no darkness. Sacrifice yourself unto Jesus, serve, and follow Him, and you will see that I told you the truth, that Jesus Christ is a magnificent Savior.

A TRUE CARRIER

Jesus Christ is a true carrier. He carries His children each and every day. He is a loving Savior. He gives us so much love that all we have to do is just relax. When it comes to His sheep, He is so soft and gentle, but to those who harm His sheep, He is a ferocious force. Jesus is Lord of everything. He is a magnificent leader. He judges everyone according to his or her works. My brothers and sisters, show Jesus love. Give Him a spiritual kiss. Jesus will carry you to the way of righteousness. As a matter of fact, He *is* the way of righteousness. He is someone that you can truly depend on. All you have to do is just be obedient to Him. It's that simple. Jesus loves all of us. He will break His neck for each and every last one of us. Ask Jesus for a pure heart, and He will give it to you. Ask Him for a gentle soul, and He will give it to you. My brothers and sisters, He is caring and a true carrier.

A TRUE ROLE MODEL

Jesus Christ is a true role model. He is a great leader to all of us that follow Him. Jesus never tells us to do wrong. He never committed a sin. Every word that comes out of His mouth is filled with grace. Everywhere He goes, He brings peace. Many people love to be around Him because He has a caring spirit. The smile on His face brightens a whole room. Jesus never brought harm to anyone. He never belittles anyone. His ways are righteous. His teachings are on the path of righteousness. Just like His Heavenly Father, Jesus has love for everyone. Jesus is love. His love is so great that He died for all of our sins. Jesus never committed adultery. He never murdered anyone. He never worshipped any false idol. Continue to walk uprightly like Jesus Christ did, for He is a true role model who does not mislead His sheep.

ADORE JESUS CHRIST

What's up, God's people? How are you doing? I love speaking to you because you are wonderful people. You are wonderful people because God created you. He created you in His and His Son's image, and knowing that He created you in their image should fill you with joy. By the way, God's Son is Jesus Christ, you know, the one who died for our sins, and knowing that He died for our sins, we need to adore Him. You see, my brothers and sisters, Jesus loves us so much that He told God that He would come down to earth and be the sacrifice for our sins (Hebrews 10). Answer these questions: Would you leave your place in the holy kingdom of heaven to come down to earth to die for people? Would you leave a holy place to come to an unholy place? Jesus Christ loves you so much that He did that. Get on your knees and thank Him. Raise your hands to praise and glorify Him. Pay your tithes and offerings to give God what's due Him. Do you think that God wanted His Son to go through that? He had to for you and me. That is how much God loves us. Adore Jesus for dying for your sins. Adore Jesus for preparing a place for you in heaven. Oh, what the heck, adore Jesus, because, believe me, He is going to absolutely adore you.

APPRECIATE JESUS CHRIST FOR BEING IN YOUR LIFE

Why not be happy about where you are at now? You always worry about what you have and don't have. Why not just appreciate Jesus Christ for being in your life? I'm here to remind you to do that. The more you appreciate Jesus Christ for being in your life, the more you will stop worrying. I'm talking to those who have Christ in their life. Those of you who don't have Christ in your life, all you have to do is repent of all of your sins and accept Jesus Christ as your personal Savior. Now, back to those who do have Christ in their life. That sound mind you have, Christ gave it to you. That pure heart and soul you have, Christ gave it to you. That wonderful spouse, children, and house you have, Christ gave it to you, so appreciate Him. He is all that you need. What more do you want? Christ made a way for you to be set down here on earth. He made a way for you to go to heaven. Christ is saying, "I'm all that you need; what more do you want? You ask, and I give, and you knock, and I open the door." Appreciate Jesus Christ for being in your life. Appreciate Him for being everywhere you go and for covering you with His blood. Love, honor, and adore Him. He is the one that cares for you. He is the one that heals and nurtures you. Thank Him for your earthly and eternal blessings. Smile, be happy, and be joyful that His light shines through you. Appreciate Jesus Christ for being in your life because when He returns with His holy angels and in all His glory and majesty, He will recognize that you were the one who showed Him great honor and respect.

AS COOL AS HE WANTS TO BE

Jesus Christ is as cool as He wants to be. He is not arrogant. He is not stuck on Himself, or as we all say, "stuck up." When Jesus was on this planet, He conversed with sinners. You have people that think that they are too holy and too righteous to talk to sinners. How are you going to get someone saved if you think that you are too holy and too righteous? Jesus did not walk around turning His nose up at people. He was meek and lowly in spirit, meaning, humble. He let people with all types of diseases and infirmities touch Him. He had friends who were prostitutes. The minute we hear someone in our church is a prostitute, we want to judge and condemn that person. Jesus is as cool as He wants to be. He was nice, kind, and compassionate to everyone, and He is still nice, kind, and compassionate to everyone. His grace and mercy are limitless. His love is limitless. What you need to do is get off your pedestal and stop thinking you are better than everyone. Jesus did not walk around thinking that He was better than everyone because He is as cool as He wants to be.

BE BOLD IN THE LORD

My brothers and sisters, are you tired of being a coward? I know that I am. I'm getting sick and tired of the enemy punking me out. I am in the Lord, and I'm going to be bold in the Lord. My brothers and sisters, Jesus does not want you to be a coward. He wants you to be bold. You have been a coward long enough. Now it's time for you to be tough. Jesus Christ was tough, and He wants you to be tough. Stop allowing the enemy to punk you out. You have power over the enemy. The enemy does not have more power than Christ does. Christ gave you the power to triumph over the enemy. Use the power that Christ has given to you. Stand tall and stand strong. When you stand tall and stand strong, the enemy will back down. The enemy is not big and bad like he proclaims that he is. Those demons were afraid of Jesus. They obeyed Jesus, and you have the same power that Jesus has, so be bold in the Lord, and your enemies will scatter.

BE CONFORMED BY CHRIST

Don't be conformed by the ways of this world but be conformed by Christ. This world is full of sin, but Christ is full of love. This world will drive you to hell, but Christ will drive you to heaven. This world does not care about you, but Christ does. Christ does not want you to live a sinful life. He wants you to live a life of holiness. Living in this world, you can easily live a sinful life. Christ does not want you to live by the ways of this world. He wants you to live by the ways of His Heavenly Father. Don't get caught up in the pleasures of this world, get caught up in the pleasures of Christ. Let Jesus give you pleasure. The pleasures of this world will not satisfy you the way Christ will. Christ does not give diseases and infirmities. He gives life. The pleasures of this world can not match up or compete with Christ. The pleasures of this world will not last because they are temporal, but the pleasures of Christ are eternal. The pleasures of Christ gives you hope. The pleasures of Christ motivate you and give you a purpose to live. Be conformed in Christ and not the ways of this world because Christ is high above, and better, than the world.

BE DOWN WITH JESUS

People, be down with Jesus. Being down with Jesus means to be cool with Him. It means to kick it with Him. Relax with Him. Being on His side does not mean to be sad in spirit. It does not mean to be in a depression pit because Jesus doesn't get down like that. Jesus does not have time for depression. He has time for joy and happiness. Being down with Jesus you are going to be happy because in Jesus there is no depression. The only way you will get depressed is if you allow yourself to get depressed. Jesus does not make people depressed. He makes them happy. Jesus Christ loves being happy. He loves having fun. Being down with Him you are going to have His joy and happiness. Don't be focused on the cares of this world; be focused on Jesus. He is eternal, but the world is temporal. Whatever you do, please don't be down with Satan. If you are down with Satan, you are down with lust, murder, hate, jealousy, seduction, evil, deception, abuse, and sin. Satan is no good for you. Being down with him doesn't get you anywhere but hell. Hell is eternal chaos and suffering. Satan doesn't care about you. Do you want to be down with someone who cares about you? Do you want to be down with someone who loves you? Sure you do, and that is why you are going to be down with Jesus because in Him you have love and eternal life.

BE FRIENDLY II

People, be friendly toward one another. Love your neighbor as you love yourself. Life is too short for us to be against each other. Speak kind words to people. We all have feelings. It does not feel good to hurt someone. Be like Jesus and walk in love. Do not belittle anyone, and do not abuse anyone. Abuse is not friendly, and abuse is not love. If someone speaks to you, speak back. Do not walk past anyone without speaking. The more you speak kindly to people, the closer the world will grow in peace. Your attitude can make you either beautiful or ugly. I choose to be beautiful, and you can too. We have to respect each other. We have to be nice to each other, so be friendly, my brothers and sisters, because it shows you are just like Christ.

BE OBEDIENT TO JESUS

My Christian saints and friends, be obedient to Jesus. It is your duty to be obedient to Him. Obedience shows that you respect Jesus as your Lord and Savior. It shows that you love Him. Jesus blesses those who obey Him. He respects those who obey Him. It is an honor and a privilege to obey Jesus. By Jesus telling or asking you to do something, that should make you make happy. By Jesus speaking to you, that should make you happy. I have nothing against Jesus. I have not always been obedient to Jesus, but I love Him. It's time for us to be obedient to Jesus. It's time for us to listen to Jesus. We have no time to waste. The enemy is out there killing, kidnapping, and murdering people. The enemy is doing it in the open. The enemy is not destroying people in secret. We as the bride of Christ have to be ready for war. We have to be ready to attack the enemy spiritually, not fleshly. The key to attacking the enemy is by obeying Christ. We can't defeat the enemy without the help of Christ. Be obedient to Jesus, for it brings blessings, respect, and victory over the enemy.

BE PREPARED

Christ is coming back, so you better be prepared. Get ready. Christ is not going to allow His people to continue to suffer. He does not like how His people are being treated. He is getting ready to come back for His people. He is ready to reward His people. He is getting tired of the ways of this world. He is ready to bring judgment to this world. He is getting sick and tired of the corruption in this world. The world has been sinning long enough. The world has been doing its wicked and evil deeds long enough. The world is getting out of hand. The world is heading for destruction. It is time for Christ to put an end to this world. It is time for Christ to come back, so get saved, follow Him, and be ready for His glorious return.

CARE ABOUT JESUS

All God wants you to do is to care about His Son Jesus. He knows that He can't force you to, but He's hoping that you do. Jesus cares about you more than anybody does. He sacrificed Himself and died for you. He resurrected from His grave and prepared a place for you, and He did not hesitate to do it. Your mother, father, sister, brother, husband, or wife do not care about you the way that Jesus does. Jesus healed your broken heart. He forgave you from all of your sins. He set you free and delivered you from bondage. Must I continue on? Whose father created you? Jesus' Father created you. Whose father adopted you into the heavenly family? Jesus' Father adopted you into the heavenly family, and it was because of Jesus. He asked His Father God if we could be adopted into the heavenly family, and God answered yes. Jesus Christ could have said "Father, let heaven just be for you and me," but instead, He said, "Father, we need more company," and that's where we came in. We are part of the heavenly family. Continue to follow Jesus. And continue to obey Him. Most of all, care about Him because He already proved at Calvary that He cares about you.

COME TO JESUS

Are you sick and tired of people telling you lies? Are you sick and tired of being deceived? Well, here is what I suggest. I suggest that you come to Jesus. Come to Jesus! He will not deceive you. He will not tell you lies. He will tell you the truth you need to know. Jesus does not believe in telling lies. He believes in telling the truth. He is full of truth. He is ready for you to come to Him. He is waiting on you. Jesus has so much to tell you. He has so much wisdom and knowledge to give to you. Don't refuse to come to Him because it is a terrible thing to waste your mind. When you refuse to come to Jesus, you are wasting your mind. Jesus will not give you false doctrine. He will give you true doctrine. What Jesus gives doesn't last temporarily. It lasts eternally. Jesus has enough knowledge to give to the universe. As a matter of truth, He has more than enough knowledge. You have to be willing to come to Him. You have to be willing to listen and hearkened unto Him. Jesus will not lie to you. He will not confuse or deceive you. He will guide you in all truth. In Jesus you will find all that is good and positive, so come to Him, and I guarantee you will find truth, love, compassion, and satisfaction.

DON'T BE A SCOFFER

I know some of you are wondering what I'm talking about, but don't be a scoffer. A scoffer is someone who denies the coming of Christ (2 Peter 3:3–4). A scoffer is someone who mocks the coming of Christ. A scoffer says that Jesus Christ is not coming back. That is why I'm warning you about being one because Jesus Christ is coming back. Jesus Christ is not a liar. When Jesus says He's coming back, know He's coming back. Scoffers are those who don't believe that He's coming back. True believers of Christ know that He's coming back. We have no doubt in our minds that He's coming back. Jesus is coming back. We don't take Jesus' words for a fantasy. We know that He is not a liar. We know that He is not a deceiver. We are waiting for His return. Scoffers are laughing at us, saying that we are only wasting our time waiting for something that is not going to happen, but I'm telling you it *is* going to happen. My brothers and sisters, this world is not going to be here for long. Jesus Christ is returning. He's gathering His angels for His glorious return. I am serious. I want you to believe in Jesus. He is going to swiftly return. I don't know when He's coming, but He's coming. Scoffers just don't know what trouble that they are going to be in. Jesus Christ takes it personally when you don't believe, so don't be a scoffer unless you want to face the wrath of God.

DON'T BETRAY JESUS

My brothers and sisters, please don't betray Jesus. That is a bad thing to do. Jesus said, it is better for a man not to be born than to betray Him. That is serious, my brothers and sisters. It is plain out ignorant and stupid to betray Jesus. Whosoever betrays Jesus is a backstabber. If you are going to betray Jesus, don't walk with Him. If you are going to betray Jesus, don't follow Him because you are a fool. You want to betray someone who loves you more than your father and mother? You want to betray someone who died for your sins? You are pathetic. Jesus cares about you. He descended from heaven to save you. He descended from heaven to consecrate and sanctify you. You don't belong to Satan. You belong to Jesus. Satan is the one that betrayed God. He turned against God in heaven. You don't have to be a fool like him. Whenever he approaches you, rebuke him and tell him, "No, I will not betray Jesus because He loves me, and I love Him."

DON'T DENY JESUS

My brothers and sisters, please don't deny Jesus. Jesus will not deny you, so why would you deny Him? The only time that Jesus will deny you is if you deny Him. Why would you want to deny Jesus anyway? Jesus is amazing. Jesus is outstanding. He cares about you, and He's not ashamed of you. He does not care how you may look on the outside because He loves you. He is here to give and show you love, so don't deny Him. When you deny Jesus, you miss out on your blessings. When you deny Jesus, you are saying that you don't know Him. Of all beings, Jesus is the one you should want to know. When you were in an abusive relationship, He delivered you out of it. When you were starving, He provided you with food. When you were on your way to being evicted, He helped you pay your bills. Jesus will not leave you hanging. He will not leave you comfortless. Don't forget what Jesus said: "Whosoever therefore shall confess me before men, him will I confess before my Father which is in heaven. But whosoever shall deny me before men, him will I also deny before my Father which is in heaven" (Matthew 10:32–33).

DON'T GET ANGRY

My brothers and sisters, don't get angry with Jesus. What did Jesus do to make you angry? All He does is speak the truth. You should be happy to hear the truth. Are you sick and tired of people telling you lies? You may not be, but I am. You see, truth is not your enemy; lies are your enemy. The one you should get angry with is Satan because he is the father of all lies (John 8:44). Besides, Jesus doesn't make people angry, He makes them happy. What book are you reading? The book I read is the Bible. It tells you all the truth about Jesus. Jesus is not angry with you. He loves you. He is slow to anger. He is not the reason for your problems. He is not the reason for your tough situations. That is life. That is the world. You see, the world does not know Jesus. The world does not understand Him. The world rejects the truth. In life, Jesus suffered. He had problems dealing with the world. But Jesus wants to be your friend. He does not want to be your enemy. He died for you, and when He died for you, He was not angry. So what you need to do is stop allowing your emotions to control you. Get to know Jesus more and more, and don't get angry with Him, because, for heaven's sake, He is not angry with you.

DON'T LET ANYONE

Don't let anyone crush your hopes and dreams. Be what you want to be in life. Go after your hopes and dreams. You have to work hard to achieve your hopes and dreams because that is the only way you are going to be successful. "Faith without works is dead also" (James 2:26). Jesus Christ didn't let anyone crush His hopes and dreams. He did not let Satan, His family, His followers, Pharisees, or Sadducees crush His hopes and dreams. His hopes and dreams were to die for everyone's sins and to resurrect from His grave, and you know what? He was successful in doing those things, and then some. Many people tried to stop Him. Even people in His own family. Many were against His teachings. Many were against Him empowering and healing people. People threw stones at Jesus, but He still pursued His dreams. Right now, He's sitting at a great position on the right-hand side of God. What I'm trying to tell you, my brothers and sisters, is, if Jesus can reach His hopes and dreams, you can to. The whole army of hell was trying to destroy Him. Some people in church hated Him. You are made in His likeness. He gave you the power to reach your hopes and dreams. You have the Christ mind, and no one has the power to control your mind because you have the Christ mind. Remember that Jesus' Spirit lives in you. Remember that He loves you. Don't let anyone crush your hopes and dreams because you have the power to go after and achieve them.

DON'T LIVE IN DARKNESS

Don't live in darkness. There is nothing but misery, sadness, and depression living in darkness. Darkness does not have anything good for you. It hates good. Its main objective is to stay away from good. Good is light. Darkness knows that it can't defeat it. The light is where Jesus dwells. Jesus said that even a little light could defeat darkness. Light contains the elements of love, peace, friendship, joy, happiness, and forgiveness; everything about Jesus. Darkness hates those things. It hates itself. What makes you think that it cares about you? Don't associate with darkness. Don't try to pull others in it. I'm telling you the truth. I used to be in darkness. I know how it feels to be in it. I care about you enough to tell you to stay away from it. I care about you enough to tell you, don't live in it. Come to the light and stay in the light because Jesus will give you all the love that you need. "I am the light of the world: he that followeth me shall not walk in darkness, but shall have the light of life" (John 8:12).

DON'T MAKE FUN

Let me holler at you for a quick second. Don't make fun of people. It's not right to make fun of people. It's not good to make fun of people. People have feelings, which means that they can get hurt by what you say about them. Some people can't help the way they look, smell, talk, or walk, and it doesn't make things better when you talk about them. Instead of talking about someone, get to know him or her. Just because you may disapprove of someone it doesn't mean that the individual is not unique. Who are you anyway? You are not Jesus Christ. Jesus Christ didn't make fun of anyone. He didn't make fun of anyone's disability or how they looked, smelled, talked, or walked. He knows that it is cruel to do that. Do you want someone to make fun of you? No, you do not, because you know your feelings will get hurt. Put yourself in that person's shoes, the one who you are making fun of. Think about how that person feels. Some people say that they don't care when someone talks about them, but they are only lying. They do care. Some people can't sleep at night because they are still thinking about what someone said about them. Thank you for that quick second, and remember . . . Don't make fun of people.

DON'T RUN FROM JESUS

Let me give you some great advice: Don't run from Jesus, but run *to* Him. How are you going to get healed or delivered if you run from Him? How are you going to get saved if you run from Him? Those are the reasons why you've got to run to Him. Jesus does not want you to be afraid of Him. He wants you to run toward Him. Like He told Peter, don't be afraid. Jesus is not here to destroy you. He is not here to condemn you. He is not an abuser, so why do you choose to run away from Him? He is here to give you life, and life more abundantly (John 10:10). Jesus loves you, and He will not do anything to harm you. He is the one that you should run to. In Jesus you'll find rest. In Jesus you'll find peace. There is no confusion in Jesus because He does not waver or is double-minded. His mind is balanced. Jesus is full of love and compassion. He wants to offer all of the benefits of heaven to you, so don't run from Jesus because in Him there is eternal life.

DON'T SERVE SIN

People, don't serve sin because sin will lead you to hell. You are already living in a world of sin, so why would you want sin to destroy you for all eternity? Sin does not care about you. That is why Jesus died for you, to release you from it. Don't allow sin to have control over you. Don't play with sin. Jesus Christ gave you the power to defeat sin. As a matter of fact, Jesus defeated sin when He died on the cross. Don't let sin be your lord; let Jesus be your lord. Don't invite sin into your heart; invite Jesus into your heart. Jesus will make you beautiful. Sin will make you ugly. Jesus wants to save your soul. Sin wants to destroy it. Jesus wants you to see God. Sin does not want you to see God. It wants you to be in bondage. It wants to hold you captive. Sin is trash. There is nothing great about sin. There is nothing good about sin, so don't serve it, for the wages of it are death (Romans 6:23).

DON'T TURN YOUR BACK ON JESUS

Savior, I appreciate you for being in my life. I do not take you for granted. I thank you for dying for my sins. I love you and will never turn my back on you. I'm going to tell my brothers and sisters to not turn their backs on you. Jesus, you never left us alone. You have always been there for us. From the beginning of time you had a plan for us. You kept us in your heart. You never forgot about us, and we gladly appreciate it. My brothers and sisters, don't turn your back on Jesus. He is the reason that you are alive. I know that it's easy to get caught up in the world because of its many pleasures. That is why you have to stay focused on Jesus. Jesus will keep your soul in right standing with God. Jesus will keep you from being deceived. He is going to bless you to be successful, so once you make it to the top, don't forget about Him. Many people have turned their backs on Jesus, but you don't have to be one of those that do it. Keep yourself in right standing with Him. When you depart from this earth, He will remember you. When you stand face-to-face with Jesus, He will tell God that you did not deny Him. Live your life for Jesus and don't turn your back on Him because He certainly did not turn His back on you when He died on the cross.

DON'T WISH BAD ON PEOPLE

My brothers and sisters, don't wish bad things to happen to others. It is not walking like Christ if you wish bad things on others. Bless and wish good things to happen to people, and not bad things. I don't care how bad a person may have hurt you, still wish good on that person. We have to forgive those who have hurt us. I know it may be hard to forgive someone or to wish good on someone, but still do it. Your blessings come through forgiveness. Your healing comes through forgiveness. I've been hurt plenty of times and had to forgive those who hurt me. I did not wish bad things to happen to them. Look what happened to Jesus. No one has ever suffered like Jesus. No one has ever been hurt like Him. What did Jesus tell God? He told God to forgive the people for they know not what they do. He did not tell God to destroy them. He did not tell God to harm them. He told God to forgive them. Jesus did not wish bad things on anyone. If Jesus can bless people, we can bless people. We are made in His likeness. Continue to walk like Christ. Continue to obey Him. Continue to adore Him, and please don't wish bad on people because Jesus did not die for you to do that.

DRINK THE LIVING WATER

My brothers and sisters, drink the living water. When you drink the living water you shall never thirst again. This living water gives you power. This living water gives you anointing. This living water also heals. I know you are wondering what I'm talking about. Well, I'm talking about Jesus Christ. Jesus Christ is the living water, and with Him you shall never thirst again. Jesus Christ will not leave you comfortless. Jesus Christ will not leave you dry. Jesus Christ will not abandon you. You can always count on Him. He will amaze you. He is not a circus act; He is the real deal. Taste the living water and you will experience what I'm writing about. I am telling you the truth. I am not here to deceive you. I love you, and I want you to drink the living water. He is here to help you. He is here to guide you. He loves you. My brothers and sisters, drink the living water, which is Jesus Christ, and you will see that you will never thirst again (John 4:14).

GET EXCITED!

My brothers and sisters, get excited! Get excited because Jesus is on His way back! He's on His way back to earth! He's coming back for you! He's ready to take you to the place that He prepared for you! He is going to show you what real peace is all about! Real peace is not temporal it is eternal. Jesus is getting sick and tired of the violence in this world. He's getting sick and tired of His people suffering. He's ready to cast wickedness in hell. He's waiting for His Father to give Him the word to come down here. Jesus is excited. He's excited that He has joint heirs to the kingdom. We are His joint heirs, and He's ready to receive us. He's ready to take us to the kingdom, and the kingdom is so glorious. I can see God sitting on His throne. I can see Jesus Christ sitting on the right-hand side of Him. God is saluting Jesus. He is saluting Jesus for stepping up to the plate and sacrificing Himself for us. He is saluting Jesus for being unselfish. If it weren't for Jesus, we would not be joint heirs to the kingdom of heaven. The joy of the Lord is waiting for us. The kingdom of heaven is waiting for us, so get excited because Jesus is on His way back to take us there eternally.

GO AFTER CHRIST

Are you sick and tired of going after things that are not worth anything? I know I am, and that is why I choose to go after Christ. Christ is worth something. He is my salvation, and there is nothing on earth more precious than that. Salvation is priceless. You can not put a price tag on it. Salvation is your key to spiritual freedom. It frees you from all that is ungodly. You get salvation by going after Christ. It is not going to be handed to you. You have to go and get it. You've got to have that hunger and thirst for it. You have to be desperate for it. There is going to come a time in your life that you are going to get tired of living by the ways of the flesh. There is going to come a time in your life that you are going to get tired of living by the ways of the world. The ways of the world will wear you out. Your spirit and your body will get tired. That's why you have to go after Christ and get saved. Once you get saved, be faithful to Christ. Don't go back out to the world to do the things that you used to do. Don't use Christ for your own lustful pleasures because He will most certainly cast you into outer darkness. Go after Christ to get saved. Go after Christ to get healed and delivered. Most of all, go after Christ so you can live with Him and God for all eternity.

GOD'S RIGHT-HAND MAN

Hello, hello, and hello! I love Father God for all eternity. You should feel the same way too. Let's talk about His right-hand man. His right-hand man is awesome and full of love. He was the one that died for all of our sins. Right now He's talking to the Father about everlasting life. He's telling the Father that He's happy He died for us. That it was worth it dying for us. He's saying that He's proud of us. Jesus is the one that is guiding us to the Father. Jesus is the one who is guiding us on that narrow pathway. His eyes are always watching us. When we fall, He is there to pick us up. He is not a liar. He does what He says. He prophesies what's going to happen, and it will come to pass. Just saying His name fills you with joy. He is the one that tells your boss to take it easy on you. He is the one that tells your teacher to treat you like he or she treats the other students. Jesus is talking to the Father about your wonderful destiny. He's talking to the Father about how great your blessings are going to be. Welcome Jesus into your hearts. He will bring life into you. He will open big doors for you. He will protect you from your enemies. My brothers and sisters, please don't be selfish with Him. Keep your mind on Him. I'd rather have my mind on Jesus than to have my mind on polluted thoughts. Love, honor, and respect Jesus for He is God's right-hand man who, God knows, won't betray Him.

HAVE SELF-CONTROL

Have self-control. Jesus Christ does not work with disorderly people. He works with people that are in order. He works with people that can control themselves. Jesus Christ is about business. He is not about foolishness. He does not have time for foolishness. On your time act like a fool, but on Jesus' time be about business. While you are acting like a fool, lives are being taken. While you are acting like a fool, lives are being destroyed. I'm not telling you not to have fun because it is okay to have fun. There is a time to have fun, and there is a time to be serious. It's not funny seeing someone getting destroyed by alcohol. It's not funny seeing someone getting destroyed by drugs. It is time to pray and to be serious. I am not going to die before my time. I am not going to perish. I am going to live. Believe me, I am going to live in Christ. I am living in Christ right now. If I am being too hard on you, good. I am hard on you because I care about you. I do not want you to perish. I want you to live, so have self-control because a person who has self-control can run a nation.

HAVING THE CHRIST MIND

Now, knowing that you have the Christ mind should motivate you to shed some light on others. People would be happy for you to shed some light on them because most of them do not have it. You see, having the Christ mind gives you the power to shed some light on others. It gives you the power to enlighten others. All people need the Christ mind. My brothers and sisters, having the Christ mind makes you walk in power. Having the Christ mind makes you walk with confidence. You know that you can do all things in Christ who strengthens you (Philippians 4:13). People wonder about you. They want to investigate you. They want to get to know you. Having the Christ mind gives you peace which surpasses all understanding (Philippians 4:7). Nothing will bother you. With God's help you know how to handle situations. Having the Christ mind is so tremendous. Before you got saved your mind was in turmoil, but once you got saved, going through the process and transformation of being part of the body of Christ, you felt that awesome change. You know that there is a God. You know that you have the grace of God. You know that God has great works for you to do. Even Jesus Christ said your works are going to be greater than His because He must return to the Father. My brothers and sisters, be happy that you have the Christ mind. Those of you who do not have it, receive it because having the Christ mind is one of the most remarkable things to have coming from the great and Almighty God.

HE DOES CARE

My brothers and sisters, I know that you are sick and tired of getting yourself hurt. You get out of one relationship, and then jump into another one. Why do you continue to do that? As long as you do that, you are going to constantly get yourself hurt. My brothers and sisters, get to know Jesus Christ for He cares about you. He will not hurt you. He will give you so much love like you never experienced before. He does not want your heart to be broken. He is the one that is going to fix your broken heart. His love is greater than your mother's, father's, sister's, brother's, grandmother's, ex's. He cares about every part of your body. He is the love that you've been waiting for. Ask Him to take you out on a date. He will pay for the movie and dinner. After the movie and dinner are over, He will take you home and will not try to get between your legs. He does not want what you have between your legs; He wants what's inside your chest, and that's your heart. I know that you are tired of getting hurt, so give Him a chance, and you will see that He does care for you. He is someone that will love you, speak kindly to you, comfort you, and protect you. Show Him love and honor. Don't worry about what people have to say about you. If they ask why you are so happy, just tell them that you are in a great relationship, and that is with Jesus Christ, so get to know Him for He does care about you, and He will not give you drama.

IT'S OKAY

People, it's okay to follow Christ. Jesus wants you to follow Him. He wants you to be with Him. He wants to see you. He wants to lead you in the right direction. Following Christ you are going in the right direction. You are not going in the wrong direction. Jesus does not believe in deceiving people. He believes in saving, delivering, and leading them. He walks on the path of truth and righteousness where there is no deception. He destroys any evil that comes His way. It's okay to follow Him because He will protect you. You are safe in His hands. He will protect you from all evil. Christ is your protector, which means you are going to be safe. Jesus does not lead people into danger; He leads them into safety. You are safe with Him. Believing in Christ you will get blessed. Serving Christ you will get blessed. Trusting Christ you will get blessed. Following Christ you will get blessed, and that is why it's okay to follow Him.

JESUS CHRIST HAS IT GOING ON

My brothers and sisters, Jesus Christ has it going on. Before He came to this planet, He had it going on, and He still does. Jesus Christ walks and talks with grace. He never intends to hurt anyone's feelings. Feel me on this. You know He had it going on when an angel came to His mother and told her that she was going to conceive a great man of God (Luke 1:35). You know He had it going on when a king was out to destroy Him when He was a young child (Matthew 2:13). You know He had it going on when the enemy was doing the best that he could to tempt Him (Matthew 4:1–11). Let me also add that He died on a cross for us, calmed the winds and the seas, and resurrected from the grave. Jesus Christ is sensational. He protected the Hebrew boys in the fiery furnace (Daniel 3:25). What more do you want me to say? Get to know Jesus Christ. Open up your heart to Him and follow Him. Then you will understand what I mean when I say Jesus Christ has it going on.

JESUS IS FEARLESS

Jesus is fearless. He's not afraid of death, pain, or suffering. He did not let fear get in His way to do God's will. He did not let fear get in His way because He was on a mission. His mission was to die for our sins, resurrect from His grave, and to be God's right-hand man, and you know what? Jesus accomplished those things. Jesus stared fear right in its eyes and punked it out. Jesus defeated fear and did not drop a sweat doing it. He sent fear running with its tail stuck between its legs. Then He beat death like it stole something. Jesus had those demons afraid of Him. He had His enemies trembling. I'm telling you all, Jesus is not afraid of anything. Let me tell you all another thing that He did. When Jesus' disciples were afraid of the big storm that came upon the sea, Jesus rebuked it and the sea became still. Read the Gospel of Jesus and you will see what I'm talking about. It's in the New Testament. Last, but not least, Jesus descended to the lower parts of the earth to preach the Gospel, and His saints that were in the lower parts of the earth rose as well. Jesus does not play. He is fearless. Read the Bible, get to know Jesus, and you will see what I'm talking about.

JESUS IS REAL

Jesus Christ is a loving Savior. He loves everyone and everything except evil. Jesus Christ is an awesome Savior. When He speaks, everyone listens, including the seas and the winds (Matthew 8:26). Some people may not understand Him because He speaks in parables, but believe me, as you get closer to Him, you will understand. Jesus Christ is the Son of God, which means that He has a huge amount of power because God anointed Him (Luke 4:18–19). Remember the way that He commanded demons out of people (Matthew 8:28–32)? Remember the way that He brought Lazarus back from the dead (John 11:43–44)? Remember the way that He was rose from His grave (Matthew 28:1–10)? Jesus is mighty, and the only way to get to God is through Him. All you have to do is believe that He died for your sins and accept Him as your personal Savior. Jesus will help you get through your trials and tribulations. He will help you triumph over your fears. When you get sick, He will heal you. If you are blind, He will bless you with sight (Matthew 9:27–31). Jesus is real. I just hope and pray that you believe it.

JESUS IS NOT EVIL

Jesus is not evil. If He were evil, He would not have thought about saving the world. If He were evil, He would not have sacrificed Himself for you and me. If He were evil, none of us would be down here. We all would be facing the wrath of God. Jesus is not a murderer. Jesus is not a destroyer. He is a savior and a deliverer. He does not kill lives, He saves lives. Jesus does not go into people's homes to kill them. He goes into their homes to save them. Jesus does not kidnap people. He does not torture people. Evil is not in His blood. When someone says that Jesus is wicked, that person is a liar. When someone says that He is the devil, that person is a fool. Jesus is too good to be the devil. He is too holy and righteous to be the devil. He hates the devil. He despises the devil. Jesus means you well. He does not mean you any harm. His love for you is larger than the universe. He would do anything to save and protect you. Jesus is full of love. He is full of peace. He is full of knowledge. Knowledge that He is willing to give to you so you can know the truth about Him. My brothers and sisters, Jesus is not evil.

JESUS IS SPECTACULAR

What a beautiful day it is! It is a beautiful day because we serve a beautiful Savior. The beautiful Savior that we serve created this beautiful day. He is spectacular. There is nothing ugly about Him. His ways are amazing. His teachings are righteous. He carries Himself in holiness the way we should carry ourselves. He lived His life in love the way each of us should live our lives. Jesus is spectacular. He did not disobey any of God's commandments. He was obedient to God from the beginning of time. Everything about Jesus is spectacular. His love is spectacular. His forgiveness is spectacular. His mercy is spectacular. His grace is spectacular. Jesus wants us to be spectacular. That is why He died for us, so we too can be spectacular. You can not be spectacular with sin living in you. You can not be spectacular with hate living in you. Jesus did not have hate or sin in Him. That's why He died for us, to cleanse us from sin. My brothers and sisters, sin brings hate. Sin brings anger and all that other ungodly stuff. Jesus does not want you to be part of that. He wants you to be sanctified, so open your hearts to Jesus and keep them open so you can be spectacular just as He is.

JESUS WILL MAKE A WAY

Good afternoon, my brothers and sisters. Today is a lovely day that God Almighty has created. I love God Almighty, and I thank Him for that phenomenal prayer that He answered for me so I can dwell eternally with Him. My brothers and sisters, I just want to tell you that Jesus will make a way. When He died on the cross, He made a way for you. My brothers and sisters, I know that it's hard living on planet Earth, but hang in there. Your blessings will be arriving shortly. Jesus Christ is your blessing. When you have Him, you have everything. He will make a way for you to get that house you desire. He will make a way for you to get your riches. He will make a way to help your family members get off drugs, alcohol, and cigarettes. He always keeps His promises. I love Him and will do anything for Him because He saved my life. Jesus Christ saved me from the gates of destruction. Don't give up, keep your head up, and walk with pride. Keep your eyes on God and know that His begotten Son will make a way. Amen.

KEEP JESUS IN YOUR HEART

Hello, my brothers and sisters. I'm glad to know that you have Jesus in your heart. My brothers and sisters, keep Him in your heart. Don't let anyone turn your heart away from Him. That person won't love you like Jesus. Jesus put that comfort in your heart. Jesus put that love and peace in your heart, so don't allow anyone to take that away from you. Stay focused on Him and continue to serve Him. Jesus didn't dump you. Jesus didn't hurt you. He didn't abuse you, so why would you not keep Him in your heart? He calms the storms and the winds in your life. He keeps you away from thuggish people. He keeps you standing. If someone loves you like that, why should you let anyone take that away from you? Leave those no-good men and women alone. Let Jesus know that you love Him. For those of you who don't have Jesus in your heart, invite Him in, and those of you who do, keep Him because Jesus is going to keep you in His.

KEEP YOUR MIND ON JESUS

Jesus is my personal Savior. Jesus is my best friend. When times get rough, I know I can depend on Him to be there for me. He will also be there for you. All you have to do is just keep your mind on Him. Jesus will open many doors for you if you would just trust Him. There are going to be times that you are going to get weak, but Jesus will be there to strengthen you. He is your key to getting closer to the Heavenly Father. To make it to God you've got to go through Jesus.

What I love about Jesus the most is that He feels your pain. He knows this earth is full of sin. Just like we go through trials and tribulations, He went through them as well. Satan also tempted Him. Jesus died for all of our sins. We have to be strong in Him. We have to believe in Him. Jesus will deliver you out of any difficult situation that you are in. Please don't take Him for granted. He is wonderful and a great master to serve. Keep your mind on Jesus for He will show you great kindness, mercy, and supply you with everything you need.

KEEP YOUR MIND RIGHT WITH JESUS

Hey, I know what you need to do. You need to keep your mind right with Jesus. Keeping your mind right with Jesus shows Him that you are serious about being spiritually minded. It shows Him that you want Him to continue to control your mind. Jesus loves your mind. He would not do anything to destroy it. You keep your mind right with Jesus by reading your Bible. You keep your mind right with Jesus by praying and fasting. It is best for you to keep your mind right with Jesus so you can have peace, and if you do not keep your mind right with Him, you are going to find yourself in a whole lot of trouble. Your mind is too precious to be caught up in confusion, stress, and frustration. Keep your mind right with Jesus so you can have a stable mind. He does not want you to be double-minded because a double-minded person won't receive anything from the Lord, and a double-minded person is unstable in all his ways (James 1:7–8). Jesus wants you to have a clean and peaceful mind. He wants your whole mind, and not half or a quarter of it. I know that you don't want your mind to be filled with junk. I know that you get sick and tired of being confused, so keep your mind right with Jesus because His mind is surely right with you.

LET JESUS

My brothers and sisters, we all have to let Jesus pour peace, love, kindness, happiness, and joy into our hearts. If we don't let Jesus pour those things into our hearts, we are going to forever be bitter, sorrowful, and angry. For us not to be bitter, sorrowful, or angry, we have to invite Jesus into our hearts. Jesus is the peacemaker. His purpose is to store peace inside of us. We have to let Jesus store peace in us by inviting Him in. Are you sick and tired of being empty on the inside? When you invite Jesus in, you will no longer be empty on the inside. He is what you are missing. He is the love that you are looking for. His love contains great benefits. Like I told you earlier, His love contains peace, kindness, happiness, and joy. What do you have to lose? Those are the things you need. Are you sick and tired of someone popping you upside your head? Are you sick and tired of someone cursing and abusing you? Get rid of that dog and invite Jesus into your hearts. Jesus Christ will treat you like the king or queen that you are. He will treat you the way that you are supposed to be treated. He will not treat you like you are an animal. He will not treat you badly. Let Jesus come into your life and you will see that I'm not lying.

LET NOT YOUR HEART BE TROUBLED

My brothers and sisters, let not your heart be troubled. You serve Jesus Christ, so there is no way that your heart should be troubled. With Jesus in your heart, it should not be troubled. Why should it be troubled? There is no reason for it to be troubled. Jesus defeated death. He defeated Satan. He overcame the world and prepared a place for you. What are you fearful about? There is no reason to be fearful. God's wrath is not upon you. God is not angry with you. He is not seeking to destroy you. What are you worried about? There is no reason to be worried. The Holy Spirit comforts your heart. The Holy Spirit controls your heart. Jesus is taking care of you, and He is going to continue to take care of you. He was the one that fed over five thousand people. He was the one that told the wind and the waves, "Peace, be still," and quiet they became. With a fool controlling your heart, that is when you should worry, but with Jesus controlling your heart, you don't have to worry. If you don't want to listen to me, listen to Jesus. "Let not your heart be troubled: ye believe in God, believe also in me" (John 14:1).

LIVE IN POWER

Live in power, and that is in Jesus Christ. Living in Jesus there is power for He is power. He is full of it. Get the power and use it because you need it. You can not survive without the power of Christ. You can not live without the power of Christ. If you think that you can, you would be only deceiving yourself. The enemy will tear you to pieces if you don't use the power of Christ. The enemy will run circles around you. He wants you to think you can make it without the power of Christ. He wants your guard to be down. That is why you've got to keep your guard up with the power of Christ. The enemy is a creeper. He is waiting for you to drop your guard. He is a venomous snake, a predator. That is why you have to be ready to put your foot on His throat. It's wonderful living in power. It's great living in power. Living in power is unique because Jesus is unique, and if Jesus is unique, you are unique because you are made in His likeness. Live in power, stay in power, and use it because Jesus is the manufacturer of it.

MAKE PEACE

Don't make war with Jesus, make peace with Him. Making war with Jesus is something that you should not do. It is something that you should not want or think about doing. It is a war that you can not win. It is a war that you will surely lose. God will put you away if you mess with His Son. God does not play that. Why should you not make peace with Jesus? Jesus is wonderful. Jesus is kind. He is beautiful. Jesus does not want you to make war with Him. He wants the two of you to be friends. He wants you all to be peacemakers. Jesus does not want you to face the wrath of God. He wants you to have the peace of God. Jesus does not want to have war with you. He loves you. He would do anything for you. He died for you, so why would He want to fight you? That would make Him foolish, something He's not. We are the ones that would be foolish if we make war with Jesus. We are the ones that will be foolish if we fight Jesus because He will wipe out all of us. My brothers and sisters, make peace with Jesus and not war because making war is simply idiotic.

MAKE YOUR MOVE

Let me ask you a question. What are you waiting for? Jesus Christ is ready to meet you, so make your move toward Him. When you make your move, don't be afraid. Jesus does not want you to be afraid. He is not a monster, so don't be afraid to approach Him. You don't have to be perfect to make your move to Jesus. He wants you to come as you are. You don't have to be holy or righteous to make your move to Him. That is the reason why Jesus wants to meet you, so He can make you holy and righteous. He does not want to meet you to destroy you. He does not want to meet you to make fun of you. He does not want to meet you to judge or condemn you. There's already too many people that are doing that to you, but don't worry because Jesus is going to handle them. There is only one judge, and that is God Almighty. Jesus is going to let you know what the true church is all about. He is going to give you a new name, a righteous name. Last, but not least, He is going to give you what you've been searching for, and that is love. Make your move to Jesus because He is waiting for you with open and caring arms.

MARRY JESUS

Marry Jesus. Why? Jesus is trustworthy. Jesus is honest. He will not break your heart. He will not commit adultery. He will not lie to you. Jesus will give you all the love that you need. He will not verbally or physically abuse you. He will not treat you like trash. He will not treat you like an animal. Jesus will give you sound advice. He will give you comfort. When you come home from a hard day at work, He will not give you drama. He will not argue or fuss with you. Jesus will not be a deadbeat dad or mom. He will help you raise the children. He will help you keep the house clean. Jesus will not flee from home, leaving you alone with the children. His love is perfect. His love is unconditional. He will not give you problems. His heart will always be open for you. His ears will always be ready to listen. What more could you ask for? Accept Jesus' proposal, and I guarantee that you will have an everlasting, loving marriage.

NEVER LEAVE NOR FORSAKE

Jesus Christ will never leave thee nor forsake thee. He cares about you, so why would He leave or forsake you? Even when you think that He's not with you, He's with you. Jesus will always be with you. Through good times and bad times He will be with you. He is the one that is going to keep you standing. He is the one that is going to keep you strong. Jesus is your strength. He is your shield and protector. He is the one that keeps you from getting deceived. He is the one that keeps you from getting harmed. Jesus is your shepherd. He loves you. He does not want you to stray away. He wants you to stay among the flock. And if you do leave the flock, He will find you because you belong to Him. You don't belong to the world. You belong to Jesus. You are His sheep. Keep holding on. Keep fighting the good fight. Keep pushing. And when times get rough, count it all joy because you know that Jesus will never leave thee nor forsake thee.

ONE OF A KIND

Listen up! Listen up! Jesus Christ is one of a kind. He is the one and only Jesus Christ. He is the one that resurrected from His grave and ascended to heaven to sit on the right-hand side of God. How many people that you know did that? By the power of God Jesus did that. He is the only one that did it. He sacrificed Himself on that cross like a soldier, and you know what? He did it for you. No one else would have done it for you, but Jesus did. Jesus is the great high priest. He is superior to the angels. He is greater than all the people of God that you read about in the Bible. As a matter of fact, He is their master and leader. God gave Jesus the right to be the head over everything. He is God's right-hand man. He is second in command, and God is the first in command. Jesus is above the clouds and the stars that you see in the sky. He commands the weather. He operates the solar system. There is nothing too hard for Him. There is nothing that He can't handle. Jesus is one of a kind, so believe me because someday you will find out.

PURSUE

My brothers and sisters, pursue Christ. Seek Christ. Christ is the top prize to your salvation. He is the #1 prize. He is the king of salvation. He is the giver of salvation. He is salvation. And when He gives it to you, it can not be taken away. It becomes signed and sealed. It becomes your heavenly birth certificate and eternal Social Security Number. It is the mark of Jesus Christ. It is not the mark of the beast. The mark of the beast is ugly, terrible, and pathetic, so when the enemy tries to offer it to you, reject it. Be willing to die for Christ. Be willing to gain your salvation. Salvation is yours for the giving. It is yours for the keeping, but to get it, you have to pursue Christ. Bump living for the world, and bump living for Satan. Pursue Christ and live for Christ. Jesus Christ is worth it. He is absolutely worth it. Pursuing Christ is not going to be easy because the serpent is lurking, and he is going to try to deceive you. He does not want you to find Christ because he knows that if you find Christ you are going to encourage others to find Christ. He does not want you to find Christ because there is power in Christ. With Christ you can, and will, defeat him. The enemy does not want to be defeated; he wants to be a conqueror. He wants to be a god. Pursue Christ and be willing to pursue Him because by God He was willing to die for you. He raced to that cross and died for you.

RESPECT JESUS

It is truly remarkable to serve someone like Jesus Christ. My brothers and sisters, you should not be hesitant when it comes to blessing Him. He is the one who is making a way for you to come to the Father, Almighty God, so you should respect Him. Jesus is not only loving and compassionate, He is also tough. It had to take someone tough and with courage to die on a cross for you. It does not feel good to have nails driven into your flesh and bones. I know that was painful. How many of you would have gone through so much for people? Jesus had to endure rejection. He had to endure persecution. That was pain and longsuffering. Many people down here on earth, including myself, think that we have gone through something bad.

None of us have suffered what Jesus Christ had suffered. Would you have died for someone who rejected you? Would you have died for someone who spit on you? Last, but not least, would you have gone to hell and saved souls? No, you would not, so respect Jesus for He is the epitome of Christian living and the resurrection of life.

SHOW JESUS CHRIST LOVE

What's up, my brothers and sisters in Christ Jesus? How are you all doing? Today is a marvelous day that Jesus Christ has created. He is a remarkable Savior. My brothers and sisters, I just want to tell you all to show Jesus Christ some love. Come on, my brothers and sisters, He deserves it. He not only humbled Himself on earth, but He also humbled Himself in heaven. He left His throne of glory to come to this sinful world. That's when He first humbled Himself to God in heaven. Then He humbled Himself to die on a cross for us, something He didn't have to do. Show Jesus some love. Love, honor, and obey Him. Show Him that you are willing to follow Him. He died for all of us. He loves us. Repent, for the kingdom of heaven is at hand and accept Jesus Christ as your personal Savior. He will take good care of you. Live to bless Jesus Christ, and live to love Him. Let His words abide in you. Keep Him first in your life. Show Him gratitude. We all have to do that. He was the one that delivered your relatives off drugs and alcohol. He was the one that delivered you from that spirit that was hindering you. Jesus is worthy to be praised. He loves being praised. Understand this, my brothers and sisters, when you bless Jesus, you are also getting blessed. He is blessing you this very hour. Follow Jesus, care for Him, respect Him, adore Him, and witness that He will not only reward you on earth, but also in heaven. Amen.

SHOW MEEKNESS

What's up, my brothers and sisters? Who do you have going on? I know who I have going on, and that is Jesus Christ. I am going to show Him meekness. Jesus is the reason why I have this joyful spirit. He is the reason why I have this caring spirit. There are too many people in the world that do not care about Jesus. There are too many people in the world that do not know Him. My job is to reach out to people so they can get to know Him. Jesus is a remarkable Savior. He is a gentle Savior. He is always there to heal someone. He is always there to bless someone, especially with His kind words. He is always there to feed someone. Jesus never abuses anyone. He never treats anyone coldly or harshly. He is what you can ask for in a best friend. Allow Jesus to be your best friend. Allow Him to be your comforter. I will not be the only one showing Him meekness. You will also show Him meekness because you will find out that He is sensational. I want everyone to show Jesus meekness. I want everyone to be humble unto Him. He is a righteous King that treats His servants with respect. He is a righteous King that rewards His servants. He will bless you with a joyful spirit. He will bless you with a caring spirit, so show Him meekness, and He will gladly show it to you.

SMOOTH SAILING

You are smooth sailing with Christ. With Christ as your captain, your ship (soul) is going to sail smoothly. Your ship (soul) is not going to sink. Surely you are going to go through some rough waves (temptations). Surely you are going to go through some storms (trials and tribulations), but don't worry because Christ knows how to control and steer a ship. He is more powerful than rough waves and storms. They don't have power over Him. With Christ as your captain, you can overcome any storm or rough wave because you have the power of Christ. Christ is a captain that is always sober. He is a captain whose mind stays focused on the destination. Christ does not need a map to get you to the final destination (heaven) because He *is* the map. You will not get lost on the way to your final destination because Christ knows the way, for He is the Way, the Truth, and the Life. When it gets dark, you don't need to fear because you are going to come across lighthouses. God is those lighthouses. He is going to make sure that His Son has a safe journey with you. I told you, you don't have to worry. Continue to follow Christ. Continue to believe in Him. Continue to obey Him as your captain, and don't fear because He is going to tell those storms and rough waves, "Peace, be still," (Mark 4:39) so you can sail smoothly.

SPEND TIME WITH JESUS

If you are bored, I know what you can do; spend time with Jesus. When you spend time with Jesus, you will not get bored. It is fun spending time with Him for He is not a boring person or a sad person. When you spend time with Jesus, you will not get angry or sad because He is filled with peace. He is also filled with joy, happiness, and love. He is fun to be around. He will make you feel good on the inside. He will make you feel good about yourself. Don't spend time with Jesus just to see what you can get from Him. Spend time with Him to love and adore Him. Spend time with Him to bless Him. And spend time with Him to give Him honor and respect. Jesus will gladly appreciate it. He looks forward to spending time with you. He looks forward to having fun with you. Jesus loves you, and you will truly find that out by spending time with Him.

STAY ON TRACK

My brothers and sisters, stay on track following Jesus. Don't let anything or anyone get you off track. Don't let anything or anyone stop you from following Him. Just because others choose not to follow Jesus doesn't mean that you have to choose not to follow Him. Just because others choose to go to hell doesn't mean that you have to choose to go there. And just because others choose not to believe in Jesus doesn't mean that you have to choose not to believe in Him. You have your own mind. I don't care how sexy a person may be, you must still stay on track of following Jesus. There are many deceivers that would try to get you off track. They are waiting, ready, and willing to deceive you. There are many things that would try to distract you. That is why the Word of God says you have to "walk circumspectly [carefully], not as fools, but as wise, Redeeming the time, because the days are evil" (Ephesians 5:15–16). Well, the days are evil. Evil is lurking. Evil is on the prowl looking for innocent people to deceive and to destroy. God doesn't want the enemy to deceive or to destroy you. The enemy doesn't care about you, but Jesus cares about you. He sacrificed His precious and sinless life for you. He prepared a place for you. He's coming back for you. My brothers and sisters, stay focused on Him and stay on track of following Him. Don't be deceived. I love you.

THE BEST HANDS TO BE IN

The best hands to be in are in the hands of the Lord Jesus Christ. Jesus Christ will never let you go. Jesus Christ will never mislead you. By you being in His hands you should have no worries. Why should you worry when everything is already taken care of for you? Jesus has everything mapped out for you. Come on, my brothers and sisters, don't worry. Jesus Christ's hands are clean. By His hands being clean yours are clean. You won't find any dirt in His hands. In His hands you are comforted. In His hands you are protected. No one will pluck you out of His hands. Be happy that you are in the hands of the Lord. Rejoice, for He will not let you go. He loves you. He doesn't mind blessing you. His hands are overflowing with blessings. The blessings from heaven flow like a waterfall. From this point on, my brothers and sisters, recognize whose hands you are in. Jesus Christ is not a small Savior. He's a big one, so be glad that you are in the hands of the Lord who won't let you go.

THE EPITOME OF RIGHTEOUSNESS

Who is the epitome of righteousness? Jesus Christ is the epitome of righteousness. He is the founder of righteousness. He *is* righteousness. Jesus lived His earthly life without sinning. He lived His earthly life without breaking God's commandments. He was always obedient to God. He lived His earthly life without being violent. That is awesome, amazing, and spectacular! What? Living a life without sinning, without breaking God's commandments, and without being violent? Everything that Jesus did was right. Are you serious? Everything He preached and taught was right. There is not a trace of evil in Him. Neither is there a trace of sin in Him. Is that so? Jesus is holy, sanctified, and magnificent. He is contagious. And once you get hooked on Him, you stay hooked. You want to stay hooked. Refuse to let go. Believe what I'm saying. Know what I'm saying. Feel what I'm saying, for Jesus is the epitome of righteousness.

I believe you, Demetrice, I believe you.

THE GREAT HIGH PRIEST

It feels so good serving Jesus Christ, knowing that He's the great High Priest. There is no priest higher than or greater than He is. Jesus is the one that is sitting on the right side of God in the glorious kingdom of heaven. He is the one who is sinless. He was the one that triumphed over death. He also defeated sin when He died on the cross for us. Jesus preaches the truth. He does not beat around the bush. He does not sugarcoat anything. He tells you how it is. It is up to you to listen to the truth. Jesus Christ does not force the truth on anyone. Those who have ears, let them hear. Jesus is not a false priest. He is a true priest. He never lied to anyone. He does not speak lies. He does not twist the Bible. He never murmurs. Take time to get to know Jesus. Open up your heart to Him. Listen to the words that He speaks, teaches, and preaches. Your heart will feel Him. Your spirit will feel Him. "Seeing then that we have a great high priest, that is passed into the heavens, Jesus the Son of God, let us hold fast our profession" (Hebrews 4:14).

THE SPIRITUAL BEAUTICIAN

What's up, God's beautiful people? How are you doing? On the outside you are beautiful, but are you beautiful in the inside? If you are not beautiful on the inside I know someone who can make you beautiful in the inside, and that someone is Jesus Christ for He is the spiritual beautician. Jesus Christ will wash the entire dirt out of you, which means He will clean all the sin out of you. Sin is not good for the body. It is pollution, which means it can kill your spirit. Sin intoxicates the inside of you. It torments you. It is your spirit's enemy. Jesus Christ does not want sin to take control over you. That is why He wants to beautify the inside of you. Sin is what causes your attitude to be ugly. Have you ever known a person who is so beautiful on the outside, but his or her attitude is ugly? That is the result of sin. Jesus Christ does not want you to be ugly on the inside. He wants you to be beautiful. He wants to beautify your spirit with love, peace, joy, happiness, and tenderness. As long as sin is in you, your spirit is not going to be beautiful. Do you get my drift? Jesus loves and cares for you. He does not want you to be walking around with an ugly spirit. He wants you to be happy. He wants you to care for others. Invite Jesus into your hearts for He is the spiritual beautician that will give your spirit an excellent makeover.

THE TRUE GUIDE

Jesus Christ is the true guide. He is guiding His people on the pathway to God. Jesus is the right pathway. He is the way, the truth, and the life. God trusts Jesus to guide His people. He has faith in Jesus. He knows Jesus is not going to disappoint Him. He knows that Jesus is not going to lead His people in a wrong fashion. Jesus is not an antichrist. He is not a deceiver. Jesus knows the wrath of God is lethal. He respects the wrath of God. That is why God chose Him to guide His people. Jesus is the guide to safety. He protects you from the fiery darts of Satan. He protects you from demonic spirits. Follow Jesus, my brothers and sisters, because He is the light of life. Follow Jesus, my brothers and sisters, because He is the map of eternal life, the true guide to the eternal and everlasting King.

THE TRUE HOOKUP

Check this out. My brothers and sisters, Jesus Christ is the true hookup. He is your hookup to all that is good. Most of all, He is your hookup to God and eternal life. My brothers and sisters, if you don't hook up with Jesus, you are not going to hook up with God. Don't get upset. It is for your own good. Jesus Christ is fabulous. You should be excited to hook up with Him. He will not judge, condemn, persecute, or abuse you. Jesus will hook you up with joy, peace, and great finances. Do you feel me? He hooked you up when He died for your sins, resurrected, and prepared a place for you. Do you believe? Believe in Jesus' faithfulness. Believe in His Word. Most of all, believe that Jesus is real because He is the true hookup to the great and Almighty God.

THE TRUE LOVE DOCTOR

Jesus is the true love doctor. He received His master's degree of love from the University of Heaven. God is His professor and guidance counselor. Jesus earned His degree because of the love that He has for people. He earned His degree because He has no hate in His heart. And He earned His degree because He heals the brokenhearted. Jesus shows everyone love. He speaks kind words to people. He speaks positively to people. Jesus heals, delivers, and saves people with His love. He comforts their hearts with His love. Believe me because I had a broken heart, and Jesus healed, fixed, and filled it with His love. He gave me a new heart. There is no hate in me. There is no hurt in me. Jesus took all the pain and hurt away. After a conversation with Jesus, you will not be the same. Just ask the woman at the well (John 4). Jesus was trained and taught by the best, which is Almighty God. Jesus told God that He is willing to give people true love. He proved it to God by putting Himself up for sacrifice. He proved it to God by dying for you. Now *that* is true love. How many people do you know that will die for you? How many people do you know that will leave their place of royalty? No one but Jesus, because He is the true and eternal love doctor.

THE TRUE TREASURE

No! I'm not searching for gold. I'm searching for Jesus Christ. Jesus is going to help me get closer to God. Jesus is the way to God because God is the treasure you should be searching for. "He is a rewarder of them that diligently seek him" (Hebrews 11:6). God is the true treasure. He is the treasure that will never rust. He is the treasure that will never run out, the treasure that can't be stolen. He is everlasting. All you have to do is keep Him in your heart. He will be with you everywhere you go. He is omnipresent. God will shine inside and outside of you. Many will want what you have. Just tell them that you have Jesus Christ. He is the reason you've got what you have. It's not easy seeking after the true treasure because you have to deal with the wiles of the devil, but don't worry because that true treasure that you are searching for will give you the power to triumph over the devil.

Don't give up on your search; keep pressing. Your reward is going to be great. Whenever you feel like giving up, just think about the great things that you are going to gain once you receive the true treasure. You will be gaining great things, such as wisdom, knowledge, understanding, peace everlasting, joy everlasting, healing, and anointing. Be just like Jesus Christ because He is a true witness that will tell you that God is the best and true treasure to search for.

THERE IS STILL HOPE

My brothers and sisters, I know that things get hard for you. I know that things may seem that they're not going to get better, but don't worry for there is still hope. Hope is Jesus Christ's middle name. He knows that you need help to be successful. He doesn't want you to feel down. He doesn't want you to give up on hope. It's not over, my brothers and sisters. Just hang in there. Don't put a gun to your head. Don't jump off of a building, and don't overdose yourself on drugs for He is with you. He is the one that's telling you to not give up. He is the one that's telling you everything is going to be all right. Continue to study, practice, exercise, and go to work and school, for He will build your strength. Don't stress yourself out. Don't let anything or anyone get to you. Keep doing what you do, and that's praying. Jesus will see your way through. Let Him handle that person that's trying to get to you. Let Him handle your problems and situations. Those types of things are His specialty. He wants to handle your burdens. Jesus will lift you up so high that your feet (spirit) will not touch the ground. Things that used to get to you will no longer get to you. People that nag you will no longer get to you. My brothers and sisters, just continue to live and do what's right. Whenever you feel down and feel like you can't go on, just know that there is still hope because Jesus Christ always lives up to His name.

THIS IS A RED ALERT!

This is a red alert for God's people: don't take heed to the antichrist. The antichrist is a false image of God. The antichrist claims to be God, but in the heart he or she is full of evil. The antichrist is here to deceive all that he can deceive, so beware. My brothers and sisters, make sure you have the Christ mind so you won't get deceived. Make sure you are rooted in Christ. Jesus Christ is the ultimate weapon against evil. With Him on your side, you don't have to worry about getting yourself into danger. He is the epitome of leadership. He is a general. The Holy Spirit will let you know who is an antichrist. My brothers and sisters, some people are wicked. Some people just don't care about your heart. They are willing to bring you down. Willing as in they desire to put you down. Whatever you do, stay happy and wear the breastplate of righteousness to protect your heart. Whatever you do, don't let anybody attack your mind and heart. Be ready for something like that. Know that Jesus is with you, and with Him on your side, you shall not be moved. So whenever an antichrist approaches you, plead the blood of Jesus, and stand for Jesus, for He is your keeper.

WASHER OF POLLUTED SOULS

It is so tremendous having Jesus Christ in your life. Jesus Christ is the washer of polluted souls. My brothers and sisters, we all live in a world of sin, and because of that our souls are polluted. "For God so loved the world that, he gave his only begotten Son, that whosoever believeth in him should not perish, but have everlasting life. For God sent not his son into the world to condemn the world; but that the world through him might be saved" (John 3:16–17). My brothers and sisters, Jesus Christ didn't die on the cross to prove to us He's a daredevil; He died on the cross to save us from sin. People, until you accept Jesus Christ into your life, your soul is going to be polluted. Jesus Christ will wash your soul from sin. Jesus Christ will protect you from infirmities and diseases. He is a perfect shield for your soul. Nothing can get through Him, and nothing can move Him. He is the rock of our salvation. He is the chief cornerstone. He is the King of kings and Lord of lords. I know that you are sick and tired of walking in sin. I know that you are tired of sin affecting your soul, so accept Jesus Christ into your life so He can wash you from your polluted soul.

WORDS DO HURT

Be careful how you talk to people because words do hurt. It's not right to hurt people. It's not kind to hurt people. Many people do not care about how they talk to others. They don't care about others' feelings. They just open their mouths and begin to tear others down. Jesus Christ does not want you to verbally abuse people. He wants you to verbally bless them. Speak kindly to people because hurting people is not the spirit of Christ. Do you love yourself? Jesus said, "Thou shalt love thy neighbor as thyself" (Matthew 19:19). You should love your neighbor as the neighbor is you. If you love yourself, love your neighbor. If you don't hurt yourself, don't hurt your neighbor. Show your neighbor kindness as you show yourself. No one likes to be around a person because he or she has a bad mouth. He or she talks too much. He or she is rude, unkind, and disrespectful. Once you start showing people respect and kindness, they will love to be in your presence. They will love to have you as company. I, personally, do not like people with rude tongues. They despise me. I care about people. I care about how I treat and talk to them. Have self-control, behave yourself, and be careful how you talk to people because words do hurt.

YOU ARE A WINNER

You are not a loser! Jesus Christ is a winner, so that makes you a winner. You are made in His image. You are made in His likeness, and in Jesus there is no darkness. We all go through trials and tribulations. We all go through storms, but when we come out, we come out as winners. Do not let anything overtake you. Do not let anything overpower you. Do not let anything trample over you. I know the enemy (Satan) is shooting fiery darts at you (Ephesians 6:16). I know people are persecuting, abusing, and setting all manner of evil against you, but don't worry because they will not prevail in destroying you (Jeremiah 1:19). You will not be destroyed. You can't be destroyed. You are a winner, and winners are tough. Winners never say die. You are in Jesus, and in Him you are victorious. In Jesus, you are more than a conqueror. In Jesus, you are a joint heir to the kingdom of heaven, and in heaven, there will be no losers, so rejoice and never quit because you are a winner.

YOU ARE CHOSEN

You are chosen, so step up to the plate and don't be afraid. Jesus has chosen you to be a disciple, so be one. Don't run away from it for there is nothing to fear. There is nothing to be afraid of because Jesus is going to give you all the power that you need. He is going to equip you with His righteousness. He is going to shield and protect you. Be happy that Christ has chosen you. You should have a smile on your face. You should be filled with joy. And you should be proud for Christ has chosen you to be part of His royal kingdom. He sees you as royalty. He sees you as prestigious. Christ wants you to reach out to people. He wants you to bring more people to Him. Christ wants His party to be crowded with millions of people, and I'm telling you, His party is going to be jamming. His party is going to be fun, and the best part about it is that it's going to be eternal. Abraham, David, Moses, Daniel, and Joshua are going to attend it. God Almighty is going to attend it. Christ's party is going to rock the heavens. And Jesus is going to greatly reward you because you dropped everything that you were doing and followed Him. I'm glad that Christ chose you.

YOU ARE NOT PERFECT

If you were perfect, Jesus Christ would have not descended from heaven to save and forgive you of your sins. All men and women have sinned, which means none of us are perfect. My friends, you are going to make mistakes, and you are going to sin because you are human. There is no one in this world that can say that he or she has never sinned. Jesus Christ is the only one that has never sinned. Though Jesus Christ was being abused, cursed at, tortured, beaten, and tempted to sin, He still did not sin. You sin even when you think that you are not. That is why we all have to get on our knees and ask Jesus for forgiveness. Jesus knows how it feels to be human. Jesus knows how it feels to be tempted. He knows that you are living in a sinful world. It is you that have to stop being hard on yourself. Jesus knows that you love Him. Jesus knows that you don't want to sin. He sees that you are making the effort not to sin, but because of human nature you are going to sin. When you ask Jesus for forgiveness, He would forgive you as though you have never sinned. Don't sin on purpose. If you have the knowledge of what is wrong, don't do the wrong. My brothers and sisters, be eager to serve Jesus, and remember that you are not perfect.

YOU CAN DO

My brothers and sisters, you can do all things through Christ which strengtheneth you (Philippians 4:13). Who or what is stopping you from doing those things? Who is hindering you? You have the power of Christ. You have the love of Christ. There is nothing that you should not be able to do. Do you believe in yourself? You have to believe in yourself. How can you believe in Jesus when you don't believe in yourself? You can't. You have to believe in Jesus, and you have to believe in yourself. It takes two to tangle. Jesus gave you the power to accomplish your goals. Jesus gave you the power to be successful. It is you that have to step out in faith and achieve them. It is you that have to get over your fears and doubts. God is not going to do all the work for you. You have to do your part. You have to get off your tail and fight for what you want. I'm not talking about a physical fight, I'm talking about a spiritual fight. You have to motivate yourself. You have to encourage yourself. God believes in you. Jesus Christ believes in you. The Holy Spirit believes in you. I believe in you. You can make it. You can do it. You can be all that you want to be. Stay in Christ.

YOU SHALL NOT BE MOVED

You shall not be moved because Christ is on your side. There is nothing that is able to move you. There is nothing that is able to shake you. There is no one more powerful than Christ. There is no one than can defeat Him. You must be a fool if you decide to jump in His face. You must be crazy if you decide to jump in His face. When someone jumps in your face, he or she is jumping in Jesus' face. When someone disrespects you, he or she is disrespecting Christ. Jesus said, "But whoso shall offend one of these little ones which believe in me, it were better for him that a millstone were hanged about his neck, and that he were drowned in the depth of the sea" (Matthew 18:6). Jesus does not want anyone messing with you. He is serious when it comes to you. He loves you, and you belong to Him. So when someone jumps in your face, tell him or her that Christ is your master, and you shall not be moved.

ABOUT THE AUTHOR

Demetrice M. Gates was born January 3, 1979, at Grady Memorial Hospital located in Atlanta, Georgia. For thirteen years he lived in a rough and violent environment, particularly in the inner-city ghetto of Atlanta. Then after the death of his father, he, along with his family, relocated to College Park, Georgia, where he attended, and graduated from, Benjamin E. Banneker High School. Demetrice is a member of World Changers Church International, which is led by Dr. Creflo and Taffi Dollar. He has a love and compassion for people, especially the youth. He has a passion to inspire, uplift, and encourage. He believes that God is the inspiration and motivation for everything. With the gift that God granted to him, he desires to touch the world.

Contact: gatesdemetrice@yahoo.com

CPSIA information can be obtained
at www.ICGtesting.com
Printed in the USA
BVHW072030120620
581302BV00002B/40